The Effective Management of Lung Cancer

Third edition

The Effective Management of Lung Cancer

Third edition

Edited by

Martin Muers MA DPhil FRCP
*Chairman, Lung Cancer Working Party of the British Thoracic Society
& Consultant Chest Physician/Lead Thoracic Oncology Physician
Leeds General Infirmary, Leeds, UK*

Ken O'Byrne MD FRCP
*Consultant Medical Oncologist
St. James Hospital, Dublin, Ireland*

Frank Wells MA MS FRCS
*Consultant Cardiothoracic Surgeon
Papworth Hospital, Cambridge, UK*

Andrew Miles MSc MPhil PhD
*Professor of Public Health Sciences
& Editor-in-Chief, Journal of Evaluation in Clinical Practice
Barts and The London,
Queen Mary's School of Medicine and Dentistry
University of London, UK*

Barts and The London
Queen Mary's School of Medicine and Dentistry

Association of
Cancer
Physicians

The Royal College
of
Radiologists

Society of
Cardiothoracic
Surgeons

British
Thoracic
Oncology Group

AESCULAPIUS MEDICAL PRESS
LONDON SAN FRANCISCO SYDNEY

Published by

Aesculapius Medical Press (London, San Francisco, Sydney)
PO Box LB48, Mount Pleasant Mail Centre, Farringdon Road, London EC1A 1LB, UK

British Library Cataloguing in Publication Data
A CIP catalogue record for this book is available from the British Library

ISBN 1 903044 42 1

While the advice and information in this book are believed to be true and accurate at the
time of going to press, neither the authors nor the publishers nor the sponsoring institutions
can accept any legal responsibility or liability for any errors or omissions that may be made.
In particular (but without limiting the generality of the preceding disclaimer) every effort
has been made to check drug usages; however, it is possible that errors have been missed.
Furthermore, dosage schedules are constantly being revised and new side effects recognised.
For these reasons, the reader is strongly urged to consult the drug companies' printed
instructions before administering any of the drugs recommended in this book.

Further copies of this volume are available from:

Claudio Melchiorri
Aesculapius Medical Press
PO Box LB48, Mount Pleasant Mail Centre, Farringdon Road, London EC1A 1LB, UK

Fax: 020 8525 8661
Email: claudio@keyadvances4.demon.co.uk
www.keyadvances.org.uk

Copy edited by The Clyvedon Press Ltd, Cardiff, UK

Typeset, printed and bound in Britain
Peter Powell Origination & Print Limited

Contents

Contributors

Peter Armstrong FMedSci, FRCP FRCR, Professor of Diagnostic Radiology, St Bartholomew's Hospital and Past President, The Royal College of Radiologists

Jesme Baird MB ChB, MBA, Director of Patient Care, The Roy Castle Lung Cancer Foundation, Glasgow

Catherine Bale MBBS MRCP, Consultant in Medical Oncology, Department of Medical Oncology, University of Newcastle upon Tyne

Tess Craig BSc RGN, Macmillan Lung Cancer Nurse Specialist, Respiratory Unit, University Hospital of North Tees, Stockton-on-Tees

Graham Dark MBBS FRCP ILTM, Senior Lecturer in Medical Oncology, Department of Medical Oncology, University of Newcastle upon Tyne

Andrew Drain MB BCh BAO MRCS (Eng), Specialist Registrar in Cardiothoracic Surgery, Papworth Hospital, Cambridge

Tim Eisen PhD FRCP, Senior Lecturer in Medical Oncology, The Royal Marsden Hospital, London and Surrey

Dean A. Fennell PhD BSc MB BS MRCP(UK), Lung Cancer and Mesothelioma Section, Department of Medical Oncology, St Bartholomew's Hospital, London

Tessa Fitzpatrick BSc RGN, Macmillan Lung Cancer Nurse Specialist, and Chair of the National Lung Cancer Forum for Nurses, Respiratory Unit, University Hospital of North Tees, Stockton-on-Tees

Jeremy George MA MSc MD FRCP, Consultant Physician, The Middlesex Hospital, London

Richard Houlston MD PhD FRCP FRCPath, Reader in Molecular and Population Genetics, Institute of Cancer Research and Honorary Consultant in Cancer Genetics, The Royal Marsden Hospital, London and Surrey

Catherine M. A. Kelly BSc MRCP, Specialist Registrar, Department of Medical Oncology, St Bartholomew's Hospital, London

Sow Ming Lee PhD FRCP, Consultant in Medical Oncology, University College London

Ethan Lyn BA MRCP FRCR, Consultant in Clinical Oncology, Mount Vernon Cancer Centre, Mount Vernon Hospital, Northwood

Athena Matakidou MB MRCP, Clinical Research Fellow, Institute of Cancer Research, Sutton

Marianne C. Nicolson MD BSc FRCP, Consultant Medical Oncologist, Aberdeen Royal Infirmary

Thomas O. Nunan FRCP FRCR, The Clinical PET Centre, Guy's and St Thomas Hospital, London

Michael D. Peake MB ChB FRCP, Consultant Physician and Honorary Senior Lecturer in Respiratory Medicine, National Clinical Lead, Lung Cancer, Cancer Services Collaborative Programme, Glenfield Hospital, Leicester

Robin Rudd MA MD FRCP, Consultant Medical Oncologist, Lung Cancer and Mesothelioma Section, Department of Medical Oncology, St Bartholomew's Hospital, London

Michèle I. Saunders MD FRCP FRCR, Windeyer Professor of Oncology, Royal Free and University college London Medical School; Consultant in Clinical Oncology, Mount Vernon Cancer Centre, Mount Vernon Hospital, Northwood

Jeremy P. C. Steele MD MRCP, Consultant and Honorary Senior Lecturer in Medical Oncology, St Bartholomew's Hospital, London

Ala Szczepura PhD, Director, Centre for Health Services Studies, University of Warwick

Eva A. Wegner FRACP, Consultant Nuclear Medicine Physician, The Clinical PET Centre, Guy's and St Thomas' Hospital, London

Frank Wells BSc MB BS MA FRCS (Eng) FECTS, Consultant Cardiothoracic Surgeon, Papworth Hospital, Cambridge

Joy Williams MSc, Research Medical Physicist, Mount Vernon Cancer Centre, Mount Vernon Hospital, Northwood

Elena Wilson BSc MRCP FRCR, Specialist Registrar in Clinical Oncology, Mount Vernon Cancer Centre, Mount Vernon Hospital, Northwood

Preface

Lung cancer, essentially a man-made disease, has grown in importance to the public health during the twentieth century, with at the time of writing an estimated 1.25 million new cases diagnosed annually on a global basis. Initially a disease of developed countries, the lung cancer burden is now approximately equally divided between developed countries and low and medium resource countries. Not only is lung cancer the commonest incident form of cancer, it is also the leading cause of cancer death world-wide claiming 1.1 million victims each year and therefore representing one of the leading public health problems of our age.

The recent assessment of the *Europe Against Cancer* target for the year 2000 demonstrated reductions in lung cancer in men in most countries of the European Union (EU) but significant increases in the death rate in women. While progress seems to be being made in tobacco control in men in the EU, it has been a distinct failure in women. The impact of sometimes subtle differences in the prevalence of cigarette smoking can cause substantial differences in lung cancer. For example, cancer mortality overall is one-sixth higher in men (and also in women) in Scotland compared to England, Wales and Northern Ireland. Almost all of this can be explained by lung cancer, which although declining in all countries is still significantly higher in Scotland that in the other home countries. The rate of lung cancer is the best index of the adverse health impact of cigarette smoking on a community.

The risk of a 35 year old dying in middle age (35–69) has been declining since 1965 in the United Kingdom and this is being driven by the declining risk of death from causes attributable to smoking. This is not a universal finding since, for example, in Hungary the risk of dying in middle age is increasing and the proportion of deaths in this age range attributable to smoking is increasing also. While cancer mortality rates are declining in the United Kingdom they are rising in Hungary and all of this increase can be directly related to the increase in cancers attributable to smoking. Such variation underlines the importance of tobacco control and why this should be the number one priority for cancer control, as emphasised in the recent revision of the *European Code Against Cancer.* Everything that can be done to prevent children and adolescents from starting smoking must be identified and implemented, but the greatest gain in public health terms in the near future will come from persuading current smokers to cease their habit.

While tobacco smoking is by far the predominant risk factor for lung cancer, it must be remembered that non-smokers can also develop this disease. By studying risk factors in lifelong non-smokers, a clearer understanding of other lung cancer risk factors and how they operate can be identified. Passive smoking, both spousal and occupational, has emerged as a risk factor for lung cancer. Studies in women in China, Taiwan and Chinese women in United States have revealed that the risk is increased by certain cooking and heating practices such as use of rapeseed oil, deep frying, also cooking without a fume extractor, burning *kang* and the use of coal. Occupational exposure to asbestos carries an increased risk and increased risk is also reported in metal and foundary workers, dry cleaners, cooks and waiters and glass workers. Residential exposure to radon is also a demonstrated risk factor for lung cancer.

While exposure to tobacco carcinogens undoubtedly contributes the greatest risk of lung cancer, there is increasing evidence that susceptibility to environmental factors for lung cancer is in part genetically determined. In the opening chapter of this volume, Matakidou, Houlston and Eisen describe how epidemiological case-control and cohort studies have consistently shown that relatives of lung cancer cases have a 2-fold increased risk of developing the disease. In order to minimise the impact of shared tobacco habits in families, a number of studies, as the authors describe, have estimated familial risks associated with non-smoker status, demonstrating similar results. Given that cigarette smoke is a rich source of chemical carcinogens and reactive oxygen species, which can damage DNA, any inherited susceptibility to lung cancer is likely to be mediated through biological differences in the bio-activation/degradation of carcinogens or cellular response to damage (DNA repair and cell-cycle control pathways). Failure to repair damage caused by free radicals and by the formation of bulky DNA adducts may produce mutations inactivating tumour suppressor genes and/or activating oncogenes, initiating a cascade of genetic events leading to lung cancer development. Despite considerable research effort, few definitive lung cancer susceptibility alleles have, as Matakidou *et al* lament, been identified to date. Further work involving large scale, genome-wide association studies are, as they emphasise, required in order to identify low penetrance susceptibility genotypes. Once these have been established, prediction of at-risk groups and prevention/early detection of lung cancer might become possible.

The underlying concept of an early lung cancer detection programme is that significantly more cures are achieved when stage I tumours are found in asymptomatic individuals, since the surgical results and 5-year survival figures are much better compared with patients not in a screening programme who often first present with symptoms. In Chapter Two, Armstrong discusses a number of prospective, non-randomised trials, particularly those published from Japan and the United States (e.g. ELCAP), that have demonstrated that low-dose spiral computed tomography (CT) of the chest can effectively detect early-stage lung cancer in high-risk individuals and that its health impact could be as great as or greater than that of breast cancer screening. Armstrong is clear that the outcome of the published studies of low-dose CT screening of asymptomatic populations for lung cancer shows that the diagnostic yield of lung cancer from CT screening is reasonable and is far superior to chest radiography, that a very high proportion of the cancers diagnosed are stage I (and that those that are stage I are almost all stage Ia), that the cancer diagnosis rate is highly dependent on the inclusion criteria with a much higher incidence of lung cancer when the age of those screened is above 60 years and that when the screening is limited to those with strong smoking history the pick-up rate of clinically insignificant benign nodules is very high and that, as expected, the pick-up rate of lung cancers and the false positive rate both drop considerably in the later rounds of screening. The central aim of any population screening programme is, of course, to do more good than harm at an acceptable cost. The potential benefits of a lung cancer CT screening programme are that it might extend life by reducing mortality due to the cancer. However, also to be considered are the potentially harmful effects including extra radiation from repetitive CT examinations and the consequences of false positive diagnoses, notably anxiety due to lead-time, anxiety and complications from unnecessary further imaging, biopsy and even surgery. It will therefore, as Armstrong points out, take a randomised controlled trial with many years of follow-up to determine any mortality reduction and until this vital piece of information is known it will not be possible to calculate the cost of such a screening programme in any meaningful way. As he concludes, important questions to answer in future large-scale studies include: does early detection using up-to-date CT techniques result in a measurable reduction in the mortality of lung cancer? Can thoracotomy be limited largely to those patients with life threatening malignancies? Can mass screening with helical CT be performed in a cost-effective manner?

Following on from Armstrong's discussion of the role of CT in screening for early lung cancer, George, writing in Chapter Three, is concerned to describe the potential role of fluorescence bronchoscopy in screening for micro-invasive carcinomas and pre-invasive lesions. These lesions are easily missed with standard white light bronchoscopy but they may be distinguished from surrounding normal tissues by exploiting differences in their properties of fluorescence when illuminated by blue light. Although pre-invasive lesions are believed to be precursors of squamous cell carcinoma, our understanding of their natural history is incomplete due to the previous difficulties of detection. Some groups advocate immediate treatment, whereas others have argued that such an approach is not justified when it is not known what proportion will progress to clinically significant cancers. George describes how, at the Middlesex Hospital, patients with pre-invasive lesions are kept under active surveillance. The lesions identified are frequently multi-focal with the capacity to progress, regress or remain indolent. In addition, the author describes how patients harbouring these lesions are at high risk of developing incidental cancers at remote sites within their lungs, in keeping with a field change effect, and how molecular biological analyses on sequential biopsy samples with the intention of identifying markers of tumour progression are being carried out with the aim of directing future treatments at lesions with genuine malignant potential.

In the final chapter of Part One of the volume, Wegner and Nunan review the place of positron emission tomography (PET) in the investigation and management of lung cancer. The main use of PET in lung cancer management, as the authors describe, is in the presurgical staging of non-small cell cancer. Many studies have shown that PET is more sensitive than CT scanning and more specific. A review by Ghambir in 2001, for example, found that in 53 studies in the literature at that stage, PET altered the patient's management in 37% of cases. A randomised study of PET versus conventional work up has shown that one in five thoracotomies for patients with lung cancer were futile as PET would have upstaged the disease. Usually PET upstages the patient but in about 10% of cases radiological abnormalities are shown to be benign and the patient is downstaged. PET is also of use in detecting recurrent disease when there are equivocal radiological findings. PET is also used, as the authors describe, in the assessment of solitary pulmonary nodules. In Europe, approximately 50% are malignant and the first line of management should be a biopsy. However in those patients in whom a biopsy has failed or who are felt to be at high risk, PET is used to determine if the lesion is metabolically active (and likely to be malignant) or not active (and thus likely to be benign). In the review by Ghambir, the overall sensitivity of PET was 96% versus 67% for CT scanning. The main problem for the UK is the lack of PET scanner provision; indeed, as Wegner and Nunn point out, there are currently only seven clinical PET scanners in the country and four of these are in London.

We have dedicated Part Two of the volume to a review of the evidence base for surgical intervention in the management of lung cancer. In the first chapter of this Part, Wells reviews current strategies for extended resection of disease and the place of reconstructive surgery. The principal advance in the improved surgical management of lung cancer has come about through a more precise system of pre-surgical and surgical staging. The more widespread application of staging techniques has allowed institutions to compare their results more accurately over time and this, as Wells discusses, has led to a refinement of the stage classification for lung cancer which has elevated certain tumour stages from an inoperable category to operable, usually in the context of ongoing clinical trials with or without neoadjuvant chemotherapy. Tumours involving direct chest wall invasion and diaphragm invasion have long been recognised as being operable. The principle in terms of an outcome for these patients is both completeness of resection and, more importantly, lymph node status - mediastinal node involvement, for example, virtually precludes likely survival. Direct mediastinal invasion in selected areas such as pericardium with left atrial encroachment has also been recognised as being resectable, but with varying long term survival reported, as Wells describes. Other direct mediastinal invasion such as to the superior vena cava or aorta has generally been regarded as being unresectable. Although reports of selected cases suggest acceptable mid-term survival, as Wells points out, most of these studies are small and retrospective. It is becoming more widely accepted that locally advanced disease within the chest, in the absence of mediastinal node spread, may well be treated surgically, but only in the context of neoadjuvant chemotherapy administered in prospective, randomised clinical trials. Undoubtedly, in the modern era of cardiothoracic surgery, heroic resections are possible with satisfactory postoperative outcomes. However, the real impact of this type of surgery in locally advanced tumours awaits availability of good quality, peer-reviewed, prospectively gathered evidence.

It has been long accepted that the only therapy that may be regarded as potentially curable for patients with lung cancer is timely and complete surgical resection. This conditional statement depends upon a working knowledge of the stage of disease. Today, professionals looking after people with lung cancer have a sophisticated array of investigations that allow a very comprehensive knowledge of the extent of tumor in each patient. We should know the cell type and the degree of differentiation of the tumor, its size, local extent and the likelihood of disease distant from the primary site. Combined PET and CT scanning will eliminate most inappropriate patients from being offered surgical treatment and the net result of this approach is to be able to select patients with cancer confined within the thorax in whom the tumour can be completely encompassed by an achievable resection. Here, then, as Drain and Wells illustrate within Chapter Six, lies the rub! What, these days, constitutes a resectable lesion, and which tumors of those that are regarded as being locally advanced, are in fact locally resectable?

Convention dictates that a tumour completely confined within a lung that is resectable by lobectomy, bilobectomy or pneumonectomy in the absence of mediastinal lymph node involvement is resectable. Local spread outside the lung, invading, chest wall, diaphragm or mediastinal structures, will inevitably mean that attempted surgical resection is much more likely to leave some disease behind. Thus, surgical resection alone cannot render a cure for patients unless parts of these vital structures are removed with the tumor 'en bloc'. Under these circumstances, surgery is usually withheld.

Is this the correct way to proceed in every case? The answer to this question is, for Drain and Wells, 'yes', unless strategies can be developed to completely encompass the disease in these more advanced cases. With modern cardiothoracic surgery, resection can be extended to include parts of the pericardium, right and left atrium, aorta and almost any part of the chest wall and diaphragm. Central airway extension can be encompassed by carinal resection and reconstruction. Truly resectable disease in this category, (T4), is relatively uncommon. It is therefore important that multi-disciplinary teams deciding upon treatment packages for such people should be aware of these more advanced surgical procedures, so as not to disadvantage patients with this late stage who may have disease that can be resected by such advanced techniques. It must be borne in mind, of course, that the involvement of N2 nodes has a disastrous effect on outcome. Obvious spread to mediastinal nodes therefore renders many of these patients inoperable, reinforcing the need for full pre-surgical nodal staging. Drain and Wells are clear that all patients put forward for such advanced surgical treatment should be managed within the context of clinical trials. They argue that the relevance of neo-adjuvant and adjuvant chemotherapy also has to be considered, as does the additional use of radiotherapy in down-staging protocols, which may allow patients who are otherwise inoperable to also benefit from advanced resection. There is no place for treating such patients outside expert units and this, they feel, is one reason for the centralization of lung cancer services in fewer units.

Having reviewed current progress in the development of surgical management of lung cancer in Part Two of this book we move in Part Three of the volume, through Chapters 7–12, to a detailed consideration of the scientific evidence and expert clinical opinion base for current management strategies in clinical and medical oncology. In the first chapter of this Part, Kelly and associates discuss the role of neoadjuvant chemotherapy in NSCLC. As they explain, radical surgery has been considered the standard of care for patients with early stage (stage I, II) and in some cases of stage III NSCLC. However long-term results remain disappointing with many patients relapsing from distant metastases. Post-operative strategies including adjuvant chemotherapy and radiotherapy have generally failed to improve survival. Promising results from several phase II preoperative (neoadjuvant) chemotherapy trials using platinum-based regimens make this approach an important area to investigate in a randomised setting. Several ongoing randomised trials investigating the role of neoadjuvant chemotherapy with surgery versus surgery alone in patients with resectable NSCLC will eventually include more than 3,000 patients worldwide. Many of these trials, as the authors describe, examine the role of the newer cytotoxic drugs (e.g. gemcitabine, paclitaxel, vinorelbine) in combination with a platinum compound which may increase further the rates of downstaging prior to surgery and long-term survival. It is important, as Kelly and her colleagues emphasise, that clinical investigators collaborate in these large clinical trials, given that the role of neoadjuvant chemotherapy has yet to be established. It is likely that further progress will come from the introduction of newer technologies (e.g. FDG-PET, oesophageal ultrasound) in order to identify NSCLC patients who have mediastinal downstaging, key-hole surgery (video-assisted) to reduce post-operative morbidity and in combining neoadjuvant chemotherapy with the large number of molecularly targeted therapies now becoming available.

The oncology community has known for a long time that the results of radical radiation therapy using a standard fractionation technique and achieving a total dose of 60Gy in 6 weeks gives poor results. Attempts have been made to improve results by altering the fractionation schedules, adding chemotherapy and dose escalation and it is within this context that Wilson and her colleagues describe the altered fractionation schedule CHART in Chapter Eight. CHART contributes significant clinical benefit in terms of survival when compared to conventional radiotherapy. Likewise, an advantage has been shown when concurrent chemotherapy is added to conventional treatment. The authors describe how, in recent years, dose acceleration using conformal therapy has been the subject of several phase I/II trials which demonstrated that the radiation dose can be escalated, providing rules are followed for the doses that can be given to the surrounding normal tissue, particularly the lung. In the studies conducted by the authors, experience was gained with CHARTWEL alone, CHARTWEL + neo-adjuvant chemotherapy and now CHARTWEL with conformal radiotherapy planning, with or without chemotherapy. These studies show that, because normal tissues are shielded, conformal therapy reduces the acute morbidity that patients endure. To date, there is no change in late morbidity although the incidence is very low. It would now be possible to considerably dose escalate with the CHARTWEL regimen in an effort to gain increased local tumour control without added morbidity.

Primary surgical resection for NSCLC offers, as described, the best chance for cure but high rates of distant relapse highlight the need for effective adjuvant therapies. Studies of neoadjuvant and adjuvant platinum based chemotherapy continue to generate interest but no standard recommendation has yet to receive universal acceptance and implementation. Several large phase III randomised trials are underway or have recently been completed and meta-analysis of their results is likely to provide definitive data for debate within the lung cancer oncology community. Other international studies using oral chemotherapy analogues and immunotherapy suggest a benefit in node negative tumours. Patients with medically inoperable early disease may also be treated effectively by a variety of radiation techniques and it is to a description of current management strategies for the treatment of early disease that Dark and Bale turn in Chapter Nine. There are several key questions regarding optimal treatment with chemotherapy in *advanced* non-small cell lung cancer and it is encouraging that well designed clinical trials are increasingly addressing the many pivotal questions relating to the optimal management of advanced disease, as Nicolson discusses within Chapter Ten.

As recently as 1995, published studies within the literature were indicating that only around 8% of patients with advanced non-small cell lung cancer were receiving chemotherapy in the UK. Nicolson is clear that when we consider whom to treat, the accumulated evidence indicates that the benefit should be queried only in the elderly and in patients with a poor performance status. As 50% of lung cancer patients are aged over 70 years and are or have been smokers, these individuals are likely to have a certain degree of co-morbidity. There is no doubt, however, that elderly patients in Europe are just as keen as patients within the United States, to receive chemotherapy with the aim of improving their quality and duration of life. Several trials have shown the clear benefit even with single agent chemotherapy in the elderly, and although toxicity is greater with combination radio- and chemotherapy in locally advanced disease, elderly patients do gain a survival benefit. Patients who are performance status 2 are more likely to have toxicity from chemotherapy and in some studies have been excluded from trials in advanced disease. There is, however, evidence that these patients stand to gain more benefit in quality of life than do the fitter PS 0 and 1 cohorts. More clinical trials for PS2 patients are required to give a definitive answer to the question, and at time of trial development careful consideration must be given of the 'acuteness' or otherwise of the poorer PS. Platinum is one of the standard chemotherapies in advanced NSCLC but toxicity of cisplatin has led investigators to evaluate non-platinum regimens. Randomised trials still seem to conclude that cisplatin or carboplatin should remain a key component of combination therapy. Combination treatment with two drugs is better than single agent treatment but three drugs seem only to increase toxicity and while, as Nicolson points out, there is conflicting evidence on whether new drugs are better than old, it is certainly true that MVP and MIC have now been definitively superceded. It is equally established that there is no benefit to prolonging therapy beyond three or four cycles. In conclusion, Nicolson notes that the addition or substitution of chemotherapy drugs with 'novel' agents is still being investigated in many clinical trials and looks forward to the results of these evaluations which may directly assist the development of the evidence base for treatment of advanced disease.

We move briefly from the major focus of this book on non-small cell lung cancer to a consideration of developments in the management of mesothelioma. As Fennell and Rudd discuss in Chapter Eleven, there are currently around 1600 new cases of mesothelioma annually in the UK and the incidence is expected to at least double over the next 15 years. This reflects the increasing use of asbestos until the mid 1970s and the long latent period between exposure and disease. Mesothelioma is generally regarded as incurable and standard treatment focuses on symptom relief, social and psychological support. Early control of pleural effusions by effective pleurodesis is important and radiotherapy to biopsy tracks has been shown to prevent seeding of tumour in the subcutaneous tissues and should be used routinely. Radiotherapy may also, as the authors discuss, relieve pain and reduce chest wall masses, but has not been shown to prolong survival. Several chemotherapy regimens have recently been shown to produce radiological responses in around 20–40% of cases and, perhaps more importantly, symptomatic benefit in 50% or more of patients. These include, as Fennell and Rudd describe, single agent vinorelbine, the combination of mitomycin, vinblastine and cisplatin, gemcitabine with cisplatin or carboplatin, and pemetrexed with cisplatin or carboplatin. The combination of pemetrexed and cisplatin improves survival compared with cisplatin alone.

The important question of whether chemotherapy confers clinically significant survival and quality of life advantages compared with active supportive care is being addressed in MSO-1, a randomised study organised by the British Thoracic Society with the Medical Research Council Cancer Trials Unit, funded by CRUK. There is renewed interest in radical surgery in selected cases, in combination with other modalities, and a randomised trial of surgery is planned (MARS). Experimental approaches include immunotherapy, angiogenesis inhibitors and gene therapy.

No volume on the effective management of lung cancer would be complete without a detailed discussion of the new, biological treatments and it is this subject which constitutes Chapter Twelve, the final chapter of Part Three of this volume. As Fennell outlines, there is a growing perception that cytotoxic therapy for advanced NSCLC has reached a therapeutic plateau. Apoptosis resistance is a major factor limiting the effectiveness of current cytotoxic therapies for NSCLC and the molecular basis of intrinsic apoptosis resistance is poorly understood in this disease. However, rapid advances in our understanding of the core cell death machinery have highlighted important processes exploited by cancer cells to evade chemotherapy induced cell death. This presents, as the author describes, a unique opportunity to drive effective drug development. Mitochondria occupy a pivotal role in apoptosis regulation. Fennell elegantly describes how chemotherapy activates a final common cytotoxic pathway in which BCL-2 family multidomain pro-apoptotic proteins BAX and BAK target mitochondria, to release specific apoptogenic factors that mediate cell suicide via activation of serine proteases, termed *caspases*. BCL-2 inhibits BAX, BAK and is therefore a novel target for ongoing clinical trials with antisense oligonucleotides. Small molecule approaches are, as Fennell illustrates, emerging as an alternative strategy for BCL-2 inhibition and are now also entering clinical trials. NSCLC cells express inhibitors of apoptosis proteins (IAPs) survivin and XIAP, which directly bind and inhibit caspases and novel small molecule approaches to block such interactions now exist and are exhibiting chemosensitizing efficacy in pre-clinical models. Several growth factor signalling pathways converge on the core apoptosis machinery, inhibiting apoptosis. Epidermal growth factor receptor (EGFR) inactivates the BAX, BAK activator, BAD, via phosphotidylinositol 3 kinase/AKT dependent phosphorylation and BAD is also inactivated by the mitogen activated protein kinase (MAPK) kinase. The implications for effectiveness of EGFR targeted therapy by small molecules and antibodies now in the clinic, also find detailed discussion within this chapter which concliudes Part Three of the volume.

We have committed Part Four of the volume, the final Part, to a review of current issues in the clinical governance of lung cancer services. In the opening chapter, Peake describes the nature and impact of the UK Cancer Services Collaborative (CSC) Programme that was established early in 2000 with the aim of improving both the outcomes and experience of care for patients with cancer. As this author reminds us, the programme has utilised the techniques of process re-engineering and lung cancer has been one of the tumour sites targeted since the process began. It has now been 'rolled out' to all 34 English Cancer Networks with the employment of staff whose role is the 'embedding' of service improvement processes with the NHS. It is estimated that currently at least one third of lung cancer patients in England have their care delivered by clinical teams whose service has been significantly improved by this programme. Many hundreds of projects of varying sizes across the UK have led to major improvements in such areas as: (a) the speed of the referral, diagnostic and management processes, (b) the percentage of patients being assessed by a specialist team, (c) high quality multi-disciplinary team working, (d) improved communication between the various health care sectors, and (e) improved patient choice, both in terms of booking of hospital visits and in the information available to make informed management choices. There is no doubt that the techniques of service re-design that the CSC has employed have led to major improvements in the standards and timeliness of care and this has, as Peake describes, been supported by patient feedback studies. To what extent such an approach will improve survival is, as yet, unknown, but high quality national comparative audit is eventually becoming a reality and should help to monitor the changes.

The year 2004 has seen further concerted effort to involve patients in shaping health services. Patient and public involvement in the development of health services, together with the interesting concept of the 'expert patient' are, in politician-speak "high on the agenda". Patients may be involved in healthcare services provision by direct involvement in the process ("user representation") and by exerting external pressure for change and improvement (media campaigning, awareness raising and political lobbying). Unlike diseases such as breast cancer and HIV/AIDS, lung cancer has not previously benefited from a strong patient voice or from high profile public awareness campaigning. In recent years, the Roy Castle Lung Cancer Foundation (RCLCF) and others have been working to change this situation, as Baird documents within Chapter Fourteen. Indeed, in 2004, the number of lung cancer patient/carer representatives directly involved in shaping services, both in communicating their views and experiences and also in key committee membership, has increased. Projects, such as CancerVOICES and the RCLCF's lung cancer "user" representative training program, have provided direction and support for patients involved in local Cancer Network Lung Cancer Groups and other strategy setting bodies. Much, however, still needs to be done to research their impact and to ensure appropriate patient representation on appropriate committees.

The role of a properly integrated and functioning multi-disciplinary team (MDT) is now well recognised as of considerable importance to the effective and efficient operation of cancer services. Lung cancer is no exception in this context and in Chapter Fifteen, Fitzpatrick and Craig discuss the role of the lung cancer clinical nurse specialist in enhancing the quality of care available to patients. As the authors point out, the pathway of care can be bewildering to the patient with referral from one specialty to another, with one investigation followed by another, and with consultation with one clinician followed by further consultations with others. Continuity of clinical relationships has been consistently highlighted by patients as an important indicator of the quality of service provision and lung cancer nurse specialists increasingly function to provide this. In the UK there are about 150 nurses whose main role is specifically to care for people with lung cancer. To do this the specialist nurse accompanies the patient and family through their 'journey of care', providing continuity, support, information and advice on how to cope. An important role of lung cancer nurses is also to advise and educate on aspects of lung cancer care such as treatments and to be involved in the breaking bad news, assisting patients in the emotional readjustments that become necessary following a cancer diagnosis and prognosis and in ensuring adequate symptom control. Fitzpatrick and Craig describe how in some centres, nurse-led clinics routinely follow patients post-radiotherapy to offer ongoing emotional and pyschological support. Lung cancer nurse specialists additionally play an active role in research aimed at improving patients' quality of life, including the continuing development of techniques to help patients alter breathing patterns and to cope psychologically with intense feelings of fear and panic.

In illustration of the nursing theory discussed, Fitzpatrick and Craig document examples of how two two nurse led initiatives in Aberdeen, Scotland, have directly influenced patient care. They describe how in their unit, a respiratory support nurse liaises very closely with consultant staff, clerks bronchoscopy patients, arranges investigations, gathers results and organises MDT meetings. In the past these 'tasks of little educational value' were reluctantly performed by inexperienced SHO's with what the authors judge as little insight into patients' fear. In conjunction with a chest physician and an IT company, a lung cancer nurse developed an electronic patient record (EPR) recording the patient's "journey" from chest clinic through investigations, treatments, follow-up and, ultimately, death. The EPR significantly improved communication with general practitioners, reduced reliance on paper notes, reduced the workload preparing for MDT meetings and provided high quality prospective audit and research data.

Rightly or wrongly, depending on one's view, the cost of service provision retains a central and indeed contentious place in clinical, political and managerial debate and it is for this reason that we have included, as the concluding chapter of this volume, a particularly thorough and thought-provoking contribution from Ala Szczepura, Professor of Health Economics at Warwick University. No matter how health services are organised and paid for, what they provide are health care interventions; specific activities meant to reduce disease risk, treat illness, or palliate the consequences of disease and disability. Debates about whether health services should provide new drugs, or about the role of hospitals versus primary care, or about preventive versus curative activities are, at bottom, debates concerning the proper use of resources. In health, as in every other sector, users want value for money – whether they pay directly or indirectly, in their roles as taxpayers or as buyers of health insurance. It is true, as the author points out, that the importance of economic evaluation has risen as expenditure on health care has increased. Initially, government strategies in the UK and elsewhere in the 1990s focused on cost containment – trying to limit the increase in expenditure on health. Increasingly, however, information on benefits gained, as well as costs, is required to decide on the most efficient use of resources.

Knowing the net cost-effectiveness of interventions – the net gain in health (compared with doing nothing) relative to the cost – can be extremely useful. Government bodies can generate such information, and then use this to determine whether a particular intervention or service should be funded: this means judging the improvement in health compared with what would have happened in the absence of action. It is in this context that Szczepura provides a detailed consideration of the improvements needed in available evidence on costs and benefits in order to be able to assess cost-effectiveness and her chapter brings this book to a close in a most thought provoking manner.

In this Third Edition volume on the effective management of lung cancer, we have aimed to provide a state-of-the-art text on investigation and management that is as succinct as possible but as detailed as necessary. Consultants in respiratory medicine, cardiothoracic surgery and clinical and medical oncology and their staff grades and trainees are likely to find the volume of considerable importance to their practice and we recommend the volume wholeheartedly to these colleagues for this purpose. We anticipate, in addition, that the book will prove of considerable interest to clinical nurse specialists working in these specialties, to oncology pharmacists and to the commissioners and planners of cancer services as part of their function in facilitating the organisation and delivery of lung cancer clinical services. Finally, we thank AstraZeneca UK Ltd, Aventis Pharma UK, Bristol-Myers Squibb UK Ltd, Lilly Oncology UK Ltd and Pierre-Fabre UK Ltd for the award of the grants of unrestricted educational sponsorship that enabled the organisation of the 3rd and 4th national Key Advances Lung Cancer update symposia at The Royal College of Physicians of London and at which synopses of the constituent chapters of this volume were presented.

Martin Muers MA DPhil FRCP
Ken O'Byrne MD FRCP
Frank Wells MA MS FRCS
Andrew Miles MSc MPhil PhD

London, April 2005

PART 1

Genetics, screening and investigation

Chapter 1

Genetics of lung cancer: current thinking on the nature and assessment of genetic predisposition to the disease

Athena Matakidou, Richard Houlston and Tim Eisen

Introduction

Lung cancer is the most common cancer in the world, representing a major public health problem. In the United Kingdom it accounts for ~19% of all cancers and ~29% of all cancer deaths, is the commonest cause of cancer death in men, and is second only to breast cancer in women (CRC 1998). Tobacco smoking is undoubtedly the major aetiological risk factor: the risk is around 10 times higher in long-term smokers compared with non-smokers (Doll and Peto 1981). Around 16% of people who smoke develop the disease (Peto *et al.* 2000), raising the possibility that individuals may have differing susceptibilities to developing lung cancer when exposed to the same carcinogens, which may in part be genetically defined. Here we review the evidence for a genetic predisposition to lung cancer and the possible molecular basis of an inherited susceptibility.

The multi-step evolution of lung cancer

Multiple morphological steps are well recognised in lung carcinogenesis (Colby *et al.* 1998). In the development of squamous carcinoma, normal epithelial cells progress through hyperplasia, metaplasia and dysplasia (pre-malignant stages) into carcinoma *in situ* and eventually frank malignancy. Adenocarcinoma is also considered to develop at least in part from premalignant precursor lesions such as atypical adenomatous hyperplasia. These preneoplastic changes are frequently detected accompanying lung cancers and in the respiratory mucosa of smokers. Molecular biological studies have demonstrated that cancers carry multiple genetic and epigenetic changes, indicating inactivation of tumour suppressor genes and activation of dominant oncogenes (Sekido *et al.* 1998). To date relatively little is known about the molecular events preceding the development of lung carcinomas and the underlying genetic basis of tobacco-related lung carcinogenesis. However, recent studies have provided evidence of a multi-step accumulation of genetic and epigenetic alterations, which often accompany the sequential morphological changes (Wistuba *et al.* 2002; Osaka and Takahashi 2002) (Figure 1.1).

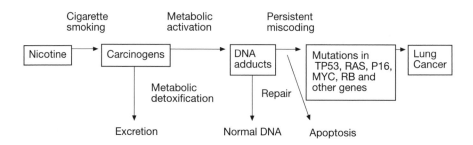

Figure 1.1 Accumulation of alterations in the multi-step progression of lung cancer carcinogenesis.

The genetic alterations accompanying lung carcinogenesis are thought to result in perturbation of the integrity of integrated signalling networks, which positively or negatively regulate various cellular processes to maintain homeostasis of the lung, leading to the carcinogenesis and progression of lung cancer. The accumulated genetic and epigenetic alterations are thought to confer various capabilities on lung cancer cells, including an escape from growth inhibitory signals and senescence events, resistance to apoptosis, sustained stimuli for proliferation and angiogenesis, and invasive and metastatic characteristics. The chronological order and catalogue of genes required to fully transform normal epithelial cells may vary among histological types of lung cancer or even within a given histological subtype.

Evidence for inherited susceptibility to lung cancer

Case-control and cohort studies

Epidemiological case-control and cohort studies have consistently shown that relatives of lung cancer cases have a twofold increased risk of developing the disease (Lee 1993; Houlston and Peto 1996). However, as most studies have been based on cases who smoked, familial aggregation of smoking habits could explain the excess risk of lung cancer in case families relative to control families. Some investigators have attempted to address this issue by taking into account smoking habits of the family members. Tokuhata and Lilienfeld (1963) found an excess risk of lung cancer in case relatives compared with control relatives irrespective of the relatives' smoking history. To minimise the impact of shared tobacco habits in families, a number of studies have estimated familial risks associated with non-smoker status (Schwartz *et al.* 1996; Wang *et al.* 1996; Wu *et al.* 1996; Mayne *et al.* 1999). Although the familial risks obtained from three out of these four studies were non-significant, pooling the data does, however, provide statistically significant support for an association between family history and lung cancer in non-smokers (OR 1.4; 95%CI: 1.0–1.9).

Twin studies

Twin studies have reported nearly equal values of familial relative risks in monozygotic (MZ) and dizygotic (DZ) pairs in males (Braun *et al.* 1994, 1995; Lichtenstein *et al.* 2000). This would suggest a strong environmental effect shared by twins (i.e. smoking behaviour) rather than a genetic component. Such data have widely been cited to counter the proposition that an inherited basis exists for lung cancer. Twin studies have, however, consistently shown greater concordance for smoking behaviour in MZ than DZ twins, suggesting that environmental exposure is being confounded by genetic influence in this study paradigm (Risch 2001). Yet, paradoxically, this concordance difference in smoking behaviour is not reflected in a concordance difference for lung cancer. A study of United States male twins found a greater concordance in smoking for MZ versus DZ twins, yet no difference in concordance for lung cancer (Goldgar *et al.* 1994). On the other hand, lung cancer in female twins (Lichtenstein *et al.* 2000), where the prevalence is much lower, did appear to follow a more conventional genetic pattern; risks in MZ were greater than in DZ twins, indicating a genetic predisposition.

Cancer syndromes predisposing to lung cancer

The only direct evidence of a genetic predisposition to date is provided by the increased risk of lung cancer associated with a number of rare Mendelian cancer syndromes. An increased lung cancer risk is observed in carriers of germ-line TP53 (Hwang *et al.* 2003) and retinoblastoma (Sanders *et al.* 1989) gene mutations, as well as in patients with xeroderma pigmentosum (Swift and Chase 1979), Bloom's syndrome (Takemiya *et al.* 1987) and Werner's syndrome (Yamanaka *et al.* 1997).

Genetic models of lung cancer susceptibility

Formal statistical modelling of the familial aggregation of lung cancer has suggested that the pattern of inheritance is best explained by a model of the co-dominant inheritance of a rare autosomal gene predisposing to the disease. Sellers *et al.* (1994) estimated that such a gene mutation could be responsible for 69% of lung cancer occurring at the age of 50 falling to 22% of cases at age 70. In an analogous situation to *BRCA1* and breast cancer, such a gene would be rare and would not account for much of the excess lung cancer risk seen in relatives of cases. However, if present, it would be associated with a large relative risk, giving rise to multigenerational families. Such highly penetrant mutations can be detected through genetic linkage (the assessment of segregation of genetic markers with disease in families). Unfortunately very few large, multi-generationally affected lung cancer families have been described and to date no genetic linkage has been established.

A polygenic mechanism might provide a more plausible explanation for the remaining familial risk. Under such a model, a large number of alleles, each conferring a small genotypic risk (perhaps of the order of 1.5–2.0), combine additively or multiplicatively to confer susceptibility. More than 100 such variants might contribute to susceptibility. Individuals carrying few such alleles would be at reduced risk, while those with many might suffer a lifetime risk as high as 50%. Such alleles will rarely cause multiple-case families and their detection is reliant on association studies (comparison of the frequency of genotypes in cases with controls).

Candidate loci for lung cancer susceptibility genes

There are more than 60 carcinogens in cigarette smoke (IARC 2002). Among these, tobacco-specific nitrosamines (such as 4-(methylnitrosamino)-1-(3-pyridyl)-1-butanone (NNK)), polycyclic aromatic hydrocarbons (such as benzo(a)pyrene) and aromatic amines probably play an important role in the development of cancer (Hecht 2003). In addition cigarette smoke is a rich source of reactive oxygen species (free radicals), which may also contribute to lung cancer pathogenesis (Pryor and Stone 1993).

Figure 1.2 shows the relationship between tobacco smoke and lung cancer. Nicotine addiction causes continual cigarette smoking and chronic exposure to carcinogens. Carcinogens such as NNK and polycyclic aromatic hydrocarbons are metabolically activated to intermediates that react with DNA, forming covalently bound products known as DNA adducts. Competing with this is the metabolic detoxification of carcinogens to harmless excreted products. If the DNA adducts are repaired by cellular repair enzymes, DNA is returned to its normal, undamaged state. However if the adducts persist during DNA replication, miscoding can occur, resulting in a permanent mutation in the DNA sequence. Cells with damaged DNA may be removed by apoptosis. If a mutation occurs in a critical region of an oncogene (RAS, MYC) or tumour suppressor gene (*TP53*), it can lead to activation/deactivation of this gene. Multiple events of this type lead to aberrant cells with loss of normal cellular growth-control regulation and, ultimately, to lung cancer development.

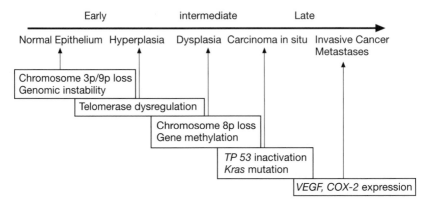

Figure 1.2 Scheme linking nicotine addiction and lung cancer through tobacco smoke carcinogens and their induction of multiple mutations in critical genes.

Any inherited susceptibility to lung cancer is likely to be mediated through biological differences in the bio-activation/degradation of carcinogens or cellular response to damage (e.g. DNA repair, cell-cycle control). It is almost inevitable that the loci currently considered as candidate low-penetrance susceptibility alleles are based on preconceptions of cancer biology and it is likely that other, as yet unrecognised, genes may influence tumour development. The number of candidate loci will inevitably increase with advances in cancer biology.

Table 1.1 summarises the genes implicated to date in lung cancer predisposition. Despite considerable research effort, few definite lung cancer susceptibility alleles have been identified. As with many other diseases, many positive associations have been reported, but few of the initial positive results have been replicated by subsequent studies (Table 1.1). The most likely explanation for this has been the inadequate sample size of most, but not all, existing studies. The inherent statistical uncertainty of case-control studies involving just a few hundred cases and controls limits their ability to reliably identify genetic determinants of modest but potentially important impact. Hence, most of the small case-control studies on the role of genetic polymorphisms and cancer risk have provided inconsistent results. The feasibility of identifying low penetrance genes through association analyses is contingent on the ascertainment and collection of a large series of lung cancer cases and controls. One such DNA collection and epidemiological database, called the Genetic Lung Cancer Predisposition Study (GELCAPS), is under construction in the United Kingdom. This study aims to collect DNA and epidemiological data from 3000 patients with lung cancer and a similar number of controls.

Conclusion

Recent technological developments have accelerated the search for genes predisposing to a variety of multifactorial diseases, including lung cancer. The completion of the human genome project has provided a vast amount of information regarding inter-individual variability at the genomic level and is providing an increasing number of candidate susceptibility loci. Recent engineering advances are yielding high-throughput genotyping technologies (Lander 1999) that have allowed rapid and highly reliable association studies to be initiated. These developments promise to advance our knowledge on lung cancer predisposition and allow the construction of individual lung cancer risk profiles. Identification of individuals at high risk of lung cancer will allow targeted screening leading to improvements in early diagnosis, intervention strategies for treatment of preneoplasia and neoplasia, and continued improvements in public health policy.

Finally it is important to note that such low-penetrance susceptibility alleles will need to be considered in the context of other risk factors. In lung cancer the risk of any low-penetrance gene studied to date is substantially less than the risk of lung cancer from smoking. Although our current data suggest the risk of lung cancer might

Table 1.1 Genes implicated in or with an established role in lung cancer

	Gene	Mechanism relevant to cancer	Details
Carcinogen metabolism	CYP1A1	Bioactivation of tobacco procarcinogens	**(=)** Le Marchand et al. (2003)
	CYP2D6		(=) Kiyohara et al. (2002)
	CYP2E1		(=) Kiyohara et al. (2002)
	CYP2C9		(=) Kiyohara et al. (2002)
	CYP2A6		(=) Kiyohara et al. (2002)
	CYP2C19		(=) Kiyohara et al. (2002)
	NAT1	Activation and inactivation of tobacco-derived aromatic amines	(=) Wilkman et al. (2001)
	NAT2		(=) Wilkman et al. (2001)
	GSTM1	Detoxification of polycyclic aromatic hydrocarbon (PAH) carcinogens	**(=)** Benhamou et al. (2002)
	GSTM4		(+) Liloglou et al. (2002)
	GSTM3		(=) Risch et al. (2001)
	GSTT1		(=) Nazar-Stewart et al. (2003)
	GSTTP1		(=) To-Figueras et al. (1999)
	SULT1A1	Bioactivation of aromatic amines	(+) Wang et al. (2002)
	mEH	Bioactivation of PAHs	**(-)** Lee et al. (2002)
	MPO	Activation of benzo(a)pyrene	(=) Feyler et al. (2002) Dally et al. (2002)
	NQO1	Activation of nitrosamines	(=) Kiyohara et al. (2002)
Methylation	MTHFR	Changes in DNA methylation (transcriptional activation/ silencing)	(+) Siemianowicz et al. (2003)
	DNMT3B		(+) Shen et al. (2002b)
Nucleotide excision repair	XPA	Repair of tobacco-related DNA adducts	(–) Wu et al. (2003)
	XPD		(+) Goode et al. (2002)
	XPG		(+) Jeon et al. (2003)
	XPC		(+) Cheng et al. (2000)
Homologous recombination	XRCC3	Repair of DNA strand breaks generated by reactive oxygen species in tobacco smoke	(=) Goode et al. (2002)
	DNA ligase I		(=) Shen et al. (2002a)
	Poly(ADP) ribose		(=) Gu et al. (1999)
Base excision repair	OGG1	Repair of DNA damage due to reactive oxygen species in tobacco smoke	(+) Goode et al. (2002)
	XRCC1		(=) Goode et al. (2002)
	APE/ref1		(=) Misra et al. (2003)
Free radical system	hGPX1	Detoxification of tobacco smoke-related free radicals	(+) Ratnasinghe et al. (2000)
	NE		(+) Taniguchi et al. (2002)
	MNSOD		(=) Lin et al. (2003)
	MMP-1		(+) Zhu et al. (2001)
	ADH3		(+) Yang et al. (2002)

(+), Suggested increased risk; (–), suggested reduced risk; (=), non-significant effect; results from meta-analyses tabulated in bold.

Table 1.1 contd.

	Gene	Mechanism relevant to cancer	Details
Apoptosis	TP53 TP73 TP21	Mediation of cellular responses to genotoxic insults by tobacco carcinogens	(=) Matakidou et al. (2003) (=) Hiraki et al. (2003) (=) Su et al. (2003)
Proto-oncogene	HRAS-VNTR L-MYC	Control of cell growth and differentiation	(=) Pierce et al. (2000) (+) Shih et al. (2002)
Other genes	AGT	Repair of DNA adducts induced by the tobacco-specific nitrosamine NNK	(+) Kaur et al. (2000)
	RAGE	Regulation of invasive process extension and cell migration in tumour cells	(+) Schenk et al. (2001)
	DRD2	Role in smoking status and addiction	(=) Qi et al. (2002)
	TNFB	Host inflammatory response to lung cancer	(–) Shimura et al. (1994)

(+), Suggested increased risk; (–), suggested reduced risk; (=), non-significant effect; results from meta-analyses tabulated in bold.

be modulated by the genetics of carcinogen metabolism and cellular repair, smoking cessation clearly decreases lung cancer risk, and so patients should not assume that they cannot affect their risk because of inheritance.

Acknowledgements

Athena Matakidou is in receipt of a fellowship by the Alan J. Lerner Fund.

References

Benhamou, S., Lee, W. J., Alexandrie, A. K., Boffetta, P., Bouchardy, C., Butkiewicz, D., Brockmoller, J., Clapper, M. L., Daly, A., Dolzan, V. *et al.* (2002). Meta- and pooled analyses of the effects of glutathione S-transferase M1 polymorphisms and smoking on lung cancer risk. *Carcinogenesis* **23**, 1343–1350.

Braun, M. M., Caporaso, N. E., Page, W. F. & Hoover, R. N. (1994). Genetic component of lung cancer: cohort study of twins. *Lancet* **344**, 440–443.

Braun, M. M., Caporaso, N. E., Page, W. F. & Hoover, R. N. (1995). A cohort study of twins and cancer. *Cancer Epidemiology, Biomarkers and Prevention* **4**, 469–473.

Cheng, L., Spitz, M. R., Hong, W.K. & Wei, Q. (2000). Reduced expression levels of nucleotide excision repair genes in lung cancer: a case-control analysis. *Carcinogenesis* **21**, 1527–1530.

Colby, T. V., Wistuba, I. I. & Gazdar, A. (1998). Precursors to pulmonary neoplasia. *Advances in Anatomic Pathology* **5**, 205–215.

CRC (1998). Cancer Research Campaign Factsheet 4: Smoking and cancer.

Dally, H., Gassner, K., Jager, B., Schmezer, P., Spiegelhalder, B., Edler, L., Drings, P., Dienemann, H., Schulz, V., Kayser, K. *et al.* (2002). Myeloperoxidase (MPO) genotype and lung cancer histologic types: the MPO -463 A allele is associated with reduced risk for small cell lung cancer in smokers. *International Journal of Cancer* **102**, 530–535.

Doll, R. & Peto, R. (1981). *The Cause of Cancer*, p. 1221. Oxford: Oxford University Press.

Feyler, A., Voho, A., Bouchardy, C., Kuokkanen, K., Dayer, P., Hirvonen, A. & Benhamou, S. (2002). Point: myeloperoxidase -463G→A polymorphism and lung cancer risk. *Cancer Epidemiology, Biomarkers and Prevention* **11**, 1550–1554.

Goldgar, D. E., Easton, D. F., Cannon-Albright, L. A. & Skolnick, M. H. (1994). Systematic population-based assessment of cancer risk in first-degree relatives of cancer probands. *Journal of the National Cancer Institute* **86**, 1600–1608.

Goode, E. L., Ulrich, C. M. & Potter, J. D. (2002). Polymorphisms in DNA repair genes and associations with cancer risk. *Cancer Epidemiology, Biomarkers and Prevention* **11**, 1513–1530.

Gu, J., Spitz, M. R., Yang, F. & Wu, X. (1999). Ethnic differences in poly(ADP-ribose) polymerase pseudogene genotype distribution and association with lung cancer risk. *Carcinogenesis* **20**, 1465–1469.

Hecht, S.S. (2003). Tobacco carcinogens, their biomarkers and tobacco-induced cancer. *Nature Reviews Cancer* **3**, 733–744.

Hiraki, A., Matsuo, K., Hamajima, N., Ito, H., Hatooka, S., Suyama, M., Mitsudomi, T. & Tajima, K. (2003). Different risk relations with smoking for non-small-cell lung cancer: comparison of TP53 and TP73 genotypes. *Asian Pacific Journal of Cancer Prevention* **4**, 107–112.

Houlston, R. S. & Peto, J. (2004). Genetics of common cancers. In *Genetic Predisposition to Cancer* (ed. R. A. Eeles, B. Ponder, D. E. Easton & A. Horwich) 2nd edition, pp. 208–226. London: Arnold.

Hwang, S. J., Cheng, L. S., Lozano, G., Amos, C. I., Gu, X. & Strong, L.C. (2003). Lung cancer risk in germline p53 mutation carriers: association between an inherited cancer predisposition, cigarette smoking, and cancer risk. *Human Genetics* **113**, 238–243.

IARC (International Agency for Research on Cancer) (2002). Tobacco smoke and involuntary smoking. *IARC Monographs on the Evaluation of Carcinogenic Risks to Humans,* vol. 83. Lyon: IARC.

Jeon, H. S., Kim, K. M., Park, S. H., Lee, S. Y., Choi, J. E., Lee, G. Y., Kam, S., Park, R. W., Kim, I. S., Kim, C. H. *et al.* (2003). Relationship between XPG codon 1104 polymorphism and risk of primary lung cancer. *Carcinogenesis* **24**, 1677–1681.

Kaur, T. B., Travaline, J. M., Gaughan, J. P., Richie, J. P. Jr, Stellman, S. D. & Lazarus, P. (2000). Role of polymorphisms in codons 143 and 160 of the O6-alkylguanine DNA alkyltransferase gene in lung cancer risk. *Cancer Epidemiology, Biomarkers and Prevention* **9**, 339–342.

Kiyohara, C., Otsu, A., Shirakawa, T., Fukuda, S. & Hopkin, J.M. (2002). Genetic polymorphisms and lung cancer susceptibility: a review. *Lung Cancer* **37**, 241–256.

Lander, E. S. (1999). Array of hope. *Nature Genetics* **21**, 3–4.

Le Marchand, L., Guo, C., Benhamou, S., Bouchardy, C., Cascorbi, I., Clapper, M. L., Garte, S., Haugen, A., Ingelman-Sundberg, M., Kihara, M. *et al.* (2003). Pooled analysis of the CYP1A1 exon 7 polymorphism and lung cancer. *Cancer Causes and Control* **14**, 339–346.

Lee, P. N. (1993). Epidemiological studies relating family history of lung cancer to risk of the disease. *Indoor Environment* **2**, 129–142.

Lee, W. J., Brennan, P., Boffetta, P., London, S. J., Benhamou, S., Rannug, A., To-Figueras, J., Ingelman-Sundberg, M., Shields, P., Gaspari, L. *et al.* (2002). Microsomal epoxide hydrolase polymorphisms and lung cancer risk: a quantitative review. *Biomarkers* **7**, 230–241.

Lichtenstein, P., Holm, N. V., Verkasalo, P. K., Iliadou, A., Kaprio, J., Koskenvuo, M., Pukkala, E., Xkytthe, Z. & Hemminki, K. (2000). Environmental and heritable factors in the causation of cancer. *New England Journal of Medicine* **343**, 78–85.

Liloglou, T., Walters, M., Maloney, P., Youngson, J. & Field, J. K. (2002). A T2517C polymorphism in the GSTM4 gene is associated with risk of developing lung cancer. *Lung Cancer* **37**, 143–146.

Lin, P., Hsueh, Y. M., Ko, J. L., Liang, Y. F., Tsai, K. J. & Chen, C. Y. (2003). Analysis of NQO1, GSTP1, and MnSOD genetic polymorphisms on lung cancer risk in Taiwan. *Lung Cancer* **40**, 123–129.

Matakidou, A., Eisen, T. & Houlston, R. S. (2003). TP53 polymorphisms and lung cancer risk: a systematic review and meta-analysis. *Mutagenesis* **18**, 377–385.

Mayne, S. T., Buenconsejo, J. & Janerich, D. T. (1999). Familial cancer history and lung cancer risk in United States non-smoking men and women. *Cancer Epidemiology, Biomarkers and Prevention* **8**, 1065–1069.

Misra, R. R., Ratnasinghe, D., Tangrea, J. A., Virtamo, J., Andersen, M. R., Barrett, M., Taylor, P. R. & Albanes, D. (2003) Polymorphisms in the DNA repair genes XPD, XRCC1, XRCC3, and APE/ref-1, and the risk of lung cancer among male smokers in Finland. *Cancer Letters* **191**, 171–178.

Nazar-Stewart, V., Vaughan, T. L., Stapleton, P., Van Loo, J., Nicol-Blades, B. & Eaton, D. L. (2003). A population-based study of glutathione S-transferase M1, T1 and P1 genotypes and risk for lung cancer. *Lung Cancer* **40**, 247–258.

Osaka, H. & Takahashi, T. (2002). Genetic alterations of multiple tumour suppressors and oncogenes in the carcinogenesis and progression of lung cancer. *Oncogene* **21**, 7421–7434.

Peto, R., Darby, S., Deo, H., Silcocks, P., Whitley, E. & Doll, R. (2000). Smoking, smoking cessation, and lung cancer in the UK since 1950: combination of national statistics with two case-control studies. *British Medical Journal* **321**, 323–329.

Pierce, L. M., Sivaraman, L., Chang, W., Lum, A., Donlon, T., Seifried, A., Wilkens, L. R., Lau, A.F. & Le Marchand, L. (2000). Relationships of TP53 codon 72 and HRAS1 polymorphisms with lung cancer risk in an ethnically diverse population. *Cancer Epidemiology, Biomarkers and Prevention* **9**, 1199–1204.

Pryor, W. A. & Stone, K. (1993). Oxidants in cigarette smoke. Radicals, hydrogen peroxide, peroxynitrate, and peroxynitrite. *Annals of the New York Academy of Sciences* **686**, 12–27.

Qi, J., Tan, W., Xing, D., Miao, X. & Lin, D. (2002). Study on the association between smoking behaviour and dopamine receptor D2 gene polymorphisms among lung cancer cases. *Zhonghua Liu Xing Bing Xue Za Zhi* **23**, 370–373.

Ratnasinghe, D., Tangrea, J. A., Andersen, M. R., Barrett, M. J., Virtamo, J., Taylor, P. R. & Albanes, D. (2000). Glutathione peroxidase codon 198 polymorphism variant increases lung cancer risk. *Cancer Research* **60**, 6381–6383.

Risch, A., Wikman, H., Thiel, S., Schmezer, P., Edler, L., Drings, P., Dienemann, H., Kayser, K., Schulz, V., Spiegelhalder, B. *et al.* (2001). Glutathione-S-transferase M1, M3, T1 and P1 polymorphisms and susceptibility to non-small-cell lung cancer subtypes and hamartomas. *Pharmacogenetics* **11**, 757–764.

Risch, N. (2001). The genetic epidemiology of cancer: interpreting family and twin studies and their implications for molecular genetic approaches. *Cancer Epidemiology, Biomarkers and Prevention* **10**, 733–741.

Sanders, B. M., Jay, M., Draper, G. J. & Roberts, E. M. (1989). Non-ocular cancer in relatives of retinoblastoma patients. *British Journal of Cancer* **60**, 358–365.

Schenk, S., Schraml, P., Bendik, I. & Ludwig, C. U. (2001). A novel polymorphism in the promoter of the RAGE gene is associated with non-small cell lung cancer. *Lung Cancer* **32**, 7–12.

Schwartz, A. G., Yang, P. & Swanson, G. M. (1996). Familial risk of lung cancer among nonsmokers and their relatives. *American Journal of Epidemiology* **144**, 554–562.

Sekido, Y., Fong, K. M. & Minna, J. D. (1998). Progress in understanding the molecular pathogenesis of human lung cancer. *Biochimica et Biophysica Acta* **1378**, F21–F59.

Sellers, T. A., Chen, P. L., Potter, J. D., Bailey-Wilson, J. E., Rothschild, H. & Elston, R. C. (1994). Segregation analysis of smoking-associated malignancies: evidence for Mendelian inheritance. *American Journal of Medical Genetics* **52**, 308–314.

Shen, H., Spitz, M. R., Qiao, Y., Zheng, Y., Hong, W. K. & Wei, Q. (2002a). Polymorphism of DNA ligase I and risk of lung cancer: a case-control analysis. *Lung Cancer* **36**, 243–247.

Shen, H., Wang, L., Spitz, M. R., Hong, W. K., Mao, L. & Wei, Q. (2002b). A novel polymorphism in human cytosine DNA-methyltransferase-3B promoter is associated with an increased risk of lung cancer. *Cancer Research* **62**, 4992–4995.

Shih, C. M., Kuo, Y. Y., Wang, Y. C., Jian, S. L., Hsu, Y. T., Wu, H. Y., Guo, M. W. & Wang, Y. C. (2002). Association of L-myc polymorphism with lung cancer susceptibility and prognosis in relation to age-selected controls and stratified cases. *Lung Cancer* **36**, 125–132.

Shimura, T., Hagihara, M., Takebe, K., Munkhbat, B., Odaka, T., Kato, H., Nagamachi, Y. & Tsuji, K. (1994). The study of tumor necrosis factor beta gene polymorphism in lung cancer patients. *Cancer* **73**, 1184–1188.

Siemianowicz, K., Gminski, J., Garczorz, W., Slabiak, N., Goss, M., Machalski, M. & Magiera-Molendowska, H. (2003). Methylenetetrahydrofolate reductase gene C677T and A1298C polymorphisms in patients with small cell and non-small cell lung cancer. *Oncology Reports* **10**, 1341–1344.

Su, L., Liu, G., Zhou, W., Xu, L. L., Miller, D. P., Park, S., Lynch, T. J., Wain, J. C. & Christiani, D. C. (2003). No association between the p21 codon 31 serine-arginine polymorphism and lung cancer risk. *Cancer Epidemiology, Biomarkers and Prevention* **12**, 174–175.

Swift, M. & Chase, C. (1979). Cancer in families with xeroderma pigmentosum. *Journal of the National Cancer Institute* **62**, 1415–1421.

Takemiya, M., Shiraishi, S., Teramoto, T. & Miki, Y. (1987). Bloom's syndrome with porokeratosis of Mibelli and multiple cancers of the skin, lung and colon. *Clinical Genetics* **31**, 35–44.

Taniguchi, K., Yang, P., Jett, J., Bass, E., Meyer, R., Wang, Y., Deschamps, C. & Liu, W. (2002). Polymorphisms in the promoter region of the neutrophil elastase gene are associated with lung cancer development. *Clinical Cancer Research* **8**, 1115–1120.

To-Figueras, J., Gene, M., Gomez-Catalan, J., Pique, E., Borrego, N., Carrasco, J. L., Ramon, J. & Corbella, J. (1999). Genetic polymorphism of glutathione S-transferase P1 gene and lung cancer risk. *Cancer Causes Control* **10**, 65–70.

Tokuhata, G. K. & Lilienfeld, A. M. (1963). Familial aggregation of lung cancer in humans. *Journal of the National Cancer Institute* **30**, 289–312.

Wang, T. J., Zhou, B. S. & Shi, J. P. (1996). Lung cancer in nonsmoking Chinese women: a case-control study. *Lung Cancer* **14**, S93–S98.

Wang, Y., Spitz, M. R., Tsou, A. M., Zhang, K., Makan, N. & Wu, X. (2002). Sulfotransferase (SULT) 1A1 polymorphism as a predisposition factor for lung cancer: a case-control analysis. *Lung Cancer* **35**, 137–142.

Wikman, H., Thiel, S., Jager, B., Schmezer, P., Spiegelhalder, B., Edler, L., Dienemann, H., Kayser, K., Schulz, V., Drings, P., Bartsch, H. & Risch, A. (2001). Relevance of N-acetyltransferase 1 and 2 (NAT1, NAT2) genetic polymorphisms in non-small cell lung cancer susceptibility. *Pharmacogenetics* **11**, 157–168.

Wistuba, I. I., Mao, L. & Gazdar, A. F. (2002). Smoking molecular damage in bronchial epithelium. *Oncogene* **21**, 7298–7306.

Wu, A. H., Fontham, E. T., Reynolds, P., Greenberg, R. S., Buffler, P., Liff, J., Boyd, J. & Correa, P. (1996). Family history of cancer and risk of lung cancer among lifetime non smoking women in the United States. *American Journal of Epidemiology* **143**, 535–542.

Wu, X., Hudmon, K. S., Detry, M. A., Chamberlain, R. M. & Spitz, M. R. (2000). D2 dopamine receptor gene polymorphisms among African-Americans and Mexican-Americans: a lung cancer case-control study. *Cancer Epidemiology, Biomarkers and Prevention* **9**, 1021–1026.

Wu, X., Zhao, H., Wei, Q., Amos, C. I., Zhang, K., Guo, Z., Qiao, Y., Hong, W. K. & Spitz, M. R. (2003). XPA polymorphism associated with reduced lung cancer risk and a modulating effect on nucleotide excision repair capacity. *Carcinogenesis* **24**, 505–509.

Yamanaka, A., Hirai, T., Ohtake, Y. & Kitagawa, M. (1997). Lung cancer associated with Werner's syndrome: a case report and review of the literature. *Japanese Journal of Clinical Oncology* **27**, 415–418.

Yang, M., Coles, B. F., Delongchamp, R., Lang, N. P. & Kadlubar, F. F. (2002). Effects of the ADH3, CYP2E1, and GSTP1 genetic polymorphisms on their expressions in Caucasian lung tissue. *Lung Cancer* **38**, 15–21.

Zhu, Y., Spitz, M. R., Lei, L., Mills, G. B. & Wu, X. (2001). A single nucleotide polymorphism in the matrix metalloproteinase-1 promoter enhances lung cancer susceptibility. *Cancer Research* **61**, 7825–7829.

Chapter 2

Population screening for lung cancer using computed tomography

Peter Armstrong

Introduction

The underlying concept of an early lung cancer detection programme is that significantly more cures are achieved when stage I tumours are found in asymptomatic individuals, since the surgical results and 5-year survival figures are much better, compared with patients not in a screening programme who often first present with symptoms. It is well accepted that 5-year survival rates for stage 1A non-small cell carcinomas are of the order of 65–75% and that survival rates are significantly worse in patients who present with higher stages. Since most patients currently present with a higher stage tumour, the average 5-year survival for lung cancer is currently approximately 15–20%.

Table 2.1 CT screening of asymptomatic individuals

	USA (Henschke 1999)	Japan (Kaneko 1996 and 2000)	Japan (Sone 2001)	Germany (Diederich 2002)	USA (Swensen 2003)
Number	1000	1669	5483	817	1520
Age	>60	>50	>40	>40	>50
Patients with lung cancer	27	15	22	11	22
Patients with lung cancer (%)	2.7	0.43	0.48	1.3	1.5
Stage I (%)	85	93	88	73	57

The outcome of the published studies of low-dose computed tomography (CT) screening of asymptomatic populations for lung cancer from the USA, Europe and Japan (Table 2.1) shows that:

- the diagnostic yield of lung cancer from CT screening is reasonable and is far superior to chest radiography
- a very high proportion of the cancers diagnosed are stage I, and those that are stage I are almost all stage IA
- the cancer diagnosis rate is, however, highly dependent on the inclusion criteria, with a much higher incidence of lung cancer when the age of those screened is

above 60, and when the screening CT is limited to those with strong smoking history
- the pick-up rate of clinically insignificant benign nodules is very high
- as expected, the pick-up rate of lung cancers and the false positive rate both drop considerably in the later rounds of screening.

Imaging algorithms to determine the nature of a small pulmonary nodule

The high false positive rate, at least in the initial screening round, is a potentially major disadvantage of screening CT. In the Early Lung Cancer Action Project (ELCAP) study (Henschke *et al.* 1999), 233 of 1000 (23.3%) patients were found to have at least one non-calcified nodule. Therefore, an algorithm was developed for nodules less than 10 mm in diameter. The algorithm uses follow-up to assess interval growth and limits biopsy to those nodules whose characteristics make lung cancer likely. Nodules larger than 10 mm are biopsied. Remarkably, using this algorithm, only 28 of the 233 patients with non-calcified nodules required biopsy. Of these nodules, all but one proved to be malignant.

It is generally regarded as unwise to follow a non-calcified nodule larger than 1 cm with imaging characteristics compatible with bronchial carcinoma, because it is believed that the delay inherent in any follow-up protocol would be detrimental to life expectancy. Follow-up, however, is the standard approach to a subcentimetre nodule detected at CT, largely because of the much higher probability of any particular nodule being an incidental benign lesion. There is, in reality, no practical alternative: such small lesions are not in general suitable for biopsy, positron emission tomography (PET) or contrast enhancement, and a large majority of patients would be severely disadvantaged by indiscriminate surgical resection. Also, with such small lesions, the hope is that the benefit of some delay, to check that the growth rate is compatible with lung cancer, thereby avoiding unnecessary surgery for benign lesions, will outweigh the disadvantage of delaying treatment for what should still be a small tumour at the time of surgery.

A variety of algorithms, which differ in points of detail, have been recommended (Yankelevitz & Henschke 2000). The approach advocated by the author is to stratify patients with non-calcified nodules into groups:

- Subjects with multiple clustered nodules, all of which are under 1cm in diameter, should be handled in the same manner as subjects who have normal chest CTs. The diagnosis is overwhelmingly likely to be old granulomatous disease.
- Single nodules up to 4 mm in diameter should be followed with repeat CT screening at 12 months. The concept behind this recommendation is that, based on the expected growth rates of non-small cell lung cancers (Garland *et al.* 1963; Spratt *et al.* 1963; Strauss 1974; Weiss 1974; Chahinian 1992), the great majority

of nodules that are in fact bronchial carcinomas will still be no larger than 10 or 11 mm in diameter.

- The shape and density of nodules between 5 and 10 mm in diameter should be assessed. If the lesion is clearly linear, Y-shaped or another specifically benign shape, then the lesion can be assumed to be benign. If none of these benign shapes is present, then follow-up CT after 3 months should be performed. The frequency of follow-up beyond 3 months should be tailored to the estimated range of possible growth rates determined at the first 3-monthly review.
- Above 1 cm in diameter, the approach is identical to that usually used for a solitary pulmonary nodule discovered on plain chest radiography.

It is possible to detect *in vivo* growth of small nodules after 30 days, even in cancers growing at average rates (Yankelevitz *et al.* 1999, 2000; Ko & Betke 2001). It is important, however, not to underestimate the difficulty in accurately determining the growth rate of nodules under 1 cm in diameter. A nodule only has to increase its diameter by 26% to double its volume. For example, a 5 mm nodule which doubles in volume during a 6-month period will increase in diameter by just 1.25 mm, a difference which requires meticulous methods of nodule measurement, preferably using dedicated software (Zhao *et al.* 1999). With appropriate software it is possible to achieve accuracies within 3% for volume measurement with phantom nodules, but inter-observer agreement *in vivo* can differ by up to 20% (Wormanns *et al.* 2000). To gain widespread application, however, the various computerised methods will need to become more widely accessible and less labour intensive.

Recent advances in technology, notably multidetector CT scanners, cine viewing, computerised nodule detection systems (Tillich *et al.* 1997; Armato *et al.* 1999; MacMahon *et al.* 1999; Reeves & Kostis 2000; Armato *et al.* 2001; Ko & Betke 2001; Wormanns *et al.* 2002) and three-dimensional reconstruction techniques, may improve the ability of low-dose helical CT to detect and accurately characterise lung nodules, but all the available systems both under- and over-diagnose nodules compared with human observers and are, therefore, used adjunctively along with radiologists.

Important biases in cancer screening programmes

The presumption that earlier diagnosis using CT necessarily equates to a decrease in mortality from lung cancer is simplistic, because there are so many variables to take into account (Black 2000; Patz *et al.* 2000; Ellis & Gleeson 2001; Ellis *et al.* 2001). Three fundamental biases need to be considered: lead-time bias, length bias and over-diagnosis bias.

The term 'lead-time bias' refers to the extra life expectancy that occurs simply from diagnosing a tumour earlier, regardless of whether or not treatment is effective. In other words, moving the time of diagnosis of a lung cancer forward inevitably improves 5-year survivals, which are calculated from the time of diagnosis, regardless of the effect on mortality.

The term 'length bias' refers to the tendency for a screening test to diagnose tumours with an inherently better prognosis, for example atypical adenomatous hyperplasia, than the usual tumours discovered by standard methods, particularly at the first examination. The volume-doubling time of the lung cancers found in one of the two large Japanese CT screening programmes (Hasegawa et al. 2000) was a mean of 15 months (range 1 to 40 months); by way of comparison the vast majority of lung cancers found by means other than CT screening double their volume with a median time of around 6 months (Garland et al. 1963; Spratt et al. 1963; Strauss 1974; Weiss 1974; Chahinian 1992; Usuda et al. 1994; Winer-Muram et al. 2002). This suggests that length bias could be a highly significant factor.

Over-diagnosis bias, namely diagnosing a benign lesion as a malignant tumour, or diagnosing a very slow-growing malignancy that would not kill the patient during his or her natural life expectancy, is an extreme form of length bias. The evidence for over-diagnosis centres on the presence of atypical adenomatous hyperplasia in a small but significant proportion of patients in all CT screening programmes (Vazquez & Flieder 2000; Kawakami et al. 2001).

These three biases can be minimised by comparing disease-specific deaths (i.e. deaths due to lung cancer) in a randomised controlled trial of a screened versus a non-screened population with sufficiently long follow-up to compensate for lead-time bias.

A fourth potential bias, namely 'selection bias' must be guarded against when designing a randomised trial. Selection bias occurs when conclusions are based on series of patients in whom the randomisation procedures did not result in truly similar groups, which may, therefore, not be representative of the population at large.

These biases explain why some screening programmes diagnose disease early, but do not necessarily lead to reduced mortality from the disease in question. Such programmes have the following characteristics when compared with historical or non-random controls:

- earlier stage at diagnosis and consequently improved resectability rates
- improved survival
- higher proportion of cancers
- no change in the number of late stage tumours
- no reduction in mortality.

There has been considerable debate regarding the advisability of introducing large scale CT screening for the early diagnosis of lung cancer (Smith 1999; Henschke & Yankelevitz 2000; Miettinen 2000; Patz et al. 2000; Aberle et al. 2001; Miettinen & Henschke 2001; Patz et al. 2001; Heffner & Silvestri 2002). The debate centres on how important the various biases are in the face of the clearly demonstrated ability of CT to detect lung cancers under a centimetre in size at a time when the tumour is still stage IA.

The need for a randomised controlled trial

The central aim of any population screening programme is to do more good than harm at an acceptable cost. The potential beneficial effects of a lung cancer CT screening programme are that it might extend life by reducing mortality due to the lung cancer. Potential harmful effects include extra radiation from repetitive CT examinations and the consequences of false positive diagnoses, notably anxiety due to lead-time, anxiety and complications from unnecessary further imaging, biopsy and even surgery. It will take a randomised control trial with many years of follow-up to determine any mortality reduction and until this vital piece of information is known it will not be possible to calculate the cost in any meaningful way. Important questions to answer in future large-scale studies include: does early detection using up-to-date CT techniques result in a measurable reduction in the mortality of lung cancer; can thoracotomy be limited largely to those patients with life-threatening malignancies; and can mass screening with helical CT be performed in a cost-effective manner?

References

Aberle, D. R., Gamsu, G., Henschke, C. I., Naidich, D. P. & Swensen, S. J. (2001). A consensus statement of the Society of Thoracic Radiology: screening for lung cancer with helical computed tomography. *Journal of Thoracic Imaging* **16**, 65–68.

Armato, S. G. III, Giger, M. L., Moran, C. J., Blackburn, J. T., Doi, K. & MacMahon, H. (1999). Computerised detection of pulmonary nodules on CT scans. *Radiographics* **19**, 1303–1311.

Armato, S. G. III, Giger, M. L. & MacMahon, H. (2001). Automated detection of lung nodules in CT scans: preliminary results. *Medical Physics* **28**, 1552–1561.

Black, W. C. (2000). Overdiagnosis: An underrecognised cause of confusion and harm in cancer screening. *Journal of the National Cancer Institute* **92**, 1280–1282.

Chahinian, P. (1992). Relationship between tumor doubling time and anatomoclinical features in 50 measurable pulmonary cancers. *Chest* **61**, 340–345.

Diederich, S., Wormanns, D., Semik, M., Thomas, M., Lenzen, H., Roos, N. & Heindel, W. (2002). Screening for early lung cancer with low-dose spiral CT: prevalence in 817 asymptomatic smokers. *Radiology* **222**, 773–781.

Ellis, J. R. & Gleeson, F. V. (2001). Lung cancer screening. *British Journal of Radiology* **74**, 478–485.

Ellis, S. M., Husband, J. E., Armstrong, P. & Hansell, D. M. (2001). Computed tomography screening for lung cancer: back to basics. *Clinical Radiology* **56**, 691–699.

Garland, L. H., Coulson, W. & Wollin, E. (1963). The rate of growth and apparent duration of untreated primary bronchial carcinoma. *Cancer* **16**, 697–707.

Hasegawa, M., Sone, S., Takashima, S., Li, F., Yang, Z.G., Maruyama, Y. & Watanabe, T. (2000). Growth rate of small lung cancers detected on mass CT screening. *British Journal of Radiology* **73**, 1252–1259.

Heffner, J. E. & Silvestri, G. (2002). CT screening for lung cancer: is smaller better? *American Journal of Respiratory and Critical Care Medicine* **165**, 433–434.

Henschke, C. I. & Yankelevitz, D. F. (2000). CT screening for lung cancer. *Radiologic Clinics of North America* **38**, 487–495, viii.

Henschke, C. I., McCauley, D. I., Yankelevitz, D. F., Naidich, D. P., McGuinness, G., Miettinen, O. S., Libby, D. M., Pasmantier, M. W., Koizumi, J., Altorki, N. K. *et al.* (1999). Early Lung Cancer Action Project: overall design and findings from baseline screening. *The Lancet* **354**, 99–105.

Kaneko, M., Eguchi, K., Ohmatsu, H., Kakinuma, R., Naruke, T., Suemasu, K. & Moriyama, N. (1996). Peripheral lung cancer: screening and detection with low-dose spiral CT versus radiography. *Radiology* **201**, 798–802.

Kaneko, M., Kusumoto, M., Kobayashi, T., Moriyama, N., Naruke, T., Ohmatsu, H., Kakinuma, R., Eguchi, K., Nishiyama, H. & Matsui, E. (2000). Computed tomography screening for lung carcinoma in Japan. *Cancer* **89**, 2485–2488.

Kawakami, S., Sone, S., Takashima, S., Li, F., Yang, Z. G., Maruyama, Y., Honda, T., Hasegawa, M. & Wang, J. C. (2001). Atypical adenomatous hyperplasia of the lung: correlation between high-resolution CT findings and histopathologic features. *European Radiology* **11**, 811–814.

Ko, J. P. & Betke, M. (2001). Chest CT: automated nodule detection and assessment of change over time – preliminary experience. *Radiology* **218**, 267–273.

MacMahon, H., Engelmann, R., Behlen, F. M., Hoffmann, K. R., Ishida, T., Roe, C., Metz, C. E. & Doi, K. (1999). Computer-aided diagnosis of pulmonary nodules: results of a large-scale observer test. *Radiology* **213**, 723–726.

Miettinen, O. S. (2000). Screening for lung cancer. *Radiologic Clinics of North America* **38**, 479–486.

Miettinen, O. S. & Henschke, C. I. (2001). CT screening for lung cancer: coping with nihilistic recommendations. *Radiology* **221**, 592–596.

Patz, E.F. Jr, Goodman, P. C. & Bepler, G. (2000). Screening for lung cancer. *New England Journal of Medicine* **343**, 1627–1633.

Patz, E.F. Jr, Black, W. C. & Goodman, P. C. (2001). CT screening for lung cancer: not ready for routine practice. *Radiology* **221**, 587–591.

Reeves, A. P. & Kostis, W. J. (2000). Computer-aided diagnosis for lung cancer. *Radiologic Clinics of North America* **38**, 497–509.

Smith, I. E. (1999). Screening for lung cancer: time to think positive. *The Lancet* **354**, 86–87.

Sone, S., Li, F., Yang, Z. G., Honda, T., Maruyama, Y., Takashima, S., Hasegawa, M., Kawakami, S., Kubo, K., Haniuda, M. *et al.* (2001). Results of three-year mass screening programme for lung cancer using mobile low-dose spiral computed tomography scanner. *British Journal of Cancer* **84**, 25–32.

Spratt, J. S., Spjut, H. J. & Roper, C. I. (1963). The frequency distribution of the rates of growth and the estimated duration of primary pulmonary carcinomas. *Cancer* **16**, 687–692.

Strauss, M. J. (1974). The growth characteristic of lung cancer and its application to treatment design. *Seminars in Oncology* **1**, 167–174.

Swensen, S. J., Jett, J. R., Sloan, J. A., Midthun, D. E., Hartman, T. E., Sykes, A. M., Aughenbaugh, G. L., Zink, F. E., Hillman, S. L., Noetzel, G. R., Marks, R. S., Clayton, A. C. & Pairolero, P. C. (2002). Screening for lung cancer with low-dose spiral computed tomography. *American Journal of Respiratory and Critical Care Medicine* **165**, 508–513.

Tillich, M., Kammerhuber, F., Reittner, P., Riepl, T., Stoeffler, G. & Szolar, D. H. (1997). Detection of pulmonary nodules with helical CT: comparison of cine and film-based viewing. *American Journal of Roentgenology* **169**, 1611–1614.

Usuda, K., Saito, Y., Sagawa, M., Sato, M., Kanma, K., Takahashi, S., Endo, C., Chen, Y., Sakurada, A. & Fujimura, S. (1994). Tumor doubling time and prognostic assessment of patients with primary lung cancer. *Cancer* **74**, 2239–2244.

Vazquez, M. F. & Flieder, D. B. (2000). Small peripheral glandular lesions detected by screening CT for lung cancer. A diagnostic dilemma for the pathologist. *Radiologic Clinics of North America* **38**, 579–589.

Weiss, W. (1974) Tumor doubling time and survival of men with bronchogenic carcinoma. *Chest* **65**, 3–8.

Winer-Muram, H. T., Jennings, S. G., Tarver, R. D., Aisen, A. M., Tann, M., Conces, D. J. & Meyer, C. A. (2002). Volumetric growth rate of stage I lung cancer prior to treatment: serial CT scanning. *Radiology* **223**, 798–805.

Wormanns, D., Diederich, S., Lentschig, M. G., Winter, F. & Heindel, W. (2000). Spiral CT of pulmonary nodules: interobserver variation in assessment of lesion size. *European Radiology* **10**, 710–713.

Wormanns, D., Fiebich, M., Saidi, M., Diederich, S. & Heindel, W. (2002). Automatic detection of pulmonary nodules at spiral CT: clinical application of a computer-aided diagnosis system. *European Radiology* **12**, 1052–1057.

Yankelevitz, D. F. & Henschke, C. I. (2000). Small solitary pulmonary nodules. *Radiologic Clinics of North America* **38**, 471–478.

Yankelevitz, D. F., Gupta, R., Zhao, B. & Henschke, C. I. (1999). Small pulmonary nodules: evaluation with repeat CT – preliminary experience. *Radiology* **212**, 561–566.

Yankelevitz, D. F., Reeves, A. P., Kostis, W. J., Zhao, B. & Henschke, C. I. (2000). Small pulmonary nodules: volumetrically determined growth rates based on CT evaluation. *Radiology* **217**, 251–256.

Zhao, B., Yankelevitz, D., Reeves, A. & Henschke, C. (1999). Two-dimensional multi-criterion segmentation of pulmonary nodules on helical CT images. *Medical Physics* **26**, 889–895.

Chapter 3

Fluorescence bronchoscopy as a tool for the detection of early malignancy and pre-invasive pulmonary lesions

Jeremy George

Introduction

Lung cancer now accounts for more deaths than any other malignancy in the UK (www.statistics.gov.uk/StatBase/xsdataset.asp?vlnk=342&More=Y). Although the prospects of cure are relatively good for patients with early stage tumours, the vast majority are diagnosed when their tumours are too advanced for curative treatment to be feasible (Mountain 1987; Bulzebruck *et al.* 1992). This has prompted the search for sensitive diagnostic tests that may detect the disease at earlier stages when treatment is more likely to be curative.

Over the last decade, fluorescence bronchoscopy has been developed with the intention of diagnosing early invasive carcinomas and pre-invasive lesions such as severe dysplasia and carcinoma-in situ (CIS). These endobronchial lesions may be difficult to distinguish from surrounding normal tissues with conventional bronchoscopes but their detection may be enhanced significantly by exploiting differences in their properties of fluorescence when illuminated by blue light (Lam *et al.* 2000).

Pre-invasive lesions are of considerable interest, as they are believed to be precursors of squamous cell carcinoma. The ultimate aim of this approach, therefore, is to detect and eradicate such lesions before they have progressed to malignancy. However, their natural history remains incompletely understood and there is no consensus on how they should be managed. This review will outline recent developments in fluorescence bronchoscopy and consider some of the controversies surrounding the management of pre-invasive lesions.

The development of fluorescence bronchoscopy

It has been known since the early part of the 20th century that tumours could be distinguished from surrounding normal tissues by their properties of fluorescence when illuminated by blue light (Sutro & Burman 1933; Herly 1943). More recently, detailed studies involving the bronchial mucosa have shown that high-grade pre-invasive lesions (severe dysplasia and CIS) and invasive carcinomas exhibit markedly reduced green fluorescence and slightly reduced red fluorescence when illuminated by blue light (Hung *et al.* 1991). Although these differences are not visible to the naked eye, they may be visualised with the use of computer enhanced imaging and optical filters.

Steven Lam's group working in Vancouver designed the first commercially available bronchoscope, known as the light induced fluorescence endoscopy (LIFE) device, which exploited these differences in tissue autofluorescence (Lam *et al.* 1993, 1998). The LIFE device employs a helium–cadmium laser to illuminate the bronchial tree with 442 nm light, and the intensities of the resulting red and green fluorescence are measured and used to create a computer-enhanced pseudo-image.

Several other systems have been developed and are now available commercially. At the Middlesex Hospital in London, we have been working with the D-light autofluorescence bronchoscope developed by Karl Storz, which employs conventional blue light emitted by a xenon arc lamp to illuminate the bronchial tree (Leonhard 1999). An optical filter, which transmits predominantly red and green wavelengths, is incorporated into the eyepiece of the bronchoscope and enables the resulting fluorescence images to be viewed directly or displayed on a monitor (see Figure 3.1).

Comparative studies with conventional white light bronchoscopy suggest that fluorescence bronchoscopy enhances the detection of severe dysplasia and CIS 1.5–6.3-fold (Lam *et al.* 1993, 1998; Ikeda *et al.* 1997; Yokomise *et al.* 1997; Venmans *et al.* 1998, 1999, 2000a; Vermylen *et al.* 1999; Hirsch *et al.* 2001). In addition, the detection of micro-invasive squamous cell carcinomas is also enhanced. Although the value of detecting invasive carcinomas cannot be questioned, the ability to detect severe dysplasia and CIS has raised an important clinical dilemma over how such lesions should be managed (Banerjee *et al.* 2003).

The clinical significance of pre-invasive lesions

Auerbach first raised the possible clinical relevance of bronchial epithelial lesions in his classic post-mortem studies (Auerbach *et al.* 1956, 1957, 1961, 1979). He demonstrated that CIS lesions were prevalent in the airways of heavy smokers and that their distribution corresponded with that seen in squamous cell carcinoma. Although these observations incriminated CIS in the development of squamous cell carcinoma, it was not possible to perform confirmatory longitudinal studies because of the difficulties in detecting these lesions with conventional bronchoscopy. However, longitudinal studies involving other organs, such as the cervix (Yajima *et al.* 1982) and mouth (Bosatra *et al.* 1997), have supported this hypothesis and suggest that squamous cell carcinoma develops via a series of morphological stages in the sequence: squamous metaplasia → dysplasia → CIS as shown in Figure 3.2.

In view of the undoubted malignant potential of pre-invasive lesions, some groups have advocated prompt treatment (Venmans *et al.* 2000b; Bota *et al.* 2001). However, careful review of the Auerbach data suggests that the majority of these lesions are

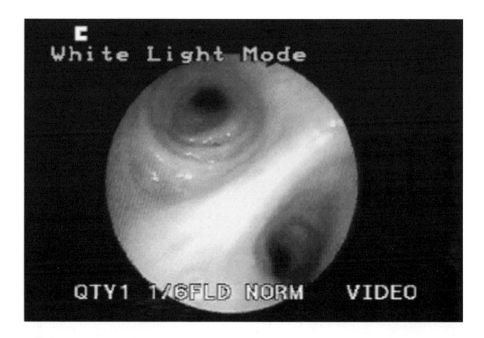

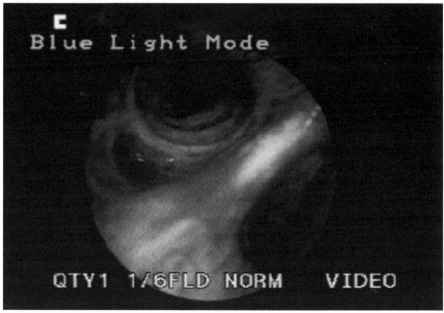

Figure 3.1 The detection of severe dysplasia with fluorescence bronchoscopy. The sub-carina between the right middle and lower lobe orifices looks normal under white light (top) but abnomal under blue light (bottom) using the Storz PDD fluorescence bronchoscope. Normal mucosa exhibits grey-blue fluorescence, whereas the area exhibiting mauve fluorescence (bottom, centre) yielded severe dysplasia on biopsy. (These illustrations are available in colour from the author).

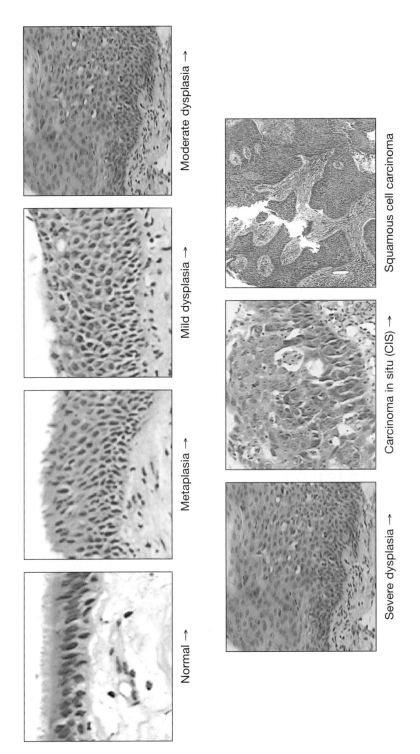

Figure 3.2 Proposed sequence of morphological stages in the pathogenesis of bronchogenic squamous cell carcinoma. (These illustrations are available in colour from the author).

unlikely to progress to malignancy. His systematic post-mortem studies demonstrated CIS in 75% of heavy smokers (Auerbach *et al.* 1961). As only 10–20% of heavy smokers actually develop clinically significant lung cancers and as CIS is only implicated in the development of squamous cell carcinoma, it could be argued that the majority will not progress to clinically significant cancers (Banerjee *et al.* 2002).

Intervention versus surveillance for pre-invasive lesions

Treatments for pre-invasive lesions vary but have included surgical resection (Saito *et al.* 1992) and endobronchial therapies (Cavaliere *et al.* 1996; Perol *et al.* 1997; van Boxem *et al.* 1998; Kato 1998; Thurer 2001). Surgery undoubtedly provides an effective method of eradicating these lesions but carries an appreciable risk, which is difficult to justify when there is no certainty that all or even some will progress. Moreover, patients harbouring pre-invasive lesions are known to be at risk of developing other cancers at remote sites within their lungs, with the result that prior lung resection may render them unfit for curative treatment when they eventually develop an invasive tumour (Pairolero *et al.* 1984).

Endobronchial treatments, such as laser coagulation (Cavaliere *et al.* 1996), electrocautery (van Boxem *et al.* 1998), cryotherapy (Thurer 2001), photodynamic therapy (PDT) (Kato 1998) and endobronchial radiotherapy (Perol *et al.* 1997), have the advantage of conserving lung tissue and have been used more extensively. Although it is claimed that these treatments are successful in up to 80% cases (Cavaliere *et al.* 1996), it is difficult to assess the value of intervention when the natural history of pre-invasive lesions remains unclear. Moreover, the detection and treatment of pre-invasive lesions on a large scale will inevitably be time-consuming and costly, particularly if they are as prevalent as suggested by Auerbach's studies, and is difficult to justify without objective evidence of clinical benefit.

At the Middlesex Hospital, we have been undertaking surveillance of patients with pre-invasive lesions. Patients found to have pre-invasive lesions initially undergo positron emission tomography (PET) and computed tomography (CT) scans and are only recruited into our surveillance programme if there is no evidence of invasive carcinoma. Depending on the severity of their lesion, fluorescence bronchoscopies are repeated at 4–6 monthly intervals enabling biopsies to be taken from sites of previously documented lesions and from any new lesions. Low dose spiral CT scans are repeated annually to exclude incidental cancers. Treatment is offered to patients at the earliest evidence of progression to invasive disease.

Preliminary findings from this long-term study are now in press (Banerjee *et al.* 2004) and suggest that approximately one in six high-grade lesions progress to invasive squamous cell carcinoma, while a similar proportion regress either to normal or to a lesser grade. The remaining high-grade lesions have persisted for up to 4 years. We have also found that new, high-grade lesions frequently develop *de novo* during surveillance and, in one patient, progressed rapidly to an invasive carcinoma (see Figure 3.3).

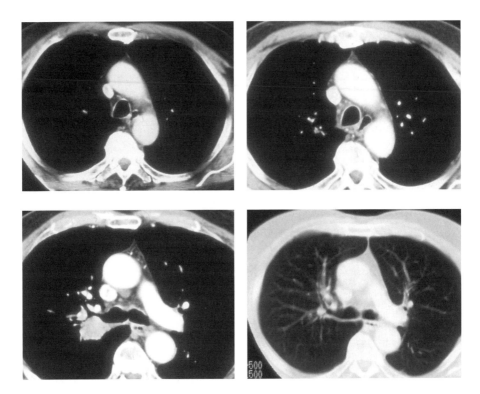

Figure 3.3 Example of a second new primary lung cancer developing during surveillance. A CT scan was obtained prior to PDT (top left) for a biopsy-proven invasive squamous cell carcinoma of the anterior trachea. This tumour had progressed from CIS but was not visible on the scan. Subsequent bronchial biopsies showed no evidence of recurrent carcinoma and the trachea remained normal on a repeat CT scan 1 year later (top right). Although routine biopsies from the right upper lobe had been entirely normal at this initial bronchoscopy, severe dysplasia developed in the area during the course of surveillance. This second lesion progressed within months to an invasive squamous cell carcinoma. Comparison between CT scans obtained at the time of this initial bronchoscopy (lower right) and 1 year later (lower left) show that this second new tumour has grown very rapidly.

Although pre-emptive endobronchial treatment might have prevented the progression to invasive carcinoma in some patients, this approach would have been difficult technically. Firstly, we have found that pre-invasive lesions are frequently multi-focal and it has not been possible to predict which of these multiple lesions will progress to carcinoma on the basis of their initial histology. Secondly, we have found that patients harbouring pre-invasive lesions are at high risk of developing incidental cancers at remote sites within their lungs, in keeping with a 'field change' effect of tobacco smoke. Ultimately, we believe that systemic treatments aimed at preventing the progression to malignancy may be more appropriate than local ablative treatments in this group of patients.

Our surveillance programme has the inherent advantages of ensuring that treatment is targeted to the most appropriate site within the airway and that incidental cancers are detected and treated promptly. It has also enabled us to establish a tissue archive so that it is now possible to make comparisons between pre-invasive lesions, which exhibit different malignant potential on follow-up. We are now undertaking detailed molecular studies on these samples with the intention of identifying markers of tumour progression. Such studies should also provide unique insights into the biology of the invasion process.

The future of fluorescence bronchoscopy in clinical practice

Although fluorescence bronchoscopy has already become established as a valuable research tool, its value in routine clinical practice remains to be seen. It is too invasive and time-consuming to be used to screen for lung cancers but it has undoubted value in locating lesions in a small number of patients serendipitously found to have abnormal sputum cytology.

If sensitive, non-invasive screening tests for lung cancer can be developed, it may become an extremely powerful clinical tool when used in conjunction with these tests. However, the establishment of an early lung cancer detection and treatment programme will inevitably be costly and laborious and it will first be necessary to define the natural history of pre-invasive lesions and then demonstrate the benefits of proactive management in large, randomised, controlled trials.

Acknowledgements

Much of the work referred to in this chapter has been performed in collaboration with Dr Pamela Rabbitts and Dr Anindo Banerjee, and has been generously supported by the UCL Hospitals Charitable Foundation. I am also indebted to Karl Storz for the loan of their D-light autofluorescence bronchoscope and for invaluable technical support.

References

Auerbach, O., Petrick, T. G., Stout, A. P., Statsinger, A. L., Muehsam, G. E., Forman, J. B. & Gere, J. B. (1956). The anatomical approach to the study of smoking and bronchogenic carcinoma. *Cancer* **9**, 76–83.

Auerbach, O., Forman, J. B., Gere, J. B., Kasscuny, D. Y., Muehsam, G. E., Petrick, T. G., Smolin, H. J. & Stout, A. P. (1957). Changes in the bronchial epithelium in relation to smoking and cancer of the lung. *New England Journal of Medicine* **256**, 97–104.

Auerbach, O., Stout, A. P., Hammond, E. C. & Garfinkel, L. (1961). Changes in bronchial epithelium in relation to cigarette smoking and in relation to lung cancer. *New England Journal of Medicine* **265**, 255–267.

Auerbach, O., Hammond, E. C. & Garfinkel, L. (1979). Changes in bronchial epithelium in relation to cigarette smoking, 1955–1960 vs. 1970–1977. *New England Journal of Medicine* **300**, 381–385.

Banerjee, A. K., Rabbitts, P. R. & George, P. J. M. (2002). Are all high-grade pre-invasive lesions pre-malignant, and should they all be treated? *American Journal of Respiratory and Critical Care Medicine* **165**, 1452–1453.

Banerjee, A. K., Rabbitts, P. R. & George, J. (2003). Fluorescence bronchoscopy: Clinical dilemmas and research opportunities. *Thorax* **58**, 266–271.

Banerjee, A. K., Rabbitts, P. H. & George, P. J. (2004). Pre-invasive bronchial epithelial lesions: surveillance or intervention? *Chest* **125**(5 Suppl.), 95S–96S.

Bosatra, A., Bussani, R. & Silvestri, F. (1997). From epithelial dysplasia to squamous carcinoma in the head and neck region: an epidemiological assessment. *Acta Oto-laryngolica Supplementum* **527**, 47–48.

Bota, S., Auliac, J. B., Paris, C., Métayer, J., Sesboüé, R., Nouvet, G. & Thiberville, L. (2001). Follow-up of bronchial precancerous lesions and carcinoma in situ using fluorescence endoscopy. *American Journal of Respiratory and Critical Care Medicine* **164**, 1688–1693.

Bulzebruck, H., Bopp, R., Drings, P., Bauer, E., Krysa, S., Probst, G., Van-Kaick, G., Muller, K. M. & Vogt-Moykopf, I. (1992). New aspects in the staging of lung cancer. Prospective validation of the International Union Against Cancer TNM classification *Cancer* **70**, 1102–1110.

Cavaliere, S., Venuta, F., Foccoli, P., Toninelli, C. & La-Face, B. (1996). Endoscopic treatment of malignant airway obstructions in 2,008 patients. [Published erratum of serious dosage error appears in *Chest* 1997 **111**(5), 1476] *Chest* **110**, 1536–1542.

Herly, L. (1943). Studies in selective differentiation of tissues by means of filtered ultraviolet light *Cancer Research* **1**, 227–231.

Hirsch, F. R., Prindiville, S. A., Miller, Y. E., Franklin, W. A., Dempsey, E. C., Murphy, J. R., Bunn, P. A. Jr. & Kennedy, T. C. (2001). Fluorescence versus white-light bronchoscopy for detection of preneoplastic lesions: a randomized study. *Journal of the National Cancer Institute* **93**, 1385–1391.

Hung, J., Lam, S., LeRiche, J. C. & Palcic, B. (1991). Autofluorescence of normal and malignant bronchial tissue. *Lasers in Surgery and Medicine* **11**, 99–105.

Ikeda, N., Kim, K., Okunaka, T., Furukawa, K., Furuya, T., Saito, M., Konaka, C., Kato, H. & Ebihara, Y. (1997). Early localisation of bronchogenic cancerous/precancerous lesions with lung imaging fluorescence endoscope. *Diagnostic and Therapeutic Endoscopy* **3**, 197–201.

Kato, H. (1998). Photodynamic therapy for lung cancer: a review of 19 years' experience. *Journal of Photochemistry and Photobiology B Biology* **42**, 96–99.

Lam, S., MacAulay, C., Hung, J., LeRiche, J., Profio, A. E. & Palcic, B (1993). Detection of dysplasia and carcinoma in situ with a lung imaging fluorescence endoscope device. *The Journal of Thoracic and Cardiovascular Surgery* **105**, 1035–1040.

Lam, S., Kennedy, T., Unger, M., Miller, Y. E., Geimont, D., Rusch, V., Gipe, B., Howard, D., LeRiche, J. C., Coldman, A. & Gazdar, A. F. (1998). Localization of bronchial intraepithelial neoplastic lesions by fluorescence bronchoscopy. *Chest* **113**, 696–702.

Lam, S., MacAulay, C., LeRiche, J. C., Palcic, B. *et al.* (2000). Detection and localization of early lung cancer by fluorescence bronchoscopy. *Cancer* **89**, 2468–2473.

Leonhard, M. (1999). New incoherent autofluorescence/fluorescence system for early detection of lung cancer. *Diagnostic and Therapeutic Endoscopy* **5**, 71–75.

Mountain, C. F. (1987). The new International Staging System for Lung Cancer. *Surgical Clinics of North America* **67**, 925–935.

Pairolero, P. C., Williams, D. E., Bergstralh, E. J., Piehler, J. M., Bernatz, P. E. & Payne, W. S. (1984). Postsurgical stage I bronchogenic carcinoma: morbid implications of recurrent disease. *Annals of Thoracic Surgery* **38**, 331–338.

Perol, M., Caliandro, R., Pommier, P., Malet, C., Montbarbon, X., Carrie, C. & Ardiet, J. M. (1997). Curative irradiation of limited endobronchial carcinomas with high-dose rate brachytherapy. Results of a pilot study. *Chest* **111**, 1417–1423.

Saito, Y., Nagamoto, N., Ota, S., Sato, M., Sagawa, M., Kamma, K., Takahashi, S., Usuda, K., Endo, C., Imal, T. & Fujimura, S. (1992). Results of surgical treatment for roentgeno-graphically occult bronchogenic squamous cell carcinoma. *Journal of Thoracic and Cardiovascular Surgery* **104**, 401–407.

Sutro, C. J. & Burman, M. S. (1933). Examination of pathologic tissue by filtered ultraviolet radiation. *Archives of Pathology* **16**, 346–349.

Thurer, R. J. (2001). Cryotherapy in early lung cancer. *Chest* **120**, 3–5.

van Boxem, T. J., Venmans, B. J., Schramel, F. M., van Mourik, J. C., Golding, R. P., Postmus, P. E. & Sutedja, T. G. (1998). Radiographically occult lung cancer treated with fibreoptic bronchoscopic electrocautery: a pilot study of a simple and inexpensive technique. *European Respiratory Journal* **11**, 169–172.

Venmans, B. J., van der Linden, H., van Boxem T. J., Postmus, P. E., Smit, E. F. & Sutedja, T. G. (1998). Early detection of pre-invasive lesions in high risk patients. *Journal of Bronchology* **5**, 280–283.

Venmans, B. J., van Boxem, A. J. & Smit, E. F. (1999). Results of two years experience with fluorescence bronchoscopy in detection of pre-invasive bronchial neoplasia. *Diagnostic and Therapeutic Endoscopy* **5**, 77–84.

Venmans, B. J., van Boxem, A. J. M., Smit, E. F., Postmus, P. E. & Sutedja, T. G. (2000a). Clinically relevant information obtained by performing autofluorescence bronchoscopy. *Journal of Bronchology* **7**, 118–121.

Venmans, B. J., van Boxem, T. J., Smit, E. F. *et al.* (2000b). Outcome of bronchial carcinoma in situ. *Chest* **117**, 1572–1576.

Vermylen, P., Pierard, P., Roufosse, C., Bosschaerts, T., Verhest, A., Sculier J. P. & Ninane, V. (1999). Detection of bronchial preneoplastic lesions and early lung cancer with fluorescence bronchoscopy: a study about its ambulatory feasibility under local anaesthesis. *Lung Cancer* **25**, 161–168.

Yajima, A., Sato, A., Mori, T., Wakisaka, T., Sato, S., Suzuki, M., Teshima, K. & Noda, K. (1982). Progression of malignancy of severe dysplasia of the uterine cervix. *Tohoku Journal of Experimental Medicine* **136**, 433–438.

Yokomise, H., Yanagihara, K., Fukuse, T., Hirata, T., Ike, O., Mizuno, H., Wada, H. & Hitomi, S. (1997). Clinical experience with lung-imaging fluorescence endoscope (LIFE) in patients with lung cancer. *Journal of Bronchology* **4**, 205–208.

Additional sources
http://www.statistics.gov.uk/StatBase/xsdataset.asp?vlnk=3342&More=Y

The role of positron emission tomography using fluorodeoxyglucose in lung cancer

Eva Wegner and Thomas Nunan

Introduction

18-Fluoro-2-deoxy-glucose (FDG) is an analogue of glucose. It has been known for over 50 years that many malignant tissues take up glucose avidly (Warburg *et al.* 1931). This raised the possibility that if a suitable analogue of glucose could be synthesised then it might be of use as a tumour marker. However the problem with labelling glucose itself is that the label would pass along the same metabolic pathways as the glucose that was metabolised. Thus an image taken would be of the tracer in all the various metabolites of glucose. FDG is taken up into cells along the glucose transporter pathways and is phosphorylated. Further degradation of FDG does not occur and it 'sticks' inside the cell. Thus it acts in a similar fashion to microspheres. This allows images to be acquired at some time after injection and thus lends itself to clinical usage. Since most physiological tissues take up relatively little glucose, the target to background ratio is favourable for tumour imaging. The exceptions to this are the brain, heart and renal tract.

Fluorine-18 decays by emitting a positron which is a form of antimatter and is a positively charged electron. This travels a few millimetres in tissue before it annihilates with a negatively charged electron. Two gamma rays are emitted which travel in opposite directions. By having a ring of detectors around the patient the source of the site of the radioactive decay can be determined. Fluorine-18 has a half-life of just under two hours and is produced by a cyclotron. As a general rule the site of FDG production needs to be less than a half-life (two hours) from the imaging site. In the UK this should not be too difficult to achieve for most of the population provided that there is an investment in cyclotron facilities. A single cyclotron can keep several positron emission tomography (PET) cameras supplied with FDG.

The physics of PET scanning enables an accurate measurement to be made of the amount of radionuclide in a particular region. This quantitative measurement is called a standardised uptake value (SUV). In order to calculate the SUV it is necessary to perform a transmission scan so that a correction for attenuation can be made. With previous generations of scanner, this was performed by external rods rotating around the patient. This was a relatively slow procedure and significantly prolonged imaging time. In recent years there has been a significant advance in PET technology. The computed tomography (CT) scanner and PET scanner are combined so that the two images are acquired sequentially without moving the patient. Modern CT scanners can acquire an image within a few minutes and this can be used to calculate the attenuation correction. There are two advantages to this: first, since the attenuation correction is acquired more quickly, the patient throughput in PET centres can be increased significantly. The second advantage is that it is possible to co-register any PET abnormalities directly on to the CT scan to localise them. Since one of the principal skills in reporting PET scans is the differentiation of physiological uptake (for instance in the ureter) from pathological uptake (in a lymph node), the co-registration of the two sets of images could significantly improve the reporting accuracy.

Positron emission tomography in pre-operative staging of non-small-cell lung cancer

The main role in PET in the staging of lung cancer is in the pre-operative assessment of patients. Patients having PET scans will all have undergone conventional work up and biopsy. Thus uptake in the primary tumour is not in itself of great significance. (There is a positive correlation between the SUV and prognosis; this is discussed below.) It is obvious that a lymph node that has only a small volume of metastatic disease is unlikely to be enlarged. It is only when the metastatic involvement reaches a significant volume that the lymph node will become enlarged. Radiological criteria traditionally have only 'called' involved nodes by virtue of their being over 1 cm in size. Thus CT scanning will be insensitive in the earlier stages of metastatic involvement of the lymph node.

One of the advantages of PET scanning as a functional imaging tool is that the size of the lymph node is not important. What is important is the volume and avidity of malignant tissue within the lymph node. As is shown below, PET can detect malignancy in normal sized lymph nodes with a high degree of accuracy. The converse also applies to enlarged lymph nodes. It is well known that not all enlarged lymph nodes are enlarged as a function of disease. One only has to look at squamous cell carcinomas with necrotic centres to appreciate the large amount of debris that is phagocytosed before clearance by normal mechanisms. It is no great surprise that lymph nodes in the draining territory of these tumours are enlarged. While PET scans can give false positive uptakes in active inflammatory disease, usually, enlarged lymph nodes that are reactive have low grade uptake and can be differentiated with some confidence from malignant disease. Gupta *et al.* (2001) compared PET, CT and invasive sampling of the mediastinal lymph nodes in 77 patients with proven or suspected lung cancer. Seven of 123 (four patients) had false negative nodes by PET scanning. Three nodes were less than 1 cm and were normal by CT criteria. However, other regions of abnormality in these patients resulted in the correct clinical staging. One hundred and twenty-five lymph nodes were greater than 1 cm and thus, by definition, CT positive; only 36 were positive pathologically.

A study by Saunders *et al.* (1999) looked at the detection of N2 and N3 mediastinal lymph node involvement by CT and PET. The sensitivity of CT was 20% versus 70.6% for PET. The specificity of the CT was 89.9% versus 97% and the overall accuracy for CT was 77% versus 91% for PET. Pieterman *et al.* (2000) studied 102 patients who all had histopathological confirmation of mediastinal metastatic disease. They found the sensitivity and specificity for PET of 91% and 86%, respectively, as opposed to 75% and 66% for CT.

A common feature of these studies is the false positive rate (2%: Saunders *et al.* 1999; 13%: Gupta *et al.* 2001). There are certain situations in which PET scanning gives false positives. FDG PET is not specific for malignant disease as other inflammatory processes will also take up the tracer. In the context of lung disease, false positives can arise with active granulomas (commonly tuberculosis (TB), less commonly sarcoidosis or silicosis) and other infections. It is important in the pre-operative staging of patients to be sure that there has been histological proof of the diagnosis. Occasionally it is not possible to obtain a pathological diagnosis except by

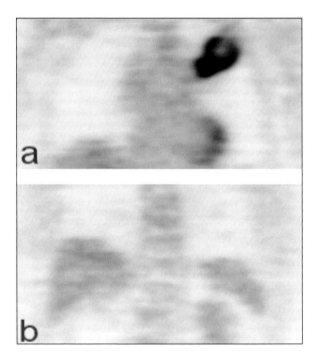

Figure 4.1 Staging: suitable for surgery (downstaged). CT showed NSCLC in the left lung, with small mediastinal nodes and mass in the right adrenal gland. PET demonstrated the tumour with no metastases in the mediastinum (a) or in the right adrenal (b).

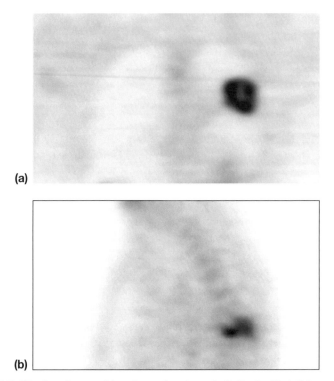

(a)

(b)

Figure 4.2 Staging: inoperable – bone (upstaged). Patient with left lung adenocarcinoma. Suitable for operation on CT. PET demonstrated the known lung cancer (a), as well as a large thoracic spine metastasis (b).

a thoracotomy. Under these circumstances so-called false positive results may occur; whether or not they are really false results is discussed in the section 'Solitary pulmonary nodules' (SPNs) below. Provided there is histology on the primary lung lesion then a false positive result is unlikely. Of course it is important to have a full patient history to ensure that such features as exposure to TB are known and considered when interpreting the PET images.

Two practical management points emerge from these studies on PET and mediastinal staging. The first is that if the PET scan shows a normal mediastinum, then it is not necessary to perform a diagnostic mediastinoscopy. The second is that if the PET is positive or equivocal in the mediastinum and the patient is otherwise a surgical candidate, then histological confirmation of the abnormality is required before the patients can be considered truly inoperable. One must remember that surgery offers potential cure of non-small-cell lung cancer (NSCLC) and thus it is important not to miss resectable disease.

Probably the most important role of FDG PET imaging in pre-operative staging is the identification of distant metastatic disease, which rules out surgery as a treatment option. It must be remembered that a normal brain takes up a significant amount of FDG. The effect of this in the context of lung cancer is to reduce the sensitivity of brain scanning in the detection of brain metastases (Larcos & Maisey 1996). However outside the brain PET scanning is both sensitive and specific for the detection of distant metastases. The study by Saunders *et al.* referred to above found unsuspected distant metastases in 17 of 97 patients. Pieterman *et al.* (2000) found distant metastases in 11 of 102 patients.

Another specific area where PET is of use is in the evaluation of equivocal radiological abnormalities. The study by Saunders *et al.* (1999) found several patients with equivocal evidence of metastases, which were negative on PET scanning. In four patients a disease was credibly excluded; in three, however, no direct biopsy was made of the site.

The PET in Lung Cancer Study (PLUS) randomised 188 patients into two groups (van Tinteren *et al.* 2002). One group had conventional work up (CWU) and the other had conventional work up with PET (CWU + PET). What the authors found was that futile thoracotomies occurred in 41% of patients in the conventional work up group, but only in 21% in the PET group. Thus one in five thoracotomies would be saved by including a PET scan in the work up. The main feature of this study was the randomisation of patients into the two groups, thus reducing selection bias. Another feature of this study was that patients were referred from nine hospitals. Thus the study represents broader practice than a single institution could provide. This study also gave some figures for disease-free survival in each group. In the CWU group 17 patients had metastases within one year of surgery. In the CWU + PET group four patients had relapsed in the first year. Since most PET studies have not had a non-PET arm, this information suggesting a disease-free survival benefit is significant.

The authors also included a cost effectiveness study using real costs rather than modelling (Verboom *et al.* 2003). They found the average costs in the conventional work up group were €9,553 per patient and in the PET group €8,284, showing that PET is cost-effective and results in a significant cost saving.

Prognostic value of positron emission tomography

Another role of PET relates to the prognostic value of the study. Several authors have shown that the higher the SUV the worse the prognosis despite treatment (Dhital *et al.* 2000; Jeong *et al.* 2002). Although the numbers were small the median survival of patients who had an SUV over 20 was only six months. Higashi *et al.* (2000) showed that the SUV correlated histologically with aggressiveness in that the more aggressive histological tumour types had higher SUVs. How this equates to clinical management of an individual patient is difficult to say. In our practice those patients with a high SUV will not be denied surgery on the basis of the SUV alone, but it is one of the many factors that contribute to the decision.

Response to treatment

Whilst the pre-treatment SUV does not *predict* the response to chemotherapy (Ryu *et al.* 2002), PET scan can *assess* the response to treatment. MacManus *et al.* (2003) studied 73 patients who had chemoradiotherapy and found that the PET response to treatment was more predictive of prognosis than CT. However their patients had radiotherapy and it is well known than radiotherapy causes increased uptake on PET scans for at least three months. Ryu *et al.* (2002) found a sensitivity of 58% for mediastinal restaging with PET; again their patients had chemoradiotherapy. Weber *et al.* (2003) studied 57 patients having chemotherapy. A highly significant correlation was found between those patients who responded on PET scanning and subsequent clinical course.

Broncho-alveolar carcinoma and small lesions

It is well known that broncho-alveolar carcinomas have a relatively low degree of uptake. The SUV is usually about 2. Thus they can be localised on PET but the low

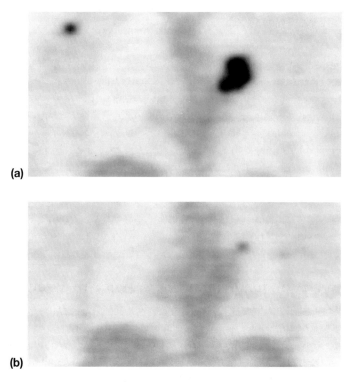

(a)

(b)

Figure 4.3 Response to chemotherapy. PET scan initially showed inoperable disease (a) primary tumour demonstrated in the left mid-zone as well as in the right shoulder. (There was metastatic disease elsewhere, not shown on this image.) Instead of surgery, the patient was given chemotherapy, subsequent PET (b) demonstrated an excellent response to chemotherapy.

uptake reduces the specificity. This is particularly the case for mediastinal disease. The background level of tracer in the mediastinum is higher than in the lungs. This makes low grade foci of uptake more difficult to interpret and thus reduces the specificity of the test. In particular, since the primary tumour takes up relatively little

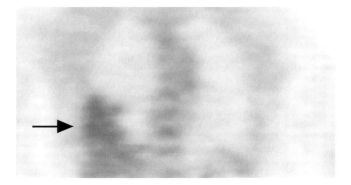

Figure 4.4 Broncho-alveolar carcinoma (indicated by arrow), considered for possible surgery if solitary. PET showed no other areas of disease; it demonstrates the low FDG uptake in the broncho-alveolar carcinoma.

FDG, mediastinal involvement is more difficult to identify. Thus if a patient has broncho-alveolar carcinoma, FDG PET is not usually used for staging.

The other area that is becoming increasingly important is in the investigation of small nodules. In order to visualise a nodule on FDG PET scanning there has to be sufficient uptake of FDG by the tumour to allow it to be seen. A small lesion must take up tracer avidly enough to allow this. Conversely a large lesion that takes up tracer to the same degree as the background cannot be identified. This is in contrast to CT or magnetic resonance imaging (MRI) in which it is just the size of the lesion that matters. Since it is not possible to know the avidity of the lesion for FDG prior to the scan, a rule of thumb has evolved that below 1 cm diameter PET is associated with a lower sensitivity. This is discussed further in the section 'Solitary pulmonary nodules' below.

Positron emission tomography in detecting recurrent disease

Scarring following surgery and radiotherapy make the diagnosis of recurrence on anatomical imaging difficult. Biopsies have a poor negative predictive value because of concerns about sampling error. The advantage of PET scanning is that the destruction of normal anatomical marks does not interfere with its ability to visualise the functioning tumour. PET has a sensitivity and specificity of 72% and 95% versus CT sensitivity and specificity of 28% and 92% (Gambhir *et al.* 2001).

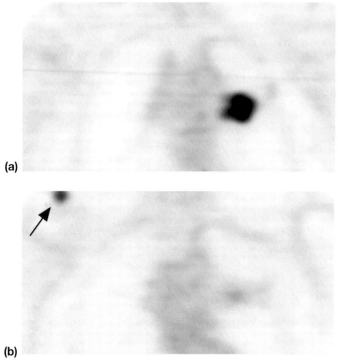

(a)

(b)

Figure 4.5 Recurrence of tumour. Patient with previous small cell lung cancer treated with chemotherapy and radiotherapy. Now has a soft tissue mass on the CT and was difficult to distinguish this from post-radiotherapy fibrosis. PET showed recurrence of tumour in the left hilum (a) and a bone metastasis in the right shoulder (b) indicated by an arrow.

Solitary pulmonary nodules

Solitary pulmonary nodules are a common problem in chest medicine. They are relatively common and affect between 0.1 and 0.2% of adults (Shulkin 1993). The clinical problem is to exclude malignant disease. Biopsy is often technically difficult and is often unsuccessful. Transthoracic needle biopsy has a sensitivity of 71 to 100% and is associated with significant morbidity. In those patients with respiratory disease, it may be felt that there is too great a risk in performing a biopsy without other evidence that the lesion needs further investigation. Bronchoscopy is also often unsuccessful because of the small size of the lesion and the fact that there is seldom an endobronchial abnormality.

The advantage of PET scanning is that it is a non-invasive tool with no morbidity. The sensitivity of PET in detecting SPNs ranges from 83 to 96% (Shon *et al.* 2002). The specificity is lower, ranging from 52 to 100%. However if one considers that, in the case of malignant SPNs, the possibility of surgical cure is greater than in other patients presenting with symptoms or signs of lung cancer, then it is important to have a test which has a high sensitivity and to accept a lower specificity. This way, patients with potentially curable cancer will not be rejected.

Much of the work on PET in SPNs has come from the USA where the incidence of benign disease is higher than in Europe. What was required of PET was to exclude those patients with benign SPNs. In Europe up to 50% of SPNs are malignant and the clinical strategy is different. This obviously affects the way in which the test is used in clinical algorithms. In a high risk (of lung cancer) group, the most cost-effective way to proceed is to get a definite diagnosis. Since PET does not have 100% sensitivity, it does not have a place in the assessment of an SPN. However a PET scan should be performed in order to assess the correct staging of the cancer if it is a non-small-cell cancer. In patients felt to be at a low risk of disease, PET is unlikely to be positive and, since the specificity is not 100%, false positives will occur and render the test less accurate. The place of PET is in the investigation of patients at an intermediate risk of lung cancer.

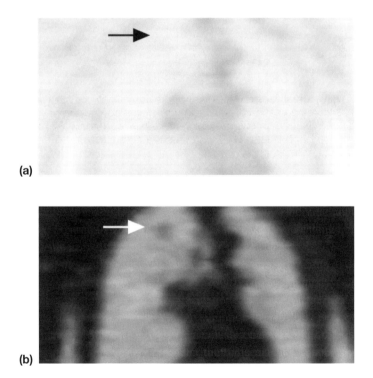

(a)

(b)

Figure 4.6 FDG negative solitary pulmonary nodule. Incidental finding on CXR. CT confirmed a solitary nodule. Bronchoscopy normal. PET demonstrated no abnormal uptake on emission scan (a), and the lesion (indicated by arrow) is identified on transmission scan (b). Likely to be a benign lesion just requiring follow up.

Gould *et al.* (2003) performed a sensitivity analysis of PET and concluded that PET should be used in intermediate cases when the pretest probability and CT results are discordant and in patients in whom there is a high risk of surgical complications.

False negative PET scans can occur in small SPNs because the volume of disease is below the threshold of the imaging technique. The introduction of CT pulmonary angiography has resulted in a greater number of small SPNs being discovered. As a rule they need to be larger than 1 cm for PET to be clinically useful. Another situation in which the sensitivity of PET is reduced is at the lung bases. PET scans take several minutes to acquire per bed position. Thus, motion in the PET scan will blur the uptake and this too will reduce the sensitivity. Finally, some lung cancers do not take up FDG; the commonest type is broncho-alveolar carcinoma, discussed above.

The fact that PET may miss small lesions indicates that in patients with a negative PET scan follow up is essential. FDG uptake and proliferation rate are linked. Those cancers with low FDG uptake are likely to have a slow proliferation rate; therefore, picking up the growth on surveillance CT scanning is likely to identify the malignancy while it is still at an early stage.

Cost-effective evaluations tend to regard false positive PET scans as a false cost. However, since most patients will have had an attempt at biopsy or a failed biopsy, a positive PET scan will indicate that the lesion is metabolically active. One of the common non-cancer causes of positive PET scans is TB. In this situation the PET scan can show that the lesion is metabolically active and that it is important to proceed to determine what the pathology is. If one asks the question, 'do I need to proceed further to investigate this mass?', then the PET scan could be regarded as a true positive.

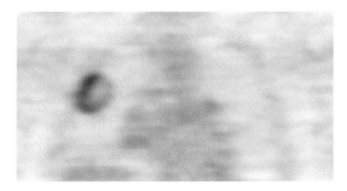

Figure 4.7 FDG positive granulomatous disease. Patient with presumed lung cancer sent for PET staging. PET demonstrated a focus with photopaenic centre, which looked like a malignancy. Follow up biopsy demonstrated granulomatous disease.

Future trends

The main development currently is in combined PET and CT scanners. These offer two advantages over the previous generation of PET scanners. In order to calculate the uptake of tracer in a tumour it is necessary to calculate the attenuation of the gamma ray in the body tissues. With the previous generation of scanners, this was performed by external radioactive rods rotating around the patients. This was a slow process and was often not performed in routine work. The combined scanner uses a CT scan to obtain the attenuation image. This can be acquired in a few minutes. Thus not only is an attenuation correction applied to the whole image, but the process is quicker allowing a significant increase in throughput. The second advantage is that the sequential acquisition of a CT and PET scan allows registration of any PET abnormalities onto the CT image. This combines the increased sensitivity of PET scanning with the resolution of CT scanning. Thus it is possible to say with confidence exactly where any PET abnormality is. Lardinois *et al.* (2003) established that the combined PET/CT scanner found additional information in 41% of patients and increased the accuracy of staging. Further, it increased the diagnostic certainty in two of eight patients.

Radiotherapy planning

An obvious topic for investigation is the potential uses of combined PET/CT in radiotherapy planning. Erdi *et al.* (2002) found, using PET/CT in 11 patients, that there was a change in planning target volume in all patients and they suggested that incorporating combined PET/CT would enable more accurate planning. Others have confirmed that there is a significant alteration of planning volumes when PET/CT is used (Mah *et al.* 2002). Another advantage of PET/CT is in the reduction of observer variation in the planning volume (Ciernik *et al.* 2003).

Having proved that PET/CT alters the planning volume, it needs to be shown that this confers a benefit in either morbidity or mortality. It is too soon to expect this type of study but it is awaited with interest.

In the UK there is great interest in the use of PET in lung cancer. The main problem at the moment is in the poor provision of PET facilities. In England at the time of writing the only clinical PET units are in London. Mobile systems are beginning to be used elsewhere. However the widespread use of PET in lung cancer and the other types of cancer where it has a proven role is yet to happen. The Department of Health is convening a working party to advise on PET provision and we can only hope it will not take too long to come to recommendations.

References

Ciernik, I. F., Dizendorf, E., Baumert, B. G., Reiner, B., Burger, C., Davis, J. B., Lutolf, U. M., Steinert, H. C., Von Schulthess, G. K. (2003) Radiation treatment planning with an integrated positron emission and computer tomography (PET/CT): a feasibility study. *International Journal of Radiation Oncology, Biology, Physics* **57**, 853–863.

Dhital, K., Saunders, C. A., Seed, P. T., O'Doherty, M. J. & Dussek, J. (2000) [(18)F]Fluorodeoxyglucose positron emission tomography and its prognostic value in lung cancer. *European Journal of Cardio-thoracic Surgery* **18**, 425–428.

Erdi, Y. E., Rosenzweig, K., Erdi, A. K., Macapinlac, H. A., Hu, Y. C., Braban, L. E., Humm, J. L., Squire, O. D., Chui, C. S., Larson, S. M. *et al.* (2002) Radiotherapy treatment planning for patients with non-small cell lung cancer using positron emission tomography (PET). *Radiotherapy and Oncology* **62**, 51–60.

Gambhir, S. S., Czernin, J., Schwimmer, J., Silverman, D. H., Coleman, R. E. & Phelps, M. E. (2001) A tabulated summary of the FDG PET literature. *Journal of Nuclear Medicine* **42** (5 Suppl.), 1S–93S.

Gould, M. K., Kuschner, W. G., Rydzak, C. E., Maclean, C. C., Demas, A. N., Shigemitsu, H., Chan, J. K. & Owens, D. K. (2003) Test performance of positron emission tomography and computed tomography for mediastinal staging in patients with non-small-cell lung cancer: a meta-analysis. *Annals of Internal Medicine* **139**, 879–892.

Gupta, N. C., Tamim, W. J., Graeber, G. G., Bishop, H. A. & Hobbs, G. R. (2001). Mediastinal lymph node sampling following positron emission tomography with fluorodeoxyglucose imaging in lung cancer staging. *Chest* **120**, 521–527.

Higashi, K., Ueda, Y., Ayabe, K., Sakurai, A., Seki, H., Nambu, Y., Oguchi, M., Shikata, H., Taki, S., Tonami, H. *et al.* (2000) FDG PET in the evaluation of the aggressiveness of pulmonary adenocarcinoma: correlation with histopathological features. *Nuclear Medicine Communications* **21**, 707–714.

Jeong, H. J., Min, J. J., Park, J. M., Chung, J. K., Kim, B. T., Jeong, J. M., Lee, D. S., Lee, M. C., Han, S. K. & Shim, Y. S. (2002) Determination of the prognostic value of [(18)F]fluorodeoxyglucose uptake by using positron emission tomography in patients with non-small cell lung cancer. *Nuclear Medicine Communications* **23**, 865–870.

Larcos, G. & Maisey, M. N. (1996) FDG-PET screening for cerebral metastases in patients with suspected malignancy. *Nuclear Medicine Communications* **17**, 197–198.

Lardinois, D., Weder, W., Hany, T. F., Kamel, E. M., Korom, S., Seifert, B., von Schulthess, G. K. & Steinert, H. C. (2003) Staging of non-small-cell lung cancer with integrated positron-emission tomography and computed tomography. *New England Journal of Medicine* **348**, 2500–2507.

MacManus, M. P., Hicks, R. J., Matthews, J. P., McKenzie, A., Rischin, D., Salminen, E. K. & Ball, D. L. (2003) Positron emission tomography is superior to computed tomography scanning for response-assessment after radical radiotherapy or chemoradiotherapy in patients with non-small-cell lung cancer. *Journal of Clinical Oncology* **21**, 1285–1292.

Mah, K., Caldwell, C. B., Ung, Y. C., Danjoux, C. E., Balogh, J. M., Ganguli, S. N., Ehrlich, L. E. & Tirona, R. (2002) The impact of (18)FDG-PET on target and critical organs in CT-based treatment planning of patients with poorly defined non-small-cell lung carcinoma: a prospective study. *International Journal of Radiation Oncology, Biology, Physics* **52**, 339–350.

Pieterman, R. M., van Putten, J. W., Meuzelaar, J. J., Mooyaart, E. L., Vaalburg, W., Koeter, G. H., Fidler, V., Pruim, J. & Groen, H. J. (2000). Preoperative staging of non-small-cell lung cancer with positron-emission tomography. *New England Journal of Medicine* **343**, 254–256

Ryu, J. S., Choi, N. C., Fischman, A. J., Lynch, T. J. & Mathisen, D. J. (2002) FDG-PET in staging and restaging non-small cell lung cancer after neoadjuvant chemoradiotherapy: correlation with histopathology. *Lung Cancer* **35**, 179–187.

Saunders, C. A., Dussek, J. E., O'Doherty, M. J. & Maisey, M. N. (1999). Evaluation of fluorine-18-fluorodeoxyglucose whole body positron emission tomography imaging in the staging of lung cancer. *Annals of Thoracic Surgery* **67**, 790–797.

Shon, I. H., O'Doherty, M. J. & Maisey, M. N. (2002) Positron emission tomography in lung cancer. *Seminars in Nuclear Medicine* **32**, 240–271.

Shulkin, A. N. (1993) Management of the indeterminate solitary pulmonary nodule: a pulmonologist's view. *Annals of Thoracic Surgery* **56**, 743–744.

van Tinteren, H., Hoekstra, O. S., Smit, E. F., van den Bergh, J. H., Schreurs, A. J., Stallaert, R. A., van Velthoven, P. C., Comans, E. F., Diepenhorst, F. W., Verboom, P. *et al.* (2002) Effectiveness of positron emission tomography in the preoperative assessment of patients with suspected non-small-cell lung cancer: the PLUS multicentre randomised trial. *The Lancet* **359**, 1388–1393.

Verboom, P., van Tinteren, H., Hoekstra, O. S., Smit, E. F., van den Bergh, J. H., Schreurs, A. J., Stallaert, R. A., van Velthoven, P. C., Comans, E. F., Diepenhorst, F. W. *et al.* (2003) PLUS study group. Cost-effectiveness of FDG-PET in staging non-small cell lung cancer: the PLUS study. *European Journal of Nuclear Medicine and Molecular Imaging* **30**, 1444–1449.

Warburg, O., Posner, K. & Negelein, E. (1931). The metabolism of the carcinoma cell. In *The Metabolism of Tumours* (ed. O. Warburg), pp. 29–169. New York: Richard R. Smith Inc.

Weber, W. A., Petersen, V., Schmidt, B., Tyndale-Hines, L., Link, T., Peschel, C. & Schwaiger, M. (2003) Positron emission tomography in non-small-cell lung cancer: prediction of response to chemotherapy by quantitative assessment of glucose use. *Journal of Clinical Oncology* **21**, 2651–2657.

PART 2

Surgical intervention

Chapter 5

Extended resection and reconstructive surgery: a review of current strategies

Francis Wells

The surgical resection rates for lung cancer in the UK remain among the lowest in Europe. Other healthcare systems achieve a resection rate of up to or just over 20%. In Britain today, the national average for most centres is under 10%. This unsatisfactory resection rate can be used as a "barometer" of care for patients with lung cancer. Not only does this fact point out the severe shortfall in services in this country, but also the needed potential in exploring surgical resection of more locally advanced tumours. Those countries with resection rates that are routinely in excess of 20% have centres that are actively engaged in down-staging chemotherapy trials and extended resections in a controlled and carefully observed environment. It is difficult to develop the more advanced surgical techniques in a constrained system.

The most important development in the surgical management of lung cancer has been the widespread introduction of tumour staging. Full prospective and retrospective post-surgical pathological staging of the tumour, in all patients, is vital if the results of extended resections are to be understood in the future. Spread of the tumour to the mediastinal lymph nodes and beyond portends a short survival time. Therefore, it is argued that the pain and risk that a patient experiences with major surgery are not justified if the chance of extended survival or cure is not significantly increased.

As data have accumulated, the understanding of the implications of mediastinal lymph node involvement has become more sophisticated. Although involvement of paratracheal and subcarinal nodes means a 5-year survival rate of less than 5% in most series, para-aortic and aortopulmonary window nodes seem to fare somewhat better (up to 25% in some series).

Direct mediastinal and chest wall invasion have also been viewed with pessimism by many physicians. However, in the absence of mediastinal lymph node involvement (groups 7, 10 and 4 particularly), selected cases can achieve worthwhile mid- and long-term survival.

In addition, although most patients with advanced local disease fare poorly, many surgeons have observed long-term survival in occasional patients with extended resection for locally advanced disease, especially in the absence of lymph node involvement. All of these observations have led to a rethink about the role of extended resection for patients with lung cancer.

In this chapter the author wishes to explore some of the possibilities for extended resection and to consider the scientific boundaries that restrict the cure rate for patients with lung cancer.

Lung cancer like breast cancer is frequently a disseminated disease at presentation. Of patients with the disease, 70–80% will have inoperable disease when first seen. This is as a result of blood-borne and lymphatic spread distant from the primary site. However, if local spread is restricted to areas that can be included within the resection, why should we not be able to expect a chance of cure? The best hope for cure still rests with surgical extirpation of the cancer.

A real concern of attending physicians and surgeons, however, is that if the use of surgery is too liberal then a significant number of patients will be subjected to unnecessary operations and the trauma that this entails.

What does extended resection mean?

Extended resection means the resection of a tumour beyond the readily accepted guidelines for staged tumours. This includes the following:

- Chest wall and diaphragmatic extension
- Superior sulcus tumours
- Involvement of the heart and/or the great vessels
- Bronchoplastic resections such as carina and main trachea
- Complete lymph node clearance within the hemi-thorax.

Some surgeons would include those patients who have other complicating factors such as advanced emphysema or coronary artery disease.

In patients with emphysema, the effect of the removal of a lobe that is badly affected by the disease may equate to the beneficial effects attributable to surgery for lung volume reduction. Hence a patient who was previously deemed to be inoperable might, with the application of that kind of lateral thought, be brought into the operable category. Similarly patients with coronary artery disease may be considered inoperable because of the extent of the coronary lesions. However, re-vascularising the heart may well render the patient operable.

Using the TNM classification, all stage I (T1N0 and T2N0) and stage II (T1N1, T2N1 and T3N0) tumours are regarded as operable. Stage IIIA (T3N1M0, T1N2M0, T2N2M0 and T3N2M0) and IIIB (T4N0 and T4N1) have not been regarded as operable by all surgical oncologists.

A T3 tumour is one of any size that directly invades the chest wall, superior sulcus, diaphragm, mediastinal pleura, parietal pericardium and main bronchus within 2 cm of the carina or with associated pulmonary collapse.

A T4 tumour is one of any size that invades the mediastinum or contents, vertebrae or carina, or has an associated pleuro-pericardial effusion of malignant origin. The presence of satellite lesions in the ipsilateral lung also falls within this category.

Identification of real mediastinal invasion preoperatively remains a significant problem. Subtle degrees of invasion or mere inflammatory adhesion of the tumour to the mediastinum is not possible to diagnose reliably on either computed tomography (CT) or magnetic resonance imaging (MRI). Often the only way forward is with surgical exploration. Indeed if a unit is not experiencing a failed thoracotomy rate of 2–3% per annum, potentially operable tumours are probably being missed.

In a recently published large study of post-surgical results, Naruke and colleagues (2001) in Tokyo have demonstrated that, in clinical stage IIIA disease, a 22.7% 5-year survival rate can be obtained. This fell to 20.1% for stage IIIB tumours. Interestingly post-surgical pathological restaging increased the survivors in the IIIA group to 23.6%, but reduced the survivors in the IIIB group to 16.5%. Superior sulcus tumours and those invading the diaphragm fared least well.

Chest wall and diaphragm invasion

A peripheral lung cancer invading the parietal pleura or deeper into the chest wall muscle or ribs can be resected very easily. Many of the smaller areas of involvement (up to 5 cm or so), especially when covered by the scapula, can be resected without reconstruction. However, if the area is larger, then the chest wall can be reconstructed using a double layer of polypropylene mesh, sandwiching a methyl methacrylate bone cement plate. This composite can be shaped to match the natural shape of the chest wall.

Similarly, invasion of the diaphragm can be dealt with by local resection and reconstruction using the same plastic mesh in a single layer. Indeed small areas of the right hemi-diaphragm do not need reconstruction at all because of the presence of the liver underneath.

These kind of extended resections have been practised since the earliest development of thoracic surgery and are relatively non-controversial. They should be part of the standard repertoire of the skilled thoracic surgeon.

The most important predictor of outcome in this situation is the presence or absence of mediastinal node invasion. In two publications (Pitz *et al.* 1996; Elia *et al.* 2001) from Italy and the Netherlands, respectively, worthwhile survival was achieved for patients with chest wall invasion in the absence of mediastinal node invasion. In both studies the presence of tumour in mediastinal nodes met with poor or no survival. In addition, the Dutch group demonstrated that spillage of tumour into the thorax during resection also resulted in a worse outcome.

Superior sulcus tumours

If tumours arising at the apex of either upper lobe invade the chest wall at an early stage, the brachial plexus, posterior angle of the first rib and/or the vertebral body may be invaded. This will result in severe local pain and referred pain from the particular nerve roots that are affected. Horner's syndrome and pain in the shoulder and arm are common and intractable. The combined use of radiotherapy and local resection has been used for some time. The results are poor for most patients in the mid to long term, but may result in the significant reduction or cessation of symptoms for a worthwhile period.

If the tumour invades within the neck of the first rib and its associated vertebral body, resection is rarely successful. Published results of very extensive local resection have met with improved results in the hands of Dartevelle and associates (1993). However, widespread adoption of these techniques is probably not wise until longer-term results are available.

Mediastinal invasion

The discovery that a tumour is invading the mediastinal structures almost invariably meets with a very nihilistic attitude. Direct spread into the mediastinal fat almost invariably means that the tumour cannot be completely removed and hence surgery should not be undertaken. However, in some circumstances resection is possible. Direct tumour extension into a mediastinal structure that can be removed with a good margin of uninvolved tissue should not deter resection, e.g. if the tumour includes pericardium that can be resected, most surgeons would do so. If the resected area is large, the defect can be repaired with a bovine pericardial patch or synthetic material. Extension into the pulmonary veins up to the left atrial wall can often be removed by extending the resection into the pericardium. Occasionally, direct invasion of the superior vena cava (SVC) can be managed by a local resection and reconstruction, as long as the extent is limited.

A recent paper from France demonstrated that worthwhile survival can be obtained by extended resection in patients with mediastinal invasion, as long as there is no significant mediastinal lymph node involvement (Doddoli *et al.* 2001). Overall 5-year actuarial survival rate in 29 patients who underwent superior vena caval (SVC) aortic, left atrial and carinal resection was 28% (median 11 months). In addition to the poor prognostic effect of positive nodal disease, incomplete resection was shown to be a disaster with early recurrence and poor mid-term outcome.

In the left side of the chest, extension into the aorta is generally considered to be unresectable, but occasionally very localised involvement can be removed and reconstructed.

The problem with all of these extended resections is that the number of properly reported cases with full staging information is limited as are the follow-up data. Case numbers are generally small and long-term follow-up reports are significantly lacking.

In any of these situations, however, if there is mediastinal lymph nodal involvement, the outlook is very poor and resection should not be undertaken.

Carinal and other bronchoplastic resections

Sleeve resection for upper lobe tumours that arise at the origin of the upper lobe bronchi is a technique that has been around for many years. In the absence of lymph node involvement, it is an excellent way of extending resection for patients with poor lung function. By reconnecting the intermediate bronchus on the left, or lower lobe bronchus on the right, back to the main bronchus, resection of tumours that are otherwise inoperable because of poor functional reserve becomes possible. They are accepted and non-controversial techniques. Surgeons who are not trained in their safe execution do their patients a disservice.

Techniques are available for resection and reconstruction of the carina for local bronchogenic carcinoma extension. These are more controversial because not only are they more difficult to complete safely, but also because there is very little data about them. However, in 1991 Grillo and Mathisen published a small series that demonstrated that the procedure was possible in skilled hands. Even this distinguished group had problems, however. Three early separations of the resected ends occurred and four patients suffered anastosmotic stenosis. There were five absolute survivors at 5 years from an original group of 37 patients, and an actuarial 5-year survival rate of 19%. Clearly, these types of procedures should be concentrated in a few skilled hands and all the data prospectively gathered.

Tumour down-staging

With the advent of modern chemotherapy protocols, there has been a reconsideration of tumours that are deemed to be inoperable as a result of mediastinal invasion. A number of patients seem to experience regression of local mediastinal invasion after completion of chemotherapy. Restaging with repeat CT may demonstrate shrinkage away from the mediastinum. There are now a number of reports of the early outcome following resection in this situation. Although these do hold some promise, there is no robust RCT data or even long-term outcome for this group of patients.

In addition, this kind of approach is not without potential additional risk. There have been a number of reports of increased pulmonary permeability following surgical resection after chemotherapy. In appraising the risk for patients the cumulative risk of both the chemotherapy regimen and the surgery have to be summated.

Conclusions

In carefully selected cases, extended resection for locally advanced disease can be achieved safely in the modern era of thoracic surgery. There are techniques that can be used to solve most of the problems that confront the surgeon. However, as with all things surgical, just because a procedure can be done it does not mean that it should be done. An unnecessary surgical assault on a patient cannot be justified.

The single most important predictor of outcome is the nodal status of the patient. Disease within the mediastinal lymph nodes represents dissemination away from the primary site and local resection alone will not cure the disease.

The effect of adjunctive chemo- and radiotherapy is under investigation, and all of these patients should be managed and studied as part of a properly constructed and well-powered clinical trial.

References

Dartevelle, P. G., Chapelier, A. R., Macchiarini, P. *et al.* (1993). Anterior thoracic approach for radical resection of lung tumors invading the thoracic inlet. *Journal of Thoracic and Cardiovascular Surgery* **105**, 1025–1034.

Doddoli, C., Rollet, G., Thomas, P. *et al.* (2001). Is lung cancer surgery justified in patients with direct mediastinal invasion? *European Journal of Cardio-thoracic Surgery* **20**, 339–343.

Elia, S., Griffo, S., Costabile, R., Ferrante, G. (2001). Surgical treatment of lung cancer invading chest wall: a retrospective analysis of 110 patients. *European Journal of Cardio-thoracic Surgery* **20**, 356–360.

Mathisen, D., Grillo, H. (1991). Carinal resection for bronchogenic carcinoma. *Journal of Thoracic and Cardiovascular Surgery* **102**, 16–23.

Naruke, T., Tsuchiya, R., Kondo, H., Asamura, H. (2001). Prognosis and survival after resection for bronchogenic carcinoma based on the 1997 TNM-staging classification: The Japanese experience. *Annals of Thoracic Surgery* **71**, 1759–1764.

Pitz, C. C., Brutel de la riviere, A., Elbers, H., Westermann, C. J., van den Bosch, M. M. (1996). Surgical treatment of 125 patients with non-small cell cancer and chest wall involvement. *Thorax* **51**, 846–850.

Chapter 6

Surgery in advanced lung cancer. Should we or shouldn't we?

Andrew Drain and Francis Wells

Introduction

It has long been accepted that the only therapy with a potential cure for patients with lung cancer is timely and complete surgical resection. This conditional statement depends upon a working knowledge of the stage of disease. Today professionals looking after people with lung cancer have a sophisticated array of investigations that allow a comprehensive knowledge of the extent of tumour in each patient. We should know the cell type and the degree of differentiation of the tumour, its size, local extent and the likelihood of disease distant from the primary site. Combined positron emission tomography (PET) and computed tomography (CT) scanning will eliminate most inappropriate patients from being offered surgical treatment. The net result of this approach is to be able to select patients with cancer confined within the thorax in whom the tumour can be completely encompassed by an achievable resection.

So what do we mean by 'advanced lung cancer'? If we assume that stage IV disease, defined as that with evidence of metastatic spread, is inoperable then we will confine ourselves in this chapter to the role of surgery in stage IIIA and IIIB non-small cell lung cancer. This, however, still leaves unanswered the question of what actually constitutes a resectable lesion, and which tumours of those that are regarded as being locally advanced, are in fact locally resectable? If tumour load has an impact on outcome then can surgery alone be enough at any stage of the disease? Lung cancer is usually a systemic disease at presentation and hence the best hope of cure lies with the control of local, regional and distant metastases. This is likely to mean the use of both systemic and local therapeutic strategies.

Resectability

Convention dictates that a tumour completely confined within a lung that can be removed by lobectomy, bilobectomy or pneumonectomy and in the absence of mediastinal lymph node involvement is resectable. Local spread outside the lung, invading, chest wall, diaphragm or mediastinal structures, will inevitably mean that attempted surgical resection is much more likely to leave some disease behind. Surgical resection alone can only render a cure for these patients if vital structures are removed with the tumour 'en bloc'.

Resection rates in the UK remain relatively low at around no more than 10%, while European and North American rates are closer to 20%. There are several reasons for this: when there is no surgeon present at multi-disciplinary meetings, operability and resectability is often decided by non-surgeons. When surgeons are present, lack of thoracic experience may lead to rigid interpretation and application of the guidelines (see British Thoracic Society and Society of Cardiothoracic Surgeons of Great Britain and Ireland Working Party (2001) guidelines for definition of operability versus resectability) and extreme scepticism regarding outcome.

While guidelines are helpful, their interpretation must be combined with an understanding of the subtleties of staging and the experience of therapeutic realism. Operative intervention does not always fit neatly into pre-defined subsets. Appropriate surgical resection can cure lung cancer and, as therapeutic strategies expand to encompass later stages of disease, biological and molecular staging improves, and refined anaesthetic and surgical techniques minimise operative complications, resection rates should increase.

But if we are to raise our resection rates to 15–20% plus, in line with Europe and North America, we will have to pick up stage I/II tumours sooner and also extend our resections into the later stages of the disease (stage IIIA/B). This should only be done if the results warrant it and the necessary surgical expertise is available. But is extended resection always the correct way to proceed?

Extended resection

The answer to this question remains no, unless strategies are utilised to completely encompass the disease in these more advanced cases. With modern cardio-thoracic surgery, resection can be extended to include parts of the pericardium, right and left atrium, aorta and almost any part of the chest wall and diaphragm. Central airway extension can even sometimes be encompassed by carinal resection and reconstruction. Therefore, it is important that multi-disciplinary teams deciding upon treatment packages for such people should contain the necessary surgical expertise and be aware of these more advanced surgical procedures, so as not to disadvantage those with advanced disease who may have meaningful resection by more extensive surgery.

Staging: clinical versus pathological

Stage grouping tumour–node–metastasis (TNM) subsets have defined limits for resectability with good evidence that N2-nodal involvement has a poor effect on outcome (Naruke *et al.* 2001; Goldstraw 1992). Obvious spread to mediastinal nodes therefore renders many of these patients inoperable, reinforcing the need for full pre-surgical nodal staging. There is a large volume of evidence that the preoperative presumption of N2 disease on CT alone is not enough, necessitating all accessible nodes to be biopsied. Some advocate mediastinoscopy for all potential resections; however the evidence for this is controversial (Canadian Lung Oncology Group

1995). The role of PET scanning for identification of mediastinal disease may supersede mediastinoscopy but has not yet become routine practice in most centres (Tinteran *et al.* 2002). To date, the only randomised trial found that routine mediastinoscopy was not superior to a selective approach guided by CT scan in the rate of thoracotomy without cure (Canadian Lung Oncology Group 1995) and selective mediastinoscopy based on CT assessment is advised.

Stage III disease

For the majority of patients with stage III disease, the picture is often one of unresectable N2 or N3 mediastinal node disease (Falk 2001). The prognosis is more favourable for stage IIIA (median survival of 12 months and a 5-year survival of 15%) compared with stage IIIB (the respective figures are 8 months and less than 5%) (Ihde & Minna 1991). Radical radiotherapy alone was for a long time the treatment of choice for these patients given the good control of symptoms (Arriagada *et al.* 1994). However, with scanty objective evidence to support this and given the heterogeneity of the group, policy is shifting towards multimodality therapy with an increasing role for surgical resection.

Surgery is mainly confined to incidental N2 disease, that is, T1-3 lesions with node negative preoperative chest x-ray, CT scan and mediastinoscopy but where N2 involvement is appreciated only during mediastinal lymph node dissection at the time of surgery. A second sub-group of IIIA who may also be considered for surgical resection are those with minimal, non-bulky N2 disease revealed by preoperative mediastinoscopy (group 5 and 6) and who are potentially resectable following induction therapy. Those with bulky N2 involvement and paratracheal nodes clearly visible on chest x-ray and CT scan or splaying of the carina at bronchoscopy are generally unresectable.

The evidence is increasingly pointing towards combined modality therapy rather than surgery alone in patients with N2 disease for both local control and treatment of early micrometastases (Pass *et al.* 1992; Rosell *et al.* 1994; Roth *et al.* 1994; Strauss 1999). Despite larger phase III trials in progress, no large, randomised study comparing chemotherapy or radiotherapy, alone or in combination with surgery is yet concluded.

Patients presenting with stage IIIB (T4 or N3) including supraclavicular or contra-lateral nodes, invasion of the spine, trachea, carina, oesophagus, aorta, or heart, or satellite lesions within the same lobe are generally considered inoperable. Satellite nodules on CT or even PET cannot be assumed to be malignant and unless there is evidence of disease elsewhere, a surgical approach offers a 5-year survival of greater than 20%, significantly better than other subsets of T4 disease (Pearson *et al.* 2002). A small number of T4 N0 tumours can be completely removed with extensive resection. As with stage IIIA, combinations of induction chemoradiotherapy and adjuvant treatment may continue to improve prognosis in combination with surgical resection; however, overstaging in these patients is a potential concern in reporting long-term survival figures and in prescribing toxic treatments for potentially totally resectable disease (Stamatis *et al.* 1999).

Lesions with carinal involvement have a poorer prognosis, highlighted in an update of the Massachusetts General experience in which 58 tracheal or sleeve resections were performed for T4 disease. It was concluded that sleeve pneumonectomy should be reserved for young, healthy patients with clinical N0 disease (as at mediastinoscopy) and completely resectable disease (Mitchell *et al.* 1999).

Chest wall and mediastinal invasion

The division between T3 and T4 lesions can sometimes be difficult to make clinically despite improved CT and magnetic resonance imaging (MRI). Observed results have shown no difference in survival between patients with T3 and T4 disease (see Figure 6.1) and inadequate differentiation in outcome between stage IIIA and IIIB (Kameyama *et al.* 2002). The heterogeneity of patients between T3 and T4 amplifies the problem in determining prognosis.

In this study, despite no statistical survival difference between IIIA and IIIB or T3 and T4 (see Figure 6.2), there was a tendency towards stepwise reduction of survival

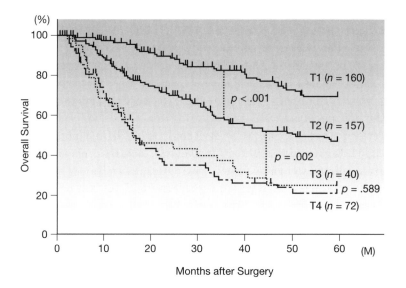

Figure 6.1 Postoperative survival curves on the basis of tumour status. There are significant differences in the prognoses between T1 and T2 groups and between T2 and T3 groups, but there is no tendency towards difference between T3 and T4 groups (Kameyama *et al.* 2002).

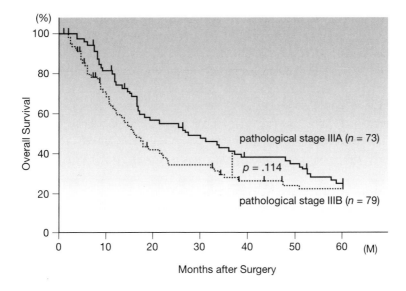

Figure 6.2 Postoperative survival curves of patients with stage IIIA and IIIB disease. There is no tendency towards difference between the prognosis of patients with stage IIIA and IIIB disease (Kameyama *et al.* 2002).

from N0 to N3 suggesting that the similarities in survival between IIIA and IIIB were due to inadequate understanding of the relevance of T3/T4 categories and inaccurate preoperative tumour staging (Kameyama *et al.* 2002). Patients with bronchial invasion and those with intra-lobar separate tumour nodules fared better than those with extrapulmonary invasion or malignant effusion. Of those with extrapulmonary disease, those with chest wall invasion also fared better, although the type of chest wall invasion is important.

Chest wall invasion is an indication for reconstruction, not a contraindication to excision (Edwards & Waller 2001). With adhesions to parietal pleura, chest wall extension is usually present and complete resection rates can be increased by up to three times if chest wall is resected en bloc, with increased 5-year survival (Albertucci *et al.* 1992).

Previous work has shown that, although stage IIIA (cT3N1 and cT1-3N2) tumours have a low chance of cure by surgery alone, surgery for chest wall invasion can give satisfactory results justified by 5-year survival rates following resection of T3N0 chest wall of 35–50% (McCuaghan 1985; Shah and Goldstraw 1995; Detterbeck and Socinski 1997; Downey *et al.* 1999). Resection of superior sulcus tumours (Pancoast) and those with vertebral involvement requiring spinal reconstruction is also possible although with a high morbidity and limited survival (Dartevelle & Macchiarini 1999; York *et al.* 1999).

In a recent review of 2738 patients with non-small cell lung cancer (NSCLC) from Milan, 146 underwent surgery with chest wall resection, of whom 77 had radical resections. Roviaro *et al.* (2003) advocate the performance of en bloc resection for chest wall resection, with decreasing morbidity and mortality over the past decade. The Mayo Clinic performed 94 chest wall resections between 1985 and 1999 with a 6.3% operative mortality and an overall 5-year actuarial survival of 38.7% (Burkhart *et al.* 2002).

The authors recently operated on a 68-year-old man with NSCLC with a T3N2 tumour extending along the pulmonary vein and involving the left atrium. The tumour was resected by a right intrapericardial pneumonectomy with resection of part of the left atrium and reconstruction of the left atrial wall with the aid of cardiopulmonary bypass. Complete tumour excision was achieved, demonstrating the full range of tools available to the thoracic surgeon. Evidence in favour of chest wall resection is now overwhelming and with mediastinal involvement the use of cardiopulmonary bypass increases the options available.

Combined multimodality treatment: the role of surgery

For patients who have disease recurrence after apparently complete tumour resection, the cause is predominantly systematic metastases, but local recurrence in the chest or a combination of both is also a problem (Aisner *et al.* 1983). Consequently and as mentioned in our introduction, the survival of these patients must be seen in the context of multimodality treatment and not just extended surgical resection. This strategy has resulted in improved survival for a substantial number of patients (Pignon *et al.* 1992; Non-Small Cell Lung Cancer Collaborative Group 1995). In particular, patients with T4 lesions with direct invasion of the vertebra, superior vena cava, oesophagus and atrium are those in whom downstaging may allow more radical resection (Rendina *et al.* 1999).

To assess this several studies are still under way. The Cleveland Clinic studied 105 patients with IIIA and IIIB NSCLC over a 6-year period who received accelerated multimodality therapy. They looked at hyperfractionated radiotherapy, concurrent chemoradiotherapy (paclitaxel and cisplatin) followed by resection and postoperative chemo-radiation. Toxic effects related to induction therapy resulting in hospital admission were 40% and treatment-related mortality 9%. But of the 77% who completed all therapy 93% were operable and 79% curatively resected. Median 2-year and 5-year survival rates were 53% and 32%, respectively. They concluded that, although this therapy was equally valuable in IIIA and IIIB NSCLC, the response to induction was unpredictable. Younger patients, non-squamous cell types, sterilised mediastinal nodes (following induction) and lower pathological tumour stage (pT) benefited the most (DeCamp *et al.* 2003).

Ichinose *et al.* (2003) assessed surgical resection performed from 3 to 6 weeks after completing induction treatment of cisplatin and concurrent radiotherapy in

22/27 patients with stage III/IV lung cancer. All who had surgery had complex procedures including resection of the superior vena cava, carina and vertebrae. Operative morbidity and mortality rates were 36% and 4%, respectively. The calculated 1-year and 3-year survival rates of all 27 patients were 73% and 56%, respectively.

The role of surgery after induction chemotherapy in stage III NSCLC was further investigated and shown to improve local control and to allow histological assessment of treatment activity with an 8-year overall survival (Bedini *et al.* 2003). In an earlier study the Cleveland Clinic had previously demonstrated the role of accelerated hyperfractionated radiation, concurrent paclitaxel/cisplatin chemotherapy and surgery for stage III NSCLC. Fourteen out of forty-five patients were downstaged to mediastinal negative lymph nodes with a 5-year survival of 29% overall and 50% 5-year survival for those with downstaging of the mediastinal nodes (Adelstein *et al.* 2002).

Following his study of 90 patients with potentially operable IIIA NSCLC who received docetaxel-cisplatin and subsequent resection, Betticher *et al.* (2003) recommends resection only for patients with mediastinal downstaging after chemotherapy. However, results of a repeat mediastinoscopy can be disappointing and it has been shown to be a not-so-effective restaging tool because of the high number of incomplete procedures and because it yields false negative results (Pitz *et al.* 2002).

Many studies looking at combined non-surgical regimes in stage III and IV NSCLC have been completed and are ongoing, with varying results (Galician Lung Cancer Group 2003; Galette 2003). As results continue to be published we will probably continue to see a trend towards surgical resection in combination with both neo-adjuvant and adjuvant chemo and radiotherapy to best manage advanced lung cancer.

Conclusions

Surgical resection for advanced lung cancer can work. Despite the plethora of trials looking at unresectable advanced lung cancer, large multi-centre trials are essential to further assess the role of surgery. This must be done in the context of the practical application of logic such as the impact of nodal downstaging. Although increased operability is surgically achievable in the appropriate unit, there is little or no standardisation in drugs, doses schedules or intensity. An expected increase in mortality and morbidity is unavoidable and therefore intellectual rigour is essential.

The relevance of neo-adjuvant and adjuvant chemotherapy as induction treatment for patients with marginally resectable stage IIIB NSCLC is feasible and promising and has to be considered in line with the additional use of radiotherapy in downstaging protocol. This may allow patients who are otherwise inoperable to benefit from advanced resection.

To achieve this, an in-depth knowledge of the implications of clinical staging is vital and the surgeon in the team must be versed in all aspects of pulmonary surgery (ability to use cardiopulmonary bypass without worrying is an advantage). All patients put forward for such advanced surgical treatment should be enrolled in clinical trials and managed in the multi-disciplinary setting.

With increasing evidence that combined multimodality treatment strategies are better than surgery alone in patients with advanced disease, there is now no place for treating such patients outside expert units. While surgical resection will continue to play a major role in advanced lung cancer, for some this will not be appropriate and aggressive surgery should be substituted by palliative care.

References

Adelstein, D. J., Rice, T. W., Rybicki, L. A., Greskovich, J. F., Ciezki, J. P., Carroll, M. A. & DeCamp, M. M. (2002). Accelerated hyperfractionated radiation, concurrent paclitaxel/cisplatin chemotherapy and surgery for stage III non-small cell lung cancer. *Lung Cancer* **36**(2):167–174.

Aisner, J., Forastierre, A. & Aroney, R. (1983). Patterns of recurrence for cancer of the lung and oesophagus. *Cancer Treatment Symposia* **2**, 87–105.

Albertucci, M., DeMeester, T. R., Rothberg, M., Hagen, J. A., Santoscoy, R. & Smyrk, T. C. (1992). Surgery and the management of peripheral lung tumours adherent to the parietal pleura. *Journal of Thoracic and Cardiovascular Surgery* **103**, 8–12; discussion 12–13.

Bedini, A. V., Tavecchio, L., Delledonne, V. & Andreani, S. M. (2003). Surgically proven complete response of stage III non-small cell lung cancer after cisplatin-enhanced radiotherapy. Clinical implications and long-term results. *Tumori* **89**(1), 16–19.

Betticher, D. C., Hsu Schmitz, S. F., Totsch, M., Hansen, E., Joss, C., von Briel, C., Schmid, R. A., Pless, M., Habicht, J., Roth, A. D., *et al.* (2003). Mediastinal lymph node clearance after docetaxel-cisplatin neoadjuvant chemotherapy is prognostic of survival in patients with stage IIIA pN2 non-small-cell lung cancer: a multicenter phase II trial. *Journal of Clinical Oncology* **21**(9), 1752–1759.

British Thoracic Society and Society of Cardiothoracic Surgeons of Great Britain and Ireland Working Party (2001). Guidelines on the selection of patients with lung cancer for surgery. *Thorax* **56**, 89–108

Burkhart, H. M., Allen, M. S., Nichols, F. C., Deschamps, C., Miller, D. L., Trastek, V. F. & Pairolero, P. C. (2002). Results of en bloc resection for bronchogenic carcinoma with chest wall invasion. *Journal of Thoracic and Cardiovascular Surgery* **123**(4), 670–675.

Canadian Lung Oncology Group. (1995). Investigation for mediastinal disease in patients with apparently operable lung cancer. *Annals of Thoracic Surgery* **60**, 1382–1389.

Dartevelle, P. & Macchiarini, P. (1999). Surgical management of superior sulcus tumours. *The Oncologist* **4**, 398.

DeCamp, M., Rice, T., David, J., Mark, A., Chidel, M., Rybicki, L., Sudish, C., Murthy, S., Eugene, H. & Blackstone, E. (2003). Value of accelerated multimodality therapy in stage IIIA and IIIB non–small cell lung cancer *Journal of Thoracic and Cardiovascular Surgery* **126**(1), 17–27.

Detterbeck. F. C. & Socinski, M. A. (1997). IIB or not IIB: the current question in staging non-small cell lung cancer. *Chest* **112**(1), 229–234.

Downey, R. J., Martini, N., Rusch, V. W., Bains, M. S., Korst, R. J. & Ginsberg, R. J. (1999). Extent of chest wall invasion and survival in patients with lung cancer. *Annals of Thoracic Surgery* **68**(1), 188–193.

Edwards, J. G. & Waller, D. A. (2001). The evidence base for surgical intervention in lung cancer. In: *The Effective Management of Lung Cancer* (Muers, M., Macbeth, F., Wells, F., and Miles, A., eds). Aesculapius Medical Press, London 2001. pp. 45–59.

Falk, S. (2001). The evidence base for radiotherapy in lung cancer In: *The Effective Management of Lung Cancer* (Muers, M., Macbeth, F., Wells, F. and Miles, A., eds). Aesculapius Medical Press, London 2001. pp. 61–70.

Galette, D., Cesario, A., Margaritora, S., Porziella, V., Macis, G., D'Angelillo, R. M., Trodella, L., Sterzi, S. & Granone, P. (2003). Enduring challenge in the treatment of non-small cell lung cancer with clinical stage IIIB: results of a trimodality approach. *Annals of Thoracic Surgery* **76**(6), 1802–1809.

Galician Lung Cancer Group (2003). Gemcitabine, cisplatin and vinorelbine as induction chemotherapy followed by radical therapy in stage III non-small-cell lung cancer: a multicentre study of galician-lung-cancer-group. *Lung Cancer* **40**(2), 215–220.

Goldstraw, P. (1992). The practice of cardiothoracic surgeons in pre-operative staging of lung cancer. *Thorax* **47**, 1–2.

Ichinose, Y., Fukuyama, Y., Asoh, H., Ushijima, C., Okamoto, T., Okamoto, J. & Sakai, M. (2003). Induction chemoradiotherapy and surgical resection for selected stage IIIB non-small-cell lung cancer. *Annals of Thoracic Surgery* **76**(6), 1810–1814.

Ihde, D. C. & Minna, J. D. (1991). Non-small cell lung cancer. Part 1: Biology diagnosis and staging. *Current Problems in Cancer* **15**, 63–104.

Kameyama, K., Huang, C., Liu, D., Okamoto, T., Hayashi, E., Yamamoto, Y. & Yokomise, H. (2002). Problems related to TNM staging: Patients with stage III non–small cell lung cancer *Journal of Thoracic Cardiovascular Surgery* **124**(3), 503–510.

Le Chevalier, M., Arriagada, R., Quoix, E., Ruffie, P., Martin, M., Douillard, J. Y., Tarayre, M., Lacombe-Terrier, M. J. & Laplanche, A. (1994). Radiotherapy alone versus combined chemotherapy and radiotherapy in unresectable non-small cell lung carcinoma. *Lung Cancer* **10**(Suppl 1), S239–S244.

McCuaghan, B. C., Martini, N., Bains, M. S. & McCormack, P. M. (1985). Chest wall invasion in carcinoma of the lung. Therapeutic and prognostic implications. *Journal of Thoracic and Cardiovascular Surgery* **89**(6) 836–841.

Mitchell, J. D., Mathisen, D. J., Wright, C. D., Wain, J. C., Donahue, D. M., Moncure, A. C. & Grillo, H. C. (1999). Clinical experience with carinal resection. *Journal of Thoracic Cardiovascular Surgery* **117**, 39.

Naruke, T., Tsuchiya, R., Kondo, H. & Asamura, H. (2001). Prognosis and survival after resection for bronchogenic carcinoma based on the 1997 TNM-staging classification: the Japanese experience *Annals of Thoracic Surgery* **71**(6), 1759–1764.

Non-Small Cell Lung Cancer Collaborative Group (1995). Chemotherapy in non-small cell lung cancer; a meta-analysis using updated data on individual patients from 52 randomised trials. *British Medical Journal* **311**, 899–890.

Pass, H. I., Pogrebniak, H. W., Steinberg, S. M., Mulshine, J. & Minna, J. (1992). Randomized control trial of neoadjuvant therpy for lung cancer: interim analysis. *Annals of Thoracic Surgery* **53**, 992–998.

Pearson, F. G., Cooper, J. D., DeSlauriers, J., Ginsberg, R. J., Heibert, C. A., Patterson, G. A. (2002). *Thoracic Surgery*. 2nd edn, 849.

Pignon, J. P., Arriagada, R., Ihde, D. C., Johnson, D. H., Perry, M. C., Souhami, R. L., Brodin, O., Joss, R. A., Kies, M. S., Lebeau, B. *et al.* (1992). A meta-analysis of thoracic radiotherapy for small cell lung cancer. *New England Journal of Medicine* **327**, 1618–1624/

Pitz, C. C., Maas, K. W., Van Swieten, H. A., de la Riviere, A.B., Hofman, P., Schtamel, F. M. (2002). Surgery as part of combined modality treatment in stage IIIB non-small cell lung cancer. *Annals of Thoracic Surgery* **74**(1), 164–169.

Rendina, E. A., Venuta, F., De Giacomo, T., Ciccone, A. M., Ruvolo, G., Coloni, G. F., Ricci, C. (1999). Induction chemotherapy for T4 centrally located non-small cell lung cancer. *Journal of Thoracic and Cardiovascular Surgery* **117**, 225–233.

Rosell, R., Maestre, J., Font, A., Moreno, I., Molina, F., Milla, A., Gomez-Codina, J., Camps, C. (1994). A randomised trial comparing preoperative chemoptherapy plus surgery with surgery alone in patients with non-small cell lung cancer. *New England Journal of Medicine* **330**, 153–158.

Roth, J. A., Fossella, F., Komaki, R., Ryan, M. B., Putnam, J. B. Jr, Lee, J. S., Dhingra, H., De Caro, L., Chasen, M., McGavran, M. *et al* (1994). A randomised trial comparing perioperative chemotherapy and surgery with surgery alone in resectable stage IIIA non-small cell lung cancer. *Journal of the National Cancer Institute* **86**, 673–680.

Roviaro, G., Varoli, F., Grignani, F., Vergani, C., Pagano, C., Maciocco, M., Romanelli, A. (2003). Non-small cell lung cancer with chest wall invasion. *Chest* **123**, 1341–1347.

Shah, S. S. & Goldstraw, P. (1995). Combined pulmonary and thoracic wall resection for stage III lung cancer. *Thorax* **50**, 782–724.

Stamatis, G., Eberhardt, W., Stuben, G., Bildat, S., Dahler, O. & Hillejan, L. (1999). Preoperative chemoradiotherapy and surgery for selected non-small cell lung cancer IIIB sub-groups: Long-term results. *Annals of Thoracic Surgery* **68**, 1144–1149.

Strauss, G. M. (1999). Role of chemotherapy in stages I to III non-small cell lung cancer. *Chest* **116**, 509S–516S.

The Canadian Lung Oncology Group (1995). Investigation for mediastinal disease in patients with apparently operable lung cancer. *Annals of Thoracic Surgery* **60**, 1382–1389.

van Tinteren, H., Hoekstra, O. S., Smit, E. F., van den Bergh, J. H., Schreurs, A. J., Stallaert, R. A., van Velthoven, P. C., Comans, E. F., Diepenhorst, F. W., Verboom, P. *et al*. (2002). Effectiveness of positron emission tomography in the preoperative assessment of patients with suspected non-small-cell lung cancer: the PLUS multicentre randomised trial. *The Lancet* **359**, 1388.

York, J. E., Walsh, G. L., Lang, F. F., Putnam, J. B., McCutcheon, I. E., Swisher, S. G., Komaki, R. & Gokaslan, Z. L. (1999). Combined chest wall resection with vertebrectomy and spinal reconstruction for the treatment of Pancoast tumours. *Journal of Neurosurgery* **91**, 74–80.

PART 3

Radiotherapy and medical oncology

Chapter 7

Neoadjuvant chemotherapy for non-small-cell lung cancer

Catherine M. A. Kelly, Siow Ming Lee and Jeremy P. C. Steele

Introduction

Surgery remains the standard of care for patients with stages I and II non-small-cell lung cancer (NSCLC) and for some subsets of stage III. The 5-year survival rates in patients with stage I and II range from 40 to 70%, but fall to less than 25% in patients with pathological stage IIIA and less than 10% in patients with unresectable stage IIIA and IIIB (Mountain 1997). One-third of patients with stage IA disease will relapse and die of their cancer within 5 years. The majority of relapses are at distant sites. In trials with longer follow-up times the brain has emerged as the most common site of relapse (Eberhardt *et al.* 2003).

In an effort to improve survival post resection of NSCLC, adjuvant and neoadjuvant combined modality strategies have been investigated. The International Adjuvant Lung Cancer Trial (IALT) identified some benefit in adjuvant cisplatin-based chemotherapy after complete resection of NSCLC in 1867 patients ($p < 0.03$) (IALT Collaborative Group 2004). A trial of such magnitude has yet to be published supporting the role of neoadjuvant chemotherapy prior to surgery for NSCLC; however, there are several ongoing trials worldwide designed to evaluate it, notably the MRC LU22 study that should report data by 2005.

The objective of neoadjuvant chemotherapy is to downstage locally advanced tumours and to reduce the risk of metastases. Mediastinal lymph node downstaging of the order of 53% was reported in one study after neoadjuvant treatment (Van Zandwijk *et al.* 2000). Advantages include a significant cytoreduction, increased resectability and conservation of functional lung parenchyma. Mediastinal lymph node clearance and complete surgical resection are strongly predictive of increased survival (Betticher *et al.* 2003). Another valid reason for giving preoperative chemotherapy is that whenever surgical resection follows chemotherapy it provides a true pathological assessment of the patient's response to induction chemotherapy, which can then be used to guide postoperative treatment (Manegold 2001).

Embarking on 3–6 cycles of neoadjuvant chemotherapy delays definitive surgery and could potentially render a previous surgical candidate unfit for resection because of treatment-related toxicities or disease progression. However, a low rate of progression has been described during induction chemotherapy in all trials: between 3 and 5% (Pisters *et al.* 2000). Phase II studies have established feasibility and safety for chemotherapy and combined chemoradiation as induction therapy. Pneumonitis and adult respiratory distress syndrome have been reported after chemotherapy alone and with combined chemoradiation induction protocols (Eberhardt *et al.* 2003).

Phase II trials of neoadjuvant chemotherapy for non-small-cell lung cancer

There have been more than 30 phase II trials (Table 7.1). Response rates have ranged from 51 to 77%. Following induction chemotherapy between 63 and 90% of patients had resectable tumours. The median survival ranged from 13 to 32 months and the 3-year and 5-year survival rates ranged from 17 to 40%. These studies have been criticised for several reasons: their size; stage heterogeneity; single centre variations in the induction chemotherapy; and the fact that some patients received preoperative chemotherapy alone whilst others received preoperative chemotherapy and radiotherapy. Patients selected for phase II trials were fit and of good performance status and therefore the results cannot be extrapolated to populations of poor performance status.

Table 7.1 Preoperative chemotherapy in stage III non-small cell lung cancer: phase II trials

Authors	Year	No. patients	CT	Overall response (%)	Resection rate %	Median survival (months)
Bitran(1)	1986	22	CAMPr	64	14	9
Burkes(2)	1992	39	MVP	64	56	18.6
Martini(8)	1993	136	MVP	77	65	19
Rusch(13)	1994	51	PE	-	88	17
Mathisen(9)	1996	40	PVF	87	100	28
Spain(14)	1988	31	MVP	73	80	19
Vokes(19)	1989	27	PEVn	48	15	8
Pisters(10)	1990	73	MPVn	77	60	19
Johnson(7)	1991	28	PV	54	40	12
Sridhar(15)	1993	35	PVF	69	81	19
Pujol(12)	1994	33	IPE	70	86	10
Elias(6)	1994	54	CAP	39	77	18
Carreta(3)	1994	32	MVP	87	75	-
Sugarbaker(16)	1995	74	VP	-	36	20
Ciriaco(4)	1995	49	MVP	84	90	9
VanKooten(18)	1999	19	GP	63	37	-
Crino(5)	1999	42	GP	62	7	-
VanZandwijk(17)	2000	47	GP	70	71	18.9
Pisters(11)	2000	94	CaT	56	86	-

CT: chemotherapy; C: cyclophosphamide; A: doxorubicin; M: mitomycin; Pr: procarbazine; V: vinblastin; P: cisplatin; E: etoposide; F: fluorouracil; Vn: vindesine; I: ifosamide; G: gemcitabine; T: taxol; Ca: carboplatin

Phase III studies

Table 7.2 Completed phase randomised trials >50 patients

Trial	Stage	Induction chemotherapy
Roth	IIIa	3 × CEP
Rosell	IIIa (T1-3, N2)	3 × MIP
Depierre	Ib, II, IIIa	2 × MIP (+2 × MIP, +RT for T3 or N2)

C: cyclophosphamide; E: etoposide; P: cisplatin; M: mitomycin; I: ifosamide

On the basis of encouraging results from phase II studies, Rosell *et al.* (1994) and Roth *et al.* (1994) conducted small, randomised trials comparing neoadjuvant chemotherapy and surgery with surgery alone. Both studies are frequently quoted in support of neoadjuvant chemotherapy for stage III NSCLC and were terminated early on the basis of interim analysis that suggested significant increases in overall survival time compared with the surgery alone arms.

In the Rosell study 60 patients with stage IIIA NSCLC were randomly assigned to receive surgery alone or induction chemotherapy consisting of three cycles of mitomycin 6 mg/m^2, ifosamide 3 g/m^2 and cisplatin 50 mg/m^2 every 3 weeks followed by surgery. All patients received mediastinal irradiation after surgery. The median survival was 26 months in the induction chemotherapy arm compared with 8 months in the surgery only arm ($p < 0.001$). The disease-free survival in the induction chemotherapy arm was 20 months compared with 5 months in the surgery only arm ($p < 0.001$). The follow-up analysis detected an overall median survival of 22 months for the neoadjuvant chemotherapy group compared with 10 months for the surgery alone group ($p < 0.005$).

Although the results are strongly supportive of neoadjuvant chemotherapy there were several flaws in the study: the sample size was small and the survival rates in the surgery alone group were very poor. Survival rates reported are similar to those among patients with metastastic NSCLC and less than previously reported survival rates in resectable stage III disease. In a review of several randomised trials involving patients with N1 or N2 squamous lung cancer treated with surgery and postoperative radiotherapy the reported 5-year survival rates ranged from 21 to 36% (Cocquyt *et al.* 1994). A further criticism focuses on the presence of k-ras gene (an adverse prognostic indicator) in 42% of the surgery alone arm compared with 15% in the induction chemotherapy plus surgery arm.

Roth *et al.* (1994) randomised 60 patients with resectable stage III NSCLC to receive either six cycles of induction chemotherapy consisting of cyclophosphamide 500 mg/m^2 day 1, cisplatin 100 mg/m^2 day 1 and etoposide 100 mg/m^2 day 1, 2 and 3, given every 28 days followed by surgery or surgery alone. Patients who responded or had stable disease received a total of three cycles. Those who progressed received no more chemotherapy. Patients who had a documented tumour regression on completion of three cycles had a further three cycles after surgery. After three cycles of chemotherapy 35% of patients had a major clinical response. Patients treated with induction chemotherapy followed by surgery had an estimated median survival of 64 months compared with 11 months for patients who had surgery alone ($p < 0.018$ by log rank test). The estimated 2-year and 3-year survival rates were 60% and 56% for the neoadjuvant chemotherapy group and 25% and 15% for those treated with surgery alone, respectively.

The later update was reported with a median time from randomisation of 82 months (Roth *et al.* 1998). The neoadjuvant chemotherapy group had a median survival of 21 months and the surgery alone group had a median survival of 14 months ($p < 0.056$ log rank test). The overall 3-year and 5-year survival rates for the neoadjuvant chemotherapy group were 43% and 36%, respectively, while those for the surgery alone group were 19% and 15%, respectively.

This study has also been criticised. As in the original study by Rosell the sample size was small. In the surgery alone arm 31% of the patients had stage IIIB tumours and 9% had stage IV disease making a total of 40% of the patients in this arm technically ineligible for this approach. In the neoadjuvant chemotherapy arm there were only three stage IIIB and no stage IV tumours.

In contrast to the above studies, a recent, large randomised phase III trial failed to report a survival advantage for stage III tumours treated with induction chemotherapy followed by surgery but reported a benefit for stages I and II. Depierre *et al.* (2002) conducted a trial to evaluate whether preoperative chemotherapy could improve survival in resectable stage I (except T1N0), II and IIIA NSCLC. A total of 355 patients were randomised. Induction chemotherapy consisted of two cycles of mitomycin 6 mg/m^2 day 1, ifosamide 1.5 g/m^2 day 1 and 3 and cisplatin 30 mg/m^2 days 1 to 3. Patients who responded were given a further two cycles postoperatively. In both arms patients with pT3 or pN3 or those who underwent incomplete surgery received thoracic radiotherapy after surgery or following postoperative chemotherapy. Response to preoperative chemotherapy was 64%. Median survival for the preoperative chemotherapy group was 37 months compared with 26 months for the surgery alone group ($p < 0.15$).

Although the trial did not demonstrate a survival advantage for the combined modality group, a subset analysis demonstrated a probable delayed survival benefit for stage I and II NSCLC. This is contrary to previously published phase III trials in that no benefit was observed for N2 disease. The study has been criticised for this reason. In analysing the two groups of N0 to N1 and N2 patients separately the authors performed a low powered, unspecified subgroup analysis. The study cannot show that induction chemotherapy is ineffective in N2 patients because it was not designed to test this hypothesis in N2 patients (De Pas *et al.* 2002). There was also significant discrepancy between clinical and postoperative pathological staging of mediastinal lymph nodes (Mok and Zee 2002).

Nagai *et al.* (2003) failed to show a survival advantage for induction chemotherapy followed by surgery in a phase III study. Induction chemotherapy consisted of a platinum agent and vindesine for three cycles followed by surgery. Sixty-two patients were enrolled. The median survival for the combined modality arm was 17 months compared with 16 months for the surgery alone arm with 3-year and 5-year survival rates of 23% and 10% for the combined modality group and 26% and 22% for the surgery only arm ($p < 0.5274$).

Radiation and chemoradiation in the induction protocol

The role of radiotherapy in the induction regimen and its impact on locoregional downstaging has not been defined; neither has the role of surgery following induction chemotherapy or chemoradiation in advanced stage III disease. Elias *et al.* (1997) in a study by the Cancer and Leukaemia Blood Group (CALBG) demonstrated no survival difference between preoperative radiotherapy (40 Gy) and high dose induction etoposide and cisplatin for two cycles. Median survival was 23 months for the preoperative radiation compared with 19 months for preoperative chemotherapy.

Results from the Radiation Oncology Group phase III study comparing concurrent chemotherapy plus radiotherapy (CT/RT) versus CT/RT followed by surgical resection for stage IIIA (pN2) NSCLC showed that induction CT/RT was feasible, and that CT/RT followed by surgery yields better progression-free survival. Longer follow-up time is required to determine whether surgery significantly prolongs overall survival in IIIA (pN2) NSCLC (Turrisi *et al.* 2003).

Taylor *et al.* (2004) reported equivalent outcomes for patients with clinical stage IIIA NSCLC treated with concurrent chemoradiation compared with induction chemotherapy followed by surgical resection. Patients undergoing induction chemotherapy followed by surgery often needed postoperative radiotherapy to achieve local control equivalent to that achieved with concurrent chemoradiation.

Ongoing trials of neoadjuvant chemotherapy

Table 7.3 Neoadjuvant chemotherapy trials in progress

Trial	Stage	Induction chemotherapy	Accrual target
US Intergroup (SWOG 9900)	Ib, II, IIIa (T3, N1)	3 × Carbo/Taxol	600
Italian (ChEST)	Ib, II, IIIa (T3, N1)	3 × Gem/Cis	700
Spanish (NATCH)	I, II, IIIa (T3, N1)	3 × Cis/Doc	628
IFCT (France)	Ia, Ib, II	Ca/T vs. GC	520
MRC LU22/EORTC	I, II, IIIa	MVP, MIC, NP	450

UK Medical Research Council LU22/EORTC (UK, Europe)

This is a randomised trial of surgical resection with or without preoperative chemotherapy in patients with operable NSCLC of any stage. To reliably detect an improvement in 3-year survival from 40% with surgery alone to 55% with chemotherapy and surgery requires 450 patients. Accrual currently stands at 420 and has increased significantly in the last year partly because of European collaboration. The trial should be complete by the end of 2004. This appears to be the largest trial of this kind and eventually a meta-analysis is planned with similar trials in the USA, Italy and Spain. Preoperative chemotherapy consists of three cycles at 3-weekly intervals of one of the chemotherapy schedules shown in Table 7.4.

Table 7.4 Preoperative chemotherapy MRC LU22/EORTC

MVP	Mitomycin 8 mg/m^2 (cycles 1 and 2 only) Vinblastine 6 mg/m^2 Cisplatin 50 mg/m^2
MIC	Mitomycin 8 mg/m^2 (cycles 1 and 2 only) Ifosamide 3 g/m^2 Cisplatin 50 mg/m^2
NP	Vinorelbine 30 mg/m^2 (days 1 and 8) Cisplatin 80 mg/m^2

The primary endpoint of the trial is survival and the secondary endpoints are quality of life, resectability rates, extent of surgery, time to and site of relapse, and clinical and pathological staging.

US Intergroup (SWOG 9900)

This is a randomised inter-group study comparing three cycles of induction chemotherapy (paclitaxel/carboplatin) and surgery and surgery alone in early stage NSCLC. Planned accrual is 600 patients.

ChEST Chemotherapy for Early Stages Trial (Italy)

This Italian trial is comparing preoperative chemotherapy consisting of gemcitabine and cisplatin in early clinical stages (T2-3 N0, T1-2 N1, T3 N1) NSCLC with surgery alone. Planned accrual is 600 patients.

IFCT (Intergroupe Francophone de Cancerologie Thoracique, France)

This is a phase III study comparing two different induction regimens: gemcitabine/cisplatin and carboplatin/paclitaxel. It is also comparing two cycles of induction chemotherapy with four cycles. The planned accrual is 520 patients.

NATCH (Neoadjuvant Carboplatin/Taxol Hope, Spain)

This trial compares neoadjuvant with adjuvant chemotherapy (paclitaxel/carboplatin) with surgery and surgery alone. The planned accrual is 628 patients with stage I, II or T3N1. The primary endpoint is survival. Genetic abnormalities in blood samples taken from the patients at baseline, 6 months and 12 months will be analysed with a view to identifying markers that may predict prognosis and chemoresistance.

Conclusion

Surgery remains the treatment of choice for early stage (stages I, II and selected IIIA) NSCLC. The standard of care for locally advanced, unresectable disease is chemotherapy and radiotherapy given sequentially or concurrently as appropriate. The role of induction chemotherapy has not been clearly defined. The impact on long-term survival remains unclear. No particular neoadjuvant chemotherapy regimen has been favoured over another and only platinum-based regimens have been extensively investigated. There are several ongoing prospective randomised trials to establish the efficacy of induction chemotherapy and answer the above questions. It is important that clinical investigators collaborate in these large trials. Further progress may come by combining neoadjuvant chemotherapy with molecular-targeted therapies, better integration of chemoradiation therapy and the identification of markers that predict prognosis and chemoresistance.

References

Betticher, D. C., Hsu Schmitz, S. F., Totsch, M., Hansen, E., Joss, C., von Briel, C., Schmid, R. A., Pless, M., Habicht, J., Roth, A. D. *et al.* (2003). Mediastinal lymph node clearance after docetaxel-cisplatin neoadjuvant chemotherapy is prognostic of survival in patients with stage IIIA pN2 non-small-cell lung cancer: a multicenter phase II trial. *Journal of Clinical Oncology* **21**, 1752–1759.

Cocquyt, V., De Neve, W. & Van Belle, S. (1994). Chemotherapy plus surgery versus surgery alone in non-small-cell lung cancer. *New England Journal of Medicine* **330**, 1756–1757.

De Pas, T., Pastorino, U., Spaggiari, L., Curigliano, G., de Braud, F. & Robertson, C. (2002). Preoperative chemotherapy in non-small-cell lung cancer: Nothing new in N2 disease. *Journal of Clinical Oncology* **20**, 2603–2604.

Depierre, A., Milleron, B., Moro-Sibilot, D., Chevret, S., Quoix, E., Lebeau, B., Braun, D., Breton, J-L., Lemarie, E. & Gouva, S. (2002). Preoperative chemotherapy followed by surgery compared with primary surgery in resectable stage I (except T1N0), II, and IIIa non-small-cell lung cancer. *Journal of Clinical Oncology* **20**, 247–253.

Eberhardt, W. E., Albain, K. S., Pass, H., Putnam, J. B., Gregor, A., Assamura, H., Mornex, F., Senan, S., Belderbos, J., Westeel, V. *et al.* (2003). Induction treatment before surgery for non-small cell lung cancer. *Lung Cancer* **42**, S9–S14.

Elias, A. D., Herndon, J., Kumar, P., Sugarbaker, D. & Green, M. R. (1997). A phase III comparison of 'best local-regional therapy' with or without chemotherapy for stage IIIA T1-3N2 non-small cell lung cancer: preliminary results. *Proceedings of the American Society of Clinical Oncology* **16**, abstract 1611.

International Adjuvant Lung Cancer Trial Collaborative Group (2004). Cisplatin-based adjuvant chemotherapy in patients with completely resected non-small cell lung cancer. *New England Journal of Medicine* **350**, 351–360.

Manegold, C. (2001). Chemotherapy in Stage I/II NSCLC and projects of the EORTC - Lung Cancer group for early stage lung cancer. *Lung Cancer* **34**, S53–58.

Mok, T. S. K., Zee, B., Depierre, A., Westeel, V., Milleron, B., Moro-Sibilot, D., Quoix, E., Braun, D. & Lebeau, B. (2002). Adequate lymph node staging is fundamental to comparative study on resectable non-small-cell lung cancer. *Journal of Clinical Oncology* **20**, 2604–2605.

Mountain, C. F. (1997). Revisions in the international staging system for lung cancer. *Chest* **111**, 1710–1717.

Nagai, K., Tsuchiya, R., Mori, T., Tada, H., Ichinose, Y., Koike, T., Kato, H., Lung Cancer Surgical Study Group of the Japan Oncology Group (2003). A randomized trial comparing induction chemotherapy followed by surgery with surgery alone for patients with stage IIIA N2 non-small cell lung cancer. *Journal of Thoracic and Cardiovascular Surgery* **125**, 254–260.

Pisters, K. M., Ginsberg, R. J., Giroux, D. J., Putnam, J. B. Jr, Kris, M. G., Johnson, D. H., Roberts, J. R., Mault, J., Crowley, J. J. & Bunn, P. A. Jr (2000). Induction chemotherapy before surgery for early-stage lung cancer: a novel approach. Bimodality Lung Oncology Team. *Journal of Thoracic and Cardiovascular Surgery* **119**, 429–439.

Rosell, R., Gomez-Codina, J., Camps, C., Maestre, J., Padille, J., Canto, A., Mate, J. L., Li, S., Roig, J. Olazabal, A. *et al.* (1994). A randomized trial comparing preoperative chemotherapy plus surgery with surgery alone in patients with non-small-cell lung cancer. *New England Journal of Medicine* **330**, 153–158.

Roth, J. A., Fossella, F., Komaki, R., Ryan, M. B., Putnam, J. B. Jr, Lee, J. S., Dhingra, H., De Caro, L., Chasen, M., McGavran, M. *et al* (1994). A randomized trial comparing perioperative chemotherapy and surgery with surgery alone in resectable stage IIIA non-small-cell lung cancer. *Journal of the National Cancer Institute* **86**, 673–680

Roth, J. A., Atkinson, E. N., Fossella, F., Komaki, R., Bernadette Ryan, M., Putnam, J. B. Jr, Lee, J. S., Dhingra, H., De Caro, L., Chasen, M. *et al.* (1998). Long-term follow-up of patients enrolled in a randomized trial comparing perioperative chemotherapy and surgery with surgery alone in resectable stage IIIA non-small-cell lung cancer. *Lung Cancer* **21**, 1–6.

Taylor, N. A., Liao, Z. X., Cox, J. D., Stevens, C., Roth, J., Walsh, G., Chang, J. Y., Guerrero, T., Jeter, M., Putnam, J. Jr *et al.* (2004). Equivalent outcome of patients with clinical stage IIIA non-small-cell lung cancer treated with concurrent chemoradiation compared with induction chemotherapy followed by surgical resection. *International Journal of Radiation Oncology, Biology, Physics* **58**, 204-212.

Turrisi, A. T., Scott, C. B., Rusch, V. R., Albain, K. S., Shepherd, F. A., Smith, C., Chen, Y., Livingston, R., Gandara, D. R., Darling, G. *et al.* (2003). Randomized trial of chemoradiotherapy to 61 Gy [no S] versus chemoradiotherapy to 45 Gy followed by surgery [S] using cisplatin etoposide in stage IIIa non-small cell lung cancer (NSCLC): intergroup trial 0139, RTOG (9309). *International Journal of Radiation Oncology, Biology, Physics* **57**, S125–126.

Van Zandwijk, N., Smit, E. F., Kramer, G. W. P., Schramel, F., Gans, S., Festen, J., Termeer, A., Schlosser, N. J. J., Debruyne, C., Curran, D. *et al.* (2000). Gemcitabine and cisplatin as induction regimen for patients with biopsy-proven stage IIIA N2 non-small-cell lung cancer: a phase II study of the European Organization for Research and Treatment of Cancer Lung Cancer Cooperative Group (EORTC 08955). *Journal of Clinical Oncology* **18**, 2658–2664.

Chapter 8

CHART to CHARTWEL with neoadjuvant chemotherapy

Elena Wilson, Ethan Lyn, Joy Williams and Michèle I. Saunders

Introduction

Patients with inoperable localised non-small cell lung cancer (NSCLC), either because of extent of disease or co-morbidity, or who decline surgery, may be suitable for treatment with radical radiotherapy. The rationale for the CHART (continuous hyperfractionated accelerated radiotherapy) fractionation regime to treat patients with inoperable NSCLC, development of the CHART weekend less (CHARTWEL) regime, where the total dose has been escalated and weekend treatment omitted, and the evidence and early results for induction chemotherapy and radiotherapy will be described. Current techniques to optimise the delivery of radiotherapy, including the use of three-dimensional conformal radiotherapy (3D CRT) with an external immobilisation device and the prevention of error due to respiratory movement with active breathing control (ABC) will be discussed.

CHART

Laboratory and clinical research has shown that human lung cancers have a capacity for rapid cellular proliferation. Growth of cancers was previously estimated using the volume doubling time (VDT), the time taken by the tumour to double in volume, which was usually weeks or months. The potential doubling time (Tpot) is the time taken by a tumour cell population to double in number, correction being made for the age distribution of the cell population. The median Tpot was 7 days in 28 human lung cancers and in some specimens it was as low as 1.6 days (Wilson *et al.* 1988). Tpot is considered to be a better reflection of the biological activity of the cancer than VDT. The implication in clinical practice of such short potential doubling times is that cancers may repopulate during a course of conventional daily radiotherapy, where 2 Gy daily fractions are given Monday to Friday with weekend breaks to a total dose of 60 Gy in 6 weeks. Acceleration of radiotherapy with earlier completion of treatment could improve results. However, experience showed that acceleration was associated with increased acute toxicity. The severity of reactions caused breaks in treatment, to allow reactions to subside before treatment could be continued, and such interruptions defeated the principle of acceleration. For CHART, hyperfractionation (the use of smaller-than-conventional fractions) was utilised to reduce the acute reactions with the additional benefit of reduced late normal tissue toxicity. In CHART 1.5 Gy fractions are administered three times per day at 0800, 1400, 2000, to a total dose of 54 Gy. Treatment is given 7 days a week without breaks for weekends and is completed in only 12 days, compared with 40–42 days for a conventional 6 week course of treatment.

At Mount Vernon Hospital, Northwood, Middlesex, UK, in a pilot study of 76 patients with NSCLC, the novel fractionation regime, CHART, showed improved local tumour control and survival compared with historical controls. The multi-centre randomised trial, conducted between 1990 and 1995, compared CHART with conventional daily radiotherapy (60 Gy in 30 fractions over 40 days) in patients with locally advanced NSCLC. Five hundred and sixty-three patients were randomised. All patients were CT (computed tomography) planned with lung correction and all participating centres were subject to quality assurance. In those patients treated with CHART there was a significant improvement of 9% in the 2-year survival (29% compared with 20%, $p = 0.008$) and a 21% reduction in the relative risk of local progression ($p = 0.033$). Subgroup analysis (predefined) showed that in those patients with squamous carcinoma (81% of cases), there was an improvement in survival of 13% (from 20 to 33%, $p = 0.0007$) at 2 years and a 27% reduction in the risk of local progression ($p = 0.012$). Furthermore, in squamous carcinoma there was a 25% reduction in the relative risk of local and/or distant progression ($p = 0.025$) and a 24% reduction in the relative risk of metastasis ($p = 0.043$). There were no important differences in acute or late morbidity (Saunders *et al.* 1997). This led the Department of Health, in its guidance for the treatment of NSCLC, to recommend CHART as the treatment of choice for early inoperable disease (NHS Executive 1998). However, since the primary tumour was the cause of death in 61% of the cases treated with CHART, there was a need to improve local control: possible methods included dose escalation, addition of cytotoxic chemotherapy and improvement in the accuracy of planning and administration of treatment.

CHARTWEL

As centres found treatment on weekends difficult to implement, the CHARTWEL regime was designed and the dose escalated. It was desirable to maintain the inter-fraction interval to allow repair of normal tissue damage, and the low dose per fraction to reduce acute and late toxicity. Dose escalation was therefore achieved by increasing the total number of fractions. As CHART was administered in only 12 days, there was scope to increase the number of fractions and overall treatment time without endangering the advantage of acceleration. In CHARTWEL treatment was given three times daily at 0800, 1400 and 2000 hrs, as in CHART, but Monday to Friday without treatment on weekends. Dose was escalated from 54 Gy in 16 days to 57 to 58.5 and then 60 Gy in an overall time of 18 days. Sixty-four patients with locally advanced NSCLC were treated. Analysis of toxicity data showed that dysphagia due to acute radiation induced oesophagitis was more severe in those patients treated with higher doses to 60 Gy but this was not clinically apparent and there was no late damage. After 6 months there was a higher incidence of Grade I pulmonary toxicity. No cases of radiation myelitis, oesophageal strictures or Grade II or III lung morbidity were seen. Retrospective comparison with the previous CHART trials indicated that the increase in overall time from 12 to 18 days did not compromise tumour control or survival (Saunders *et al.* 1998).

Chemotherapy

Chemotherapy may be combined with radiotherapy in an attempt to improve local tumour control, eradicate latent metastatic disease and improve survival. The chemotherapy may be neoadjuvant, concomitant, adjuvant or a combination.

Adjuvant chemotherapy after CHARTWEL was not intended, as any viable disease remaining after radical radiotherapy was unlikely to be eradicated by chemotherapy: the tumour blood flow may be impaired by the radiotherapy, reducing drug access to the primary tumour; and perturbation of the tumour cell population by the radiotherapy may also lead to resistance to the chemotherapy.

Three meta-analyses of phase III randomised trials evaluating chemotherapy and radiation versus radiation alone were performed in the mid-1990s (Marino *et al.* 1995; NSCLC Collaborative Group 1995; Pritchard & Anthony 1996). These analyses provided evidence in support of the utilisation of induction cisplatin-containing chemotherapy followed by radiation compared with radiation alone. It was also observed in these studies that the incidence of distant metastases was significantly lower in the chemoradiation-treated group, suggesting that chemotherapy was affecting distant micrometastatic disease sufficiently to improve overall survival. Local control, however, remained a major problem, requiring better systemic therapy or more effective radiotherapy.

Several randomised trials, initiated in the mid-1980s, have tested the use of induction chemotherapy followed by definitive radiation compared with radiation alone as a curative approach in patients with previously untreated stage III NSCLC (Le Chevalier *et al.* 1991, 1994; Dillman *et al.* 1996; Sause *et al.* 2000). All were modest in size but did report a survival benefit for sequential chemoradiation. The Cancer and Leukaemia Group B (CALGB) 8433 trial, reported by Dillman *et al.* (1996) and the Radiotherapy Oncology Group/Eastern Co-operative Group (RTOG) 8808/ECOG 4588 trial reported by Sause *et al.* (2000) showed 5-year survival rates of only 19% and 8%, respectively, while the trial reported by Le Chevalier (1991, 1994) gave a 2-year survival of 21%. The results are summarised in Table 8.1.

Table 8.1 Neoadjuvant chemotherapy and thoracic radiotherapy

Trial	No. Patients	RT (Gy)	Chemotherapy	Survival (%)
CALGB 8433 Dillman *et al.* 1996	155	60 60	None Weekly vinblastine for 5 wks and cisplatin wk 1 and 5	7 (5yr)/6 (7yr) 19 (5yr)/13 (7yr) $p = 0.007$
RTOG 8808 ECOG 4588 Sause *et al.* 2000 Ph III	458	60 60 69.6	None Weekly vinblastine for 5 wks and cisplatin wk 1 and 5 Weekly vinblastine for 5 wks and cisplatin wk 1 and 5	5 (5yr) 8 (5yr) 6 (5yr) $p = 0.04$
Le Chevalier *et al.* 1994	353	65 65	None Induction vindesine, cyclophosphamide, cisplatin, CCNUx3,+ x3 post RT	14 (2yr) 21 (2yr) $p = 0.02$

Concurrent chemo-radiotherapy may be superior to sequential treatment, but in those trials with positive findings (Schaake-Koning *et al.* 1992; Jeremic *et al.* 1996), the results may be specific to the chemotherapy and radiotherapy regimes used and did not necessarily prove the principle. Toxicity was markedly increased with concurrent treatment, with about 30% of patients suffering grade 3 or 4 toxicity, and long-term survival was only similar to or less than that for accelerated radiotherapy alone.

Hypothetically, the optimal plan could be neoadjuvant chemotherapy followed by concomitant chemo-radiotherapy. However, the studies indicated that toxicity may be markedly increased.

At Mount Vernon Hospital, three courses of mitomycin, ifosfamide and cisplatin (MIC) were administered at 21-day intervals prior to treatment with CHARTWEL to 60 Gy. The MIC regime was chosen as it had been thoroughly tested by Cullen and response rates and toxicity were known (Cullen 1995). The treatment was well tolerated but when a randomised trial was proposed it was pointed out that the use of a combination of 'older' drugs would have led to problems with international comparison.

In the 1990s paclitaxel and carboplatin had become a popular combination in the United States. Choy in 1998, reported a pilot study of 23 patients treated with weekly paclitaxel and carboplatin concomitant with 2 Gy daily fractions to 60 Gy followed by 2 further courses of paclitaxel and carboplatin at 21-day intervals. Response rate was good at 61% but 45% suffered grade 3 and grade 4 oesophageal toxicity. Choy performed a similar study with hyperfractionated radiotherapy: 69.6 Gy in 1.2 Gy fractions given twice per day in 6 weeks. In 42 patients the response rate was 78.6% but 26% suffered grade 3/4 oesophagitis (Choy *et al.* 1998).

Wagner reported a Phase I study, CP/HART, where 2 courses of paclitaxel and carboplatin were given at 21-day intervals, followed by HART: 57.6 Gy in 1.6 Gy fractions three times daily over 12 days. The dose of paclitaxel was escalated from 175 mg/m^2 to 225 mg/m^2. Twenty-two patients were treated; the response rate was 55%. Eleven patients suffered grade 3 oesophagitis and one grade 4 oesophagitis. Six patients were hospitalised because of the oesophagitis and two because of febrile neutropaenia (Wagner *et al.* ASCO 1998).

ECOG proposed a randomised trial on similar lines. However, two courses of chemotherapy may not be enough to produce a systemic effect or judge response to chemotherapy, but more than three courses would risk toxicity and might endanger radiotherapy, the definitive treatment. In the Mount Vernon trial it was decided to give three courses of paclitaxel and carboplatin at 21-day intervals followed by CHARTWEL to 60 Gy. In view of the toxicity found in other studies it was decided to proceed cautiously and gradually escalate the dose of paclitaxel from 150 to 225 mg/m^2 in 25 mg/m^2 increments in groups of six patients.

Chemotherapy given concurrently with CHARTWEL may result in additive or synergistic effects on normal tissues precipitating more severe early and/or late morbidity (Ball *et al.* 1999). It was therefore planned to investigate neoadjuvant chemotherapy followed by CHARTWEL to 60 Gy and if treatment was tolerated and results acceptable then neoadjuvant chemotherapy followed by concomitant chemo-radiotherapy with CHARTWEL could be investigated.

Accelerated radiotherapy is completed quickly, within 2 weeks for CHART and 3 weeks for CHARTWEL to 60 Gy. Should concurrent chemotherapy be given at the beginning of each week of treatment or as a once-daily dose the total dose of chemotherapy given would be low and although there might be enhancement of the radiotherapy with improved local control, systemic effect may not be achieved. Initial efforts have therefore been concentrated on combining neoadjuvant chemotherapy with CHARTWEL.

Neoadjuvant chemotherapy

Administration of the chemotherapy in the neoadjuvant setting would allow full doses of chemotherapy and radiotherapy to be given. In a pilot study, three courses of neoadjuvant chemotherapy were given prior to radical radiotherapy to the chest with CHARTWEL. Overall survival at three years was 47% for the 33 patients who had been treated with neoadjuvant chemotherapy and CHARTWEL and 30% for the 55 patients treated with CHARTWEL alone. There was no significant increase in dysphagia (Saunders *et al.* 2002). There is now a need to test neoadjuvant chemotherapy with CHARTWEL in a randomised controlled trial.

Three-dimensional conformal radiotherapy

Three-dimensional conformal radiotherapy (3D CRT) for patients with locally advanced, inoperable NSCLC allows shaping of treatment fields and dose distribution to the target volume with the aim of delivering a high dose to the disease and minimal dose to adjacent normal tissues: lung, spinal cord and oesophagus.

Two-dimensional (2D) radiotherapy treatment planning was used in the CHART trial (Saunders *et al*. 1997) and in the initial CHARTWEL experience (Saunders *et al*. 1998). In 2D planning a composite volume as defined in ICRU 29 (ICRU 1978), allowing a margin for microscopic extension, organ motion and set-up errors, was drawn around disease on a central or near central slice of the planning CT scan. The 2D volumes were usually only drawn on a few slices and there was no interaction between the information on the different slices to account for electron scatter. It has been suggested that improving local control by optimisation of the radiotherapy, with better localisation and delivery of dose to tumour and further sparing of normal tissues, could have a greater effect on survival than trying to improve the treatment of microscopic metastases with chemotherapy (Suit 1982).

In 3D CRT the gross tumour volume (GTV) and clinical target volume (CTV) are as defined in ICRU 50 (ICRU 1993). Regions of interest (disease, areas thought to contain disease and normal tissues) are marked on every slice of the planning CT scan. The 3D planning system creates a complete picture of the disease that may be viewed in three dimensions. The GTV is then automatically expanded, to create a margin for microscopic extension, defining the CTV which is then expanded further to create the planning target volume (PTV) which allows for variations in tissue position, size and shape, as well as for variations in patient and beam position. The PTV has been defined with greater precision in ICRU 62 (ICRU 1999) with the internal margin (IM) taking account of physiological uncertainties such as those due to organ movements during breathing along with variation in the size, shape and position of the CTV during treatment, and the set-up margin (SM) taking account of all uncertainties in patient positioning and alignment of the therapeutic beams during treatment planning and treatment sessions. Segregating the IM and SM within the PTV reflects the differences in the source of uncertainties. Underdosage of the CTV may result if inadequate margins are used (geometric miss). Errors caused by inaccurate set-up and organ motion have necessitated the use of greater PTV margins at the expense of normal tissues.

Divergent customised blocks or multi-leaf collimators (MLCs) are used to provide conformal shielding. The treatment planning to ensure optimum positioning of shielding is performed using beam's eye view (BEV) apertures and suitable field positioning to provide adequate dosimetric coverage of the PTV and optimal sparing of normal tissues. Three-dimensional CRT planning systems make it possible to view the relationship between normal structures and target volumes throughout the entire region being treated; 3D CRT uses the CT-based anatomical data to reconstruct organs within the computer system. The BEV facility is able to rotate the reconstructed patient within the computer and enable the planner to view the patient in the same orientation as a radiation beam pointed in that direction (Goitein *et al*. 1983). Thus, by rotating the patient and examining the corresponding graphic displays, beam orientations and shapes can be selected to ensure that the target volume is covered by the beams and the normal tissues excluded as much as possible.

The potential advantages of 3D technology, in addition to more accurate assessment of the tumour volume, include better coverage by external beams, improved assessment of doses to critical normal structures and disease from dose-volume histograms (DVH) and tools to compare and assess rival plans (Emami 1996; McGibney *et al.* 1999). It is hoped that the use of 3D CRT with accelerated radiotherapy may further improve cure rate and reduce normal tissue morbidity by more accurate dose delivery to disease, thereby facilitating dose escalation. In order to achieve this accuracy, treatment errors related to set-up and organ motion must be addressed.

Set-up and organ motion error evaluation

Rudat *et al.* (1994) measured positioning errors in 43 patients, of which 26 had intrathoracic neoplasms, by comparing simulator films with corresponding portal films. All underwent 3D conformal radiotherapy without the use of immobilisation devices. The mean positioning error in all three dimensions varied between 4 and 5 mm. As a consequence, changes in the respective dose-volume histograms (DVHs) resulted in a loss of tumour control probability (TCP) of 5%. From these results it appeared that immobilisation may be of value and data on the improvement that could be achieved by using immobilisation devices was needed.

Lung tumours move significantly during quiet respiration, causing potential inaccuracies in treatment delivery. Ross *et al.* (1990), in an analysis of movement of intrathoracic neoplasms using ultrafast CT, found that tumour motion heavily depended on tumour location: whilst upper lobe tumours were almost always fixed, hilar and lower lobe tumours showed significant lateral motion (average 9.2 mm) for the former and cranio-caudal motion for the latter. All three major geographic misses occurred in patients whose tumours moved 15 to 22 mm due to cardiac or respiratory motion. However, Stevens *et al.* (2001) did not find tumour motion to be predictable by size or location of the tumour, or pulmonary function test results. Seppenwoolde *et al.* (2002) also investigated 3D motion of lung tumours during radiotherapy in real time with fiducial markers implanted in or near the tumour, and also found that tumour motion was greatest (12 mm ± 2 mm SD) in the cranio-caudal direction for tumours situated in the lower lobes and not attached to rigid structures such as the chest wall or vertebrae. For the lateral and anterior–posterior directions, tumour motion was small for both upper and lower lobe tumours (2 ± 1 mm).

For tumours near the heart or attached to the aortic arch a measurable motion in the range of 1–4 mm was caused by the cardiac beat. Chest wall movement also causes reference points to move which may lead to set-up errors.

Techniques to improve set-up and organ motion errors
Immobilisation

Patients with NSCLC are usually treated in the supine position as this gives greater stability. It is now generally accepted that, when treatment is being planned with the accuracy of 3D CRT, patients should not be planned or treated without reliable and reproducible immobilisation, but no standard has been stipulated. Methods include immobilisation with an Alpha Cradle®, VacFix®, thermoplast and evacuated bags filled with beads or granular materials. There is no published data comparing immobilisation devices in the treatment of lung or other intrathoracic cancers with radiotherapy.

At Mount Vernon Hospital, a customised immobilisation frame is now in routine use for patients with NSCLC being treated with CHARTWEL. The metal immobilisation frame was designed to improve set-up reproducibility and built in the bioengineering department at Mount Vernon Hospital. The frame was made to be attached to the CT, simulator and treatment machine couches and to be accommodated within the CT aperture. Arms are supported and held in shoulder and elbow flexion by forearm rests adjustable for forearm length and in horizontal separation for shoulder width. Rotation of the forearm rests for comfort is possible. Vertically adjustable handgrips are attached separately to the main frame. All movements are infinitely adjustable, and once optimal positions are achieved for an individual patient, settings from attached scales are recorded. Support for mouthpieces and tubing used for ABC and abort switches have been incorporated into the frame.

Reproducibility of the frame has been assessed using CT scans (Williams *et al.* 2001). Planning CT scans were performed, before and after neoadjuvant chemotherapy, for the group positioned without immobilisation and for the group positioned in the immobilisation frame. Comparison was made of the CT scans taken with and without the frame by fusing the pre- and post-chemotherapy scans (achieved by manually aligning the vertebral bodies) for each patient. In those patients scanned without the frame, although skin and surface markers (tattoos) aligned, the internal anatomy of mediastinum and tumour were concordant in only two of five cases. When the frame was used, both external and internal anatomy agreed in five of five cases.

Organ motion

Methods of minimising error due to respiratory movement include gating, tracking, deep inspiration breath hold (DIBH) and active breathing control (ABC).

Gating, or synchronising radiotherapy with a patient's breathing, may be done either by controlling the patient's breathing or through activation of the treatment beam at a point in the patient's breathing cycle in which the position of intrathoracic stuctures is believed to be known (Ohara *et al.* 1989; Sontag & Burnham 1998; Tada *et al.* 1998). Researchers at the University of California Davis Cancer Centre and Varian Associates have developed a breathing synchronised radiotherapy (BSRT) system, consisting of a breathing monitoring system (BMOS) and linear accelerator gating hardware and software (Kubo *et al.* 2000). The ideal treatment point where organ motion is stationary is defined from the BMOS signals and fluoroscopy. The authors have proposed that the BSRT system can be used to gate radiotherapy at breath hold (BH) or free breathing (FB). However, there will still be some movement of the tumour while gating with FB, which would need to be taken into account.

The deep inspiration breath hold (DIBH) technique has been performed using a slow vital capacity manoeuvre with a spirometer. Published results on seven patients receiving a total of 164 treatment sessions have shown that DIBH alone, without alteration of margins, potentially allowed dose escalation from 69.4 to 87.9 Gy through a reduced dose to normal lung (Rosenzweig *et al.* 2000).

Barnes *et al.* (2001), in a dosimetric evaluation of lung tumour immobilisation using BH at deep inspiration (DI), found that, compared with FB conditions, at DIBH there was a mean reduction in V20 of 14.3% with the increase in lung volume alone, 22.1% with tumour immobilisation alone and 32.5% with the combined effect. This appeared to be patient dependent and due to both the increased lung volume seen at DI and the PTV margin reduction with tumour immobilisation. However, DIBH could be uncomfortable for patients to maintain.

The technique of ABC, developed at the William Beaumont Hospital by John Wong and colleagues, is to arrest respiration, and hence tumour movement, temporarily at a chosen point in the respiratory cycle by inflation of a balloon valve which occludes the airway for an adjustable period of time (Wong *et al.* 1999). Usually 75–80% of the vital capacity is chosen as this has been found to be comfortable for lung cancer patients to maintain during the BH period of up to 20 seconds. Twenty seconds were considered an adequate BH as a planning scan of the chest could be performed in three BHs and a whole segment of a fraction of radiotherapy could be given in one BH. As both scanners and treatment machines have become faster, shorter BHs are acceptable. Treatment planning and delivery may then be delivered in identical breathing conditions, with minimal margins to account for breathing motion. By reducing motion artefact, the size and shape of the GTV may also be reduced, with consequent reductions in PTV and doses to normal tissues. A feasibility study of ABC performed at Mount Vernon Hospital has shown the procedure to be reproducible and well tolerated by patients. Lung volumes have been maintained over several weeks with ABC and by increasing the lung volume with moderate deep inspiration the V20 has been reduced. For tumours that were not fixed to the mediastinum, which was usually the case, tumour movement anteriorly away from the spinal cord has reduced the spinal cord dose (Wilson *et al.* 2001). These dose reductions may enable more patients to be treated radically and may also facilitate dose escalation.

Conclusion

Survival for patients with inoperable NSCLC, suitable for treatment with radical radiotherapy, has been significantly improved by treatment with CHART. Dose escalation with CHARTWEL in combination with neoadjuvant chemotherapy has given promising results without significant increase in morbidity. It is anticipated that 3D CRT, used with effective immobilisation and techniques to overcome respiratory movement, may add to the benefits already achieved with CHART and release the full potential of the fractionation.

References

Ball, D., Bishop, J., Smith, J., O'Brien, P., Davis, S., Ryan, G., Olver, I., Toner, G., Walker, Q. & Joseph, D. (1999). A randomized phase III study of accelerated or standard fraction radiotherapy with or without concurrent carboplatin in inoperable non-small cell lung cancer: final report of an Australian multi-centre trial. *Radiotherapy and Oncology* **52**, 129–136.

Barnes, E. A., Murray, B. R., Robinson, D. M., Underwood, L. J., Hanson, J. & Roa, W. H. (2001). Dosimetric evaluation of lung tumor immobilization using breath-hold at deep inspiration. *International Journal of Radiation Oncology, Biology, Physics* **50**, 1091–1098.

Choy, H., Akerley, W. & Devore, R. (1998). Paclitaxel, carboplatin, and radiation therapy for non-small cell lung cancer. *Oncology* **12**(suppl 2), 80–86.

Cullen, M. H. (1995). Trials with mitomycin, ifosfamide and cisplatin in non-small cell lung cancer. *Lung Cancer* **12**(suppl 1), S95–106.

Dillman, R. O., Herndon, J., Seagren, S. L., Eaton, W. L. Jr & Green, M. R. (1996). Improved survival in stage III non-small cell lung cancer: Seven year follow-up of Cancer and Leukemia Group B trial 8433. *Journal of the National Cancer Institute* **88**, 1210–1215.

Emami, B. (1996). Three dimensional conformal radiation therapy in bronchogenic carcinoma. *Seminars in Radiation Oncology* **6**, 92–97.

Goitein, M., Abrams, M., Rowell, D., Pollari, H. & Wiles, J. (1983). Multi-dimensional treatment planning: II. Beam's eye-view, back projection through CT sections. *International Journal of Radiation Oncology, Biology, Physics* **9**, 789–797.

ICRU (International Commission on Radiation Units and Measurements) (1978). *Dose Specification for Reporting External Beam Therapy with Photons and Electrons*, ICRU Report 29. Bethesda, Maryland: International Commission on Radiation Units and Measurements.

ICRU (International Commission on Radiation Units and Measurements) (1993). *Prescribing, Recording, and Reporting Photon Beam Therapy*, ICRU Report 50. Bethesda, Maryland: International Commission on Radiation Units and Measurements.

ICRU (International Commission on Radiation Units and Measurements) (1999). *Prescribing, Recording, and Reporting Photon Beam Therapy*, ICRU Report 62 (supplement to ICRU Report 50). Bethesda, Maryland: International Commission on Radiation Units and Measurements.

Jeremic, B., Shibamoto, Y., Acimovic, L., Milicic, B. & Milisavljevic, S. (1996). Hyperfractionated radiation therapy with or without concurrent low-dose daily carboplatin/etoposide for stage III non-small cell lung cancer: a randomized study. *Journal of Clinical Oncology* **14**, 1065–1070.

Kubo, H. D., Len, P. M., Minohara, S. & Mostafavi, H. (2000). Breathing synchronized radiotherapy program at the University of California Davis Cancer Center. *Medical Physics* **27**, 346–353.

Le Chevalier, T., Arriagada, R., Quoix, E., Ruffie, P., Martin, M., Tarayre, M., Lacombe-Terrier, M. J., Douillard, J. Y. & Laplanche, A. (1991). Radiotherapy alone versus combined chemotherapy and radiotherapy in nonresectable non-small-cell lung cancer: First analysis of a randomized trial in 353 patients. *Journal of the National Cancer Institute* **83**, 417–423.

Le Chevalier, T., Arriagada, R., Quoix, E., Ruffie, P., Martin, M., Tarayre, M., Lacombe-Terrier, M. J., Douillard, J. Y. & Laplanche, A. (1994). Radiotherapy alone versus combined chemotherapy and radiotherapy in unresectable non-small cell lung carcinoma. *Lung Cancer* **10**(suppl 1), S239–S244.

Marino, P., Preatoni, A. & Cantoni, A. (1995). Randomized trials of radiotherapy alone versus combined chemotherapy and radiotherapy in stages IIIA and IIIB non-small cell lung cancer. *Cancer* **76**, 593–601.

McGibney, C., Holmberg, O., McClean, B., Williams, C., McCrea, P., Sutton, P. & Armstrong, J. (1999). Dose escalation of chart in non-small-cell lung cancer: is three-dimensional conformal radiation therapy really necessary? *International Journal of Radiation Oncology, Biology, Physics* **45**, 339–350.

National Health Service Executive (1998). *Guidance on Commissioning Services in Lung Cancer, Improving Outcomes in Lung Cancer: The Research Evidence. The Manual.* London: NHS Executive.

Non-Small Cell Lung Cancer Collaborative Group (1995). Chemotherapy in non-small cell lung cancer: a meta-analysis using updated data on individual patients from 52 randomized clinical trials. *British Medical Journal* **311**, 899–909.

Ohara, K., Okumura, T., Akisada, M., Inanda, T., Mori, T., Yokota, H. & Calaguas, M. J. (1989). Irradiation synchronized with respiration gate. *International Journal of Radiation Oncology, Biology, Physics* **17**, 853–857.

Pritchard, R. S. & Anthony, S. P. (1996). Chemotherapy plus radiotherapy compared to radiotherapy alone in the treatment of locally advanced, unresectable, non-small cell lung cancer: A meta-analysis. *Annals of Internal Medicine* **125**, 723–729.

Rosenzweig, K. E., Hanley, J., Mah, D., Mageras, G., Hunt, M., Toner, S., Burman, C., Ling, C. C., Mychalczak, B., Fuks, Z. *et al.* (2000). The deep inspiration breath-hold technique in the treatment of inoperable non-small cell lung cancer. *International Journal of Radiation Oncology, Biology, Physics* **48**, 81–87.

Ross, C. S., Hussey, D. H., Pennington, E. C., Stanford, W. & Doornbos, J. F. (1990). Analysis of movement of intrathoracic neoplasms using ultrafast computerized tomography. *International Journal of Radiation Oncology, Biology, Physics* **18**, 671–677.

Rudat, V., Flentje, M., Oetzel, D., Menke, M., Schlegel, W. & Wannenmacher, M. (1994). Influence of positioning error on 3D conformal dose-distributions during fractionated radiotherapy. *Radiotherapy and Oncology* **33**, 56–63.

Saunders, M., Dische, S., Barrett, A., Harvey, A., Griffiths, G. & Palmer, M. (1997). Continuous hyperfractionated accelerated radiotherapy (CHART) versus conventional radiotherapy in non-small cell lung cancer: a randomised multicentre trial. *The Lancet* **350**, 161–165.

Saunders, M. I., Rojas, A., Lyn, B. E., Pigott, K., Powell, M., Goodchild, K., Hoskin, P. J., Phillips, H. & Verma, N. (1998). Experience with dose escalation using CHARTWEL (continuous hyperfractionated accelerated radiotherapy weekend less) in non-small cell lung cancer. *British Journal of Cancer* **78**, 1323–1328.

Saunders, M. I., Rojas, A., Lyn, B. E., Wilson, E. & Phillips, H. (2002). Dose-escalation with CHARTWEL (Continuous Hyperfractionated Accelerated Radiotherapy Week-End Less) combined with neo-adjuvant chemotherapy in the treatment of locally advanced non-small cell lung cancer. *Clinical Oncology* **14**, 352–360.

Sause, W., Kolesar, P., Taylor, S. I. V., Johnson, D., Livingston, R., Komaki, R., Emami, B., Curran, W. Jr, Byhardt, R., Dar, A. R. *et al.* (2000). Final results of a phase III trial in regionally advanced unresectable non-small cell lung cancer. Radiation Therapy Oncology Group, Eastern Cooperative Oncology Group, and Southwest Oncology Group. *Chest* **117**, 358–364.

Schaake-Koning, C., van den Bogaert, W., Dalesio, O., Festen, J., Hoogenhout, J., van Houtte, P., Kirkpatrick, A., Koolen, M., Maat, B., Nijs, A. *et al.* (1992). Effects of concomitant cisplatin and radiotherapy on inoperable non-small cell lung cancer. *New England Journal of Medicine* **326**, 524–530.

Seppenwoolde, Y., Shirato, H., Kitamura, K., Shimizu, S., van Herk, M., Lebesque, J. V. & Miyasaka, K. (2002). Precise and real-time measurement of 3D tumor motion in lung due to breathing and heartbeat, measured during radiotherapy. *International Journal of Radiation Oncology, Biology, Physics* **53**, 822–834.

Sontag, M. & Burnham, B. (1998). Design and clinical implementation of a system for respiratory gated radiotherapy. *Medical Physics* **25**, D1–07.

Stevens, C. W., Munden, R. F., Forster, K. M., Kelly, J. F., Liao, Z., Starkschall, G., Tucker, S. & Komaki, R. (2001). Respiratory-driven lung tumour motion is independent of tumor size, tumor location, and pulmonary function. *International Journal of Radiation Oncology, Biology, Physics* **51**, 62–68.

Suit, H. D. (1982). The American Society of Therapeutic Radiologists Presidential Address: October 1981. Potential for improving survival rates for the cancer patient by increasing the efficacy of treatment of the primary lesion. *Cancer* **50**, 1227–1234.

Tada, T., Minakuchi, K., Fujioka, T., Sakurai, M., Koda, M., Kawase, I., Nakajima, T., Nishioka, M., Tonai, T. & Kozuka, T. (1998). Lung cancer: Intermittent irradiation synchronised with respiratory motion. Results of a pilot study. *Radiology* **207**, 779–783.

Wagner, H., Antonia, S., Shaw, G., Garland, L., Williams, C., Ellis, C., Heise, M., Meulemans, L., Robinson, L., Hubble, D. *et al.* (1998). Induction chemotherapy (IC) with carboplatin and paclitaxel followed by hyperfractionated accelerated radiation therapy (CP/HART) for patients with unresectable stage IIIA and IIIB non-small cell lung cancer. 1998 ASCO Annual Meeting, Abstract No: 1804.

Williams, J., Wilson, E., Lyn, E. & Aird, E. (2001). Feasibility of a custom made immobilisation frame for treatment of patients with locally advanced non-small cell lung cancer (NSCLC) with CHART weekend less (CHARTWEL). *Radiotherapy and Oncology* **61**(Suppl. 1), S66.

Wilson, E., Williams, J., Lyn, E. & Aird, E. (2001). Active breathing control (ABC) in the treatment of non-small cell lung cancer (NSCLC) with CHART weekend less (CHARTWEL). *Radiotherapy and Oncology* **61**(Suppl 1), S63.

Wilson, G. D., McNally, N. J., Dische, S., Saunders, M. I., Des Rochers, C., Lewis, A. A. & Bennett, M. H. (1988). Measurement of cell kinetics in human tumours in vivo using bromodeoxyuridine incorporation and flow cytometry. *British Journal of Cancer* **58**, 423–431.

Wong, J. W., Sharpe, M. B., Jaffray, D. A., Kini, V. R., Robertson, J. M., Stromberg, J. S. & Martinez, A. A. (1999). The use of active breathing control (ABC) to reduce margin for breathing motion. *International Journal of Radiation Oncology, Biology, Physics* **44**, 911–919.

Chapter 9

Evidence and opinion for medical intervention in early disease

Graham Dark and Catherine Bale

Introduction

The prognosis for patients with lung cancer remains poor, with overall 5-year survival rates strongly related to the stage of the disease at the time of diagnosis, varying from 12–15% in the USA to 5% in Scotland (Mountain 1997; Gregor *et al.* 2001). At the time of initial diagnosis 50% of patients have clinically detectable disease outside the chest, 10–15% have locally advanced unresectable disease and 25% of patients develop recurrent disease either locally or at a distant site after surgery. Surgery is regarded as the best treatment option in patients with early stage non-small-cell lung cancer (NSCLC); however, less than 20% of tumours are suitable for potentially curative resection (11% in Scotland (Gregor *et al.* 2001)) and only about a third of these survive for 5 years. More than 75% of patients with NSCLC are potential candidates for systemic chemotherapy alone or with radiotherapy at some point in the course of their disease. The aims of systemic therapy (outlined in Table 9.1) differ depending on the indication.

Table 9.1 Treatment domains and their primary objectives

Treatment domain	Primary objective of therapy
Metastatic disease	Palliation of symptoms
Adjuvant therapy	Increased disease-free and overall survival
Primary medical therapy (neoadjuvant)	Reduction in surgery or to become operable Defining goals for adjuvant therapy Translational research
Prevention of disease	Role not yet well defined

In the traditional development of chemotherapy regimens, patients with advanced or metastatic disease are included in the initial clinical trials. However, there is evidence that early tumours are more chemosensitive than advanced tumours, and demonstrate a higher response rate: the response rate to MIC (mitomycin C, ifosfamide, cisplatin) chemotherapy is 54% in regionally advanced NSCLC, but 32% in advanced disease (Cullen *et al.* 1999). Furthermore, the development of regimens with a particular patient population may produce evidence that cannot be extrapolated into the patients with early disease, or into a neoadjuvant setting. Most of the studies that have evaluated adjuvant chemotherapy for NSCLC have used regimens previously shown to be effective in metastatic disease, and an active drug in an adjuvant clinical trial is UFT, which has only minimal activity in metastatic disease (Shimizu *et al.* 1986; Langer 1999; Kato *et al.* 2004).

In several tumour types, adjuvant and neoadjuvant chemotherapy have substantially improved the cure rates obtained by surgery or radiotherapy alone. Moreover, the effects of chemotherapy for NSCLC in an adjuvant setting are similar to those demonstrated for other diseases, and yet the use of adjuvant treatment for this disease is not as widespread as for other tumour types.

This chapter will discuss the role of systemic chemotherapy in the management of early NSCLC by reviewing the role of multi-treatment modalities combining surgery, chemotherapy and radiotherapy, in the adjuvant and neoadjuvant setting.

Role of surgery

All patients with early NSCLC (stage I and II) should be treated with complete surgical resection whenever possible (Korst and Ginsberg 2001). Up to 20% of patients present with tumours that may be suitable for potentially curative resection, but only 11% are currently operated on in the UK (Gregor *et al.* 2001). Although surgery achieves long-term survival in some patients, a significant proportion experience locoregional or distant recurrence (Pisters 2000). Five-year survival rates range from 60% for stage IA (T1N0M0) to 23% for stage IIB (T3N0M0 or T2N1M0) (Mountain 1997). The results of surgery in stage III patients are poor, especially for patients with N2 disease, of whom 85% will die from their disease in the 2 years after surgery. There is therefore scope to improve on the results of surgery, even in patients with stage I disease. Treatment failure is attributable to local recurrence in 30% of patients with the remainder re-presenting with metastatic disease.

Rationale for postoperative chemotherapy

There is increasing evidence to suggest that NSCLC is a systemic disease from presentation, and that this results in the high local and distant recurrence rates after surgery with curative intent. As with other cancers, micrometastases can be detected in the bone marrow in 54% of N0 patients (Pantel *et al.* 1996) and in the lymph nodes of 63% of patients with node negative tumours (Chen *et al.* 1993). An effective treatment should be capable of eradicating these micrometastases and ideally the chemotherapy should demonstrate a response rate of approximately 50% in advanced disease, with some demonstration of complete responses. However, the more active regimens currently available produce response rates of between 35 and 50% in patients with advanced disease and complete responses are rare. It is not surprising that, when the primary aim of adjuvant treatment is an improvement in disease-free and overall survival, a major impact has not been demonstrated.

Surgery and postoperative chemotherapy

The modest long-term survival rates obtained with surgery alone in early stage NSCLC, with the likelihood of residual microscopic disease, prompted early studies of adjuvant (postoperative) chemotherapy (see Table 9.2).

Table 9.2 Summary of clinical trials of adjuvant chemotherapy for non-small-cell lung cancer

Study	Stage	Treatment	No. pt	MS (mo)	1-yr	2-yr	3-yr	5-yr
(Holmes et al. 1985)	Stage II-III completely resected	CAP BCG	62 68	23 16	75 64	41 30	- -	
(Lad et al. 1988)	Stage I-III incompletely resected	CAP-RT RT	78 86	20 13	60 54	41 32	24 20	
(Feld et al. 1994)	T2N0, T1N1 completely resected	CAP No Rx	136 133	76 83	89 88	80 73	- -	60 52
(Niiranen et al. 1992)	T1-3N0 completely resected	CAP No Rx	54 56	7+yr 5+yr	- -	- -	- -	67 56
(Dautzenberg et al. 1995)	Stage I-III completely resected	COPAC-RT RT	138 129	15/14 26/10	- -	38/36 54/22	17/19 34/6	
(Ohta et al. 1993)	Stage III completely resected	Vind No Rx	90 91	31 37	- -	- -	- -	35 41
(Wada et al. 1996)	Stage I-III completely resected	CVUFT UFT No Rx	115 108 100	- - -	- - -	- - -	- - -	61 64 49

CAP, cyclophosphamide, doxorubicin, cisplatin; BCG, Bacillus Calmette–Guérin; RT, radiotherapy; No Rx, no treatment control arm; Vind, vindesine; COPAC, cyclophosphamide, vincristine, cisplatin, doxorubicin, CCNU; CVUFT, cisplatin, vindesine, uracil, tegafur; UFT, tegafur, uracil.

A meta-analysis including data from eight cisplatin-based trials involving 1394 patients examined the effects of chemotherapy when combined with local treatment (surgery or radiotherapy). The hazard ratio for patients receiving adjuvant cisplatin-based treatment was 0.87 (95% CI 0.74–1.02, $p = 0.08$), but demonstrated a 5% improvement in survival at 5 years. In trials using long-term alkylating agents, adjuvant chemotherapy was detrimental to survival, with a hazard ratio of 1.15 (95% CI 1.04–1.27, $p = 0.005$), leading to a 4% survival reduction at 2 years. Most of the individual trials were too small for reliable detection of any significant differences between treatments, and the meta-analysis is often considered inconclusive. Several randomised clinical trials have been published and are outlined in Table 9.2; however, most focus on stage II disease (T1-2, N1), completely resected stage III (T3N0 and T1-3,N1-2) or stage I (T2N0).

A number of studies evaluating adjuvant chemotherapy in early stage NSCLC did not include a no treatment control arm, which may make any real difference between the study arms less detectable (Holmes *et al.* 1985; Lad *et al.* 1988; Dautzenberg *et al.* 1995). The Lung Cancer Study Group compared postoperative CAP chemotherapy (cisplatin, doxorubicin and cyclophosphamide) against immunotherapy with Bacillus Calmette–Guérin (BCG) in patients with completely resected stage II or III adenocarcinoma or large cell carcinoma. Relapse-free survival was significantly improved in the chemotherapy arm but, despite a 7-month improvement in median survival, the differences did not reach statistical significance (Holmes *et al.* 1985). The same group evaluated CAP chemotherapy with radiotherapy against radiotherapy alone in patients with an incomplete resection and again an improvement in median survival of 7 months was demonstrated with the 3-year survival equivalent in both arms (Lad *et al.* 1988).

Encouraging results were found in a Finnish study which randomised 110 patients with stage I NSCLC to treatment with CAP chemotherapy or no additional treatment after radical surgery. Progression rates were lower in the chemotherapy arm (31% vs. 48%, $p = 0.01$) and the survival rate at 5 years was higher in the chemotherapy arm (67% vs. 56%, $p = 0.05$) (Niiranen *et al.* 1992). However, the same treatment randomisation was also used for a Lung Cancer Study Group trial that also included patients with N1 disease. This larger study showed no improvement in either median or long-term survival (Feld *et al.* 1994). Of particular note with this study, only 53% of the eligible patients received all four courses of CAP, and only 57% of such patients received all four cycles on time. Among the patients who had recurrences, 74% had their initial recurrence at a distant site. The CAP regimen was extended with the addition of vincristine and lomustine (CCNU), but this too did not produce a significant advantage (Dautzenberg *et al.* 1995).

A Japanese study gave three cycles of vindesine with cisplatin followed by 1 year of tegafur and uracil, with two control arms of tegafur and uracil and no treatment (Wada *et al.* 1996). The 5-year survival rates, respectively, were 60.6%, 64.1% and 49% ($p = 0.053$) and when the two chemotherapy arms were combined and compared with no treatment, a significant advantage was demonstrated ($p = 0.022$) (Wada *et al.* 1996). This trial suggests that researchers should not extrapolate their experience in the management of metastatic disease into the adjuvant setting as, clearly, UFT appears to confer significant advantage and yet it has only minimal activity in metastatic disease (Shimizu *et al.* 1986; Langer 1999). The role of vindesine and cisplatin was evaluated further in patients with completely resected stage II disease, and again an improvement in median survival was demonstrated, but the long-term survival was not significantly improved (Ohta *et al.* 1993). A further study suggests that postoperative chemotherapy adds no advantage in patients who have had a pathological complete resection (Ichinose *et al.* 2001); 119 patients with stage IIIA, N2 NSCLC were radically resected, and then randomised to receive three cycles of cisplatin/vindesine chemotherapy or no additional treatment. The median survival (35 months) and 3-year survival rate (49%) were identical in the two groups. A number of large adjuvant studies have now been reported and are outlined in Table 9.3.

Table 9.3 Summary of recent clinical trials of adjuvant chemotherapy for NSCLC.

Study	No. Patients	Treatment	Stage	MS (mo)	HR	p	5-yr OS
(Keller et al. 2000)	242 246	XRT (50.4 Gy) PE+XRT	II–IIIA	39 38	0.93 (0.74–1.18)	0.56	39% 33%
(Waller et al. 2004)	189 192	No Rx PVind, MIC, MVP, PVri	I–III		1.0 (0.75–1.35)	0.98	
(Scagliotti et al. 2003)	603 606	No Rx MVP	I–IIIA	48 55.2	0.96 (0.81–1.13)	0.589	+1%
(Arriagada et al. 2004)	935 932	No Rx PE, PVind, PVrl, PVinb	I–IIIA		0.86 (0.76–0.98)	<0.03	40.4% 44.5%
(Kato et al. 2004)	488 491	No Rx UFT	Ia/b only	–	0.71 (0.52–0.98)	0.04	85.4% 87.9%
(Strauss et al. 2004)	171 173	No Rx CarboPac	Ib	–	0.62 (0.41–0.95)	0.028	59% 71% (4-yr OS)
(Winton et al. 2004)	239 243	No Rx PVrl	Ib/II	–	0.69	0.011	54% 69%

PE: cisplatin, etoposide; MIC: mitomycin C, ifosfamide, cisplatin; RT: radiotherapy; No Rx: no treatment control arm; PVind: cisplatin, vindesine; PVrl: cisplatin, vinorelbine; MVP: mitomycin C, vinblastine, cisplatin; CarboPac: carboplatin, paclitaxel; CVUFT: cisplatin, vindesine, uracil, tegafur; UFT: tegafur, uracil.

The Adjuvant Lung Project Italy compared MVP chemotherapy (mitomycin C, vindesine, cisplatin (100 mg/m^2)) with no treatment and showed a hazard ratio of 0.96 (95% CI 0.81–1.13, p = 0.585) (Italy 2002). Radiotherapy was permitted and therefore this was not a true assessment of the impact of chemotherapy. In this study 34% of patients completed the intended chemotherapy, 36% completed treatment with a dose reduction, 21% stopped early and 9% never started the intended chemotherapy. Overall, 70% of patients did not receive the intended treatment. There were fewer recurrences (199 vs. 238) but more early deaths (90 vs. 69) in the chemotherapy arm. Given that the benefit of adjuvant chemotherapy is likely to be between 5 and 10% at 5 years, if the intended treatment cannot be delivered in the majority of patients, it is unlikely that such a trial will demonstrate the intended benefit.

ECOG 3509 used a lower dose of cisplatin compared to other studies and combined radiotherapy with chemotherapy, which produced increased toxicity (Keller *et al.*

2000). The Big Lung Trial started before third generation drugs were introduced into clinical practice and more non-cancer deaths were noted in the treatment arm (Waller *et al.* 2004). Unfortunately, there is limited follow up, variable quality of the surgery and underpowered subgroup analysis, which all impact on the validity of the findings.

More recent studies have utilised a more optimal dose of cisplatin (20–30 mg/m²/week) in combination with second and third generation agents. The International Adjuvant Lung Cancer Trial (IALT) included stage I–III and demonstrated a 4.1% improvement in overall survival at 5 years (Arriagada *et al.* 2004). JBR10 and CALGB 9633 have both only been reported in abstract form but focus on early stage disease (I–II and Ib respectively), but both show a significant improvement in survival of 15% and 12% respectively (Strauss *et al.* 2004; Winton *et al.* 2004). Furthermore, 74% of patients in IALT received more than 240 mg/m² of cisplatin and 65% or patients in JBR10 received 3 or 4 cycles of treatment.

Where does this leave postoperative chemotherapy?

Based on the current evidence, postoperative chemotherapy appears to offer a small but significant benefit to patients with NSCLC. The benefits of cisplatin-based chemotherapy are, in order of magnitude, comparable to those achieved in other tumour types including ovarian, breast and colon cancer. All of the studies to date have flaws that hamper analysis and there is significant statistical heterogeneity between the studies, most of which have been under-powered to detect a 5–10% survival difference. Suboptimal drug delivery has also been a problem for the majority of patients and this may have had a significant effect on outcome. In order to demonstrate a small but clinically important survival advantage, clinical trials will require between 1500 and 2000 patients in each arm and should utilise chemotherapy combinations that are most effective in early disease. The assumption that treatment with activity in patients with advanced disease can be used for adjuvant trials may not necessarily be correct and more research in this area is required. Factors to be considered in the design and analysis of adjuvant studies are outlined in Table 9.4. The activity of treatments in a neoadjuvant setting may help to inform this process.

Table 9.4 Factors for consideration in the design and analysis of clinical trials of adjuvant chemotherapy

Trial design	Trial reporting
Appropriate preoperative evaluation to exclude metastasis	Intention to treat analysis
Complete surgical resection, negative pathological margins	Compliance and toxicity of adjuvant therapy
Careful intraoperative staging, extensive node sampling	
Tissue banking for analysis of biological markers	Disease-free and overall survival rates
Untreated control arm	
Stratification for known prognostic markers	Recurrence patterns: local, distant, or both
Randomisation after pathological staging and clinical recovery	Second primary tumour rates
Optimal chemotherapy regimen	

Rationale for preoperative chemotherapy

The concept of postoperative chemotherapy is attractive because it does not delay the definitive treatment or increase the morbidity of surgery, although it does make assessment of response difficult as patients will not have measurable disease. Preoperative or neoadjuvant chemotherapy has a number of theoretical advantages over adjuvant treatments which include: the ability to measure objective response rates in order to determine the success of treatments; the outcome of treatment can be assessed on a pathological specimen and provides opportunity for translational research on the resected specimen (see Table 9.5).

Table 9.5 Potential advantages of neoadjuvant chemotherapy

Early eradication of distant metastases
Better drug delivery through intact vasculature
Improved resectability (most patients still die of distant failure)
Improved local tumour control
Pathological assessment of induction treatment (*in vivo*)
Offers the possibility of predictive markers: clinical, pathological, biological
Could lead to individualised treatment
Less toxicity than in advanced disease
More rapid development of new therapies

Furthermore, the shrinkage of the tumour may make a patient resectable where they were not before chemotherapy; and, before an operation, the vasculature is intact and this may enhance the drug delivery to the tumour and expose micrometastases to drugs as early as possible (Green *et al.* 1994; Pastorino 1996).

Surgeons have been understandably sceptical about the risks of delaying surgery and increasing perioperative morbidity and mortality. The studies to date have shown that preoperative chemotherapy is feasible and, although some tumours will progress despite early chemotherapy and may become unresectable, such aggressive tumours are unlikely to be cured by surgery alone anyway, which identifies patients that would have relapsed early. Another difficulty is in what to resect in cases where there has been significant tumour shrinkage with chemotherapy, possibly even a complete remission at pathological review.

Surgery and preoperative chemotherapy

Numerous phase II feasibility studies of preoperative chemotherapy have been published, and included a mixed population of IIIA and IIIB tumours. Preoperative chemotherapy may increase resection rates in stage IIIA disease, but there are no well-defined criteria for resectability, nor is there a consensus about the best schedule for preoperative chemotherapy. Four randomised studies comparing cisplatin-based chemotherapy plus surgery versus surgery alone in stage IIIA disease have been

Where does this leave preoperative chemotherapy?

Based on current evidence, preoperative chemotherapy is not recommended for routine use, but all operable patients should be offered the opportunity of discussing ongoing clinical trials, such as the UK Medical Research Council LU22 study.

The clinical trials completed to date have demonstrated a significant advantage for chemotherapy before surgery over surgery alone. This is despite the fact that the studies are small, the chemotherapy regimens are not standardised and some patients had both chemotherapy and radiotherapy before surgical intervention. Nevertheless, these data confirm that the response rates for early disease (39–76%) are significantly higher than for patients with stage IV disease and that pathological responses are seen in up to 15% of patients.

This small collection of studies used a very select group of patients and those with poor prognostic features would have been excluded. Long-term survival and cure rates are difficult to interpret from these data. No chemotherapeutic regimen has shown advantage over another, but the studies do demonstrate the feasibility of this approach and indicate an opportunity for translation research to analyse the effectiveness in a more objective manner.

Remaining questions include: is surgery the best treatment after chemotherapy for patients with resectable stage IIIA disease or could radiotherapy be equally effective? Can the patients with a complete pathological response be identified preoperatively, and do they still require an operation?

Biological agents in early non-small-cell lung cancer

Lung cancer arises from a multistep process resulting in the accumulation of a number of alterations in cells (Hirsch *et al.* 2001, 2002). Both genetic (e.g. allelic losses at chromosomes 3p, 9p, 8p, 17p and MYC, RAS and TP53 mutations) and epigenetic alterations (e.g. inactivating methylation of tumour-suppressor genes) are thought to occur. In the future, it is likely that molecular information will be incorporated into staging and possibly treatment decisions at the time of diagnosis. Molecular markers that can be used to detect minimal residual disease following treatments may also identify specific patients that require additional treatments. The genotypical abnormalities in an individual tumour (such as TP53, EGFR or CYP3A status) may predict not only overall prognosis, but also the likelihood of response to particular cytotoxics or biological agents. With a greater understanding of the biological and molecular processes in this disease, new targets for therapy are being discovered, but these agents will require careful evaluation with validation of their effects on the designated target and correlation with pharmacodynamic parameters.

Several biological agents have been studied in the treatment of early stage NSCLC, including BCG (Bacillus Calmette–Guérin), levamisole, *Corynebacterium parvum*, interferons, tumour necrosis factor (TNF) and specific lymphokine-activated cell therapy; however, results to date have been disappointing (Table 9.7) (Shepherd 1997). Current research is focusing on the development of signal transduction inhibitors, cell cycle regulatory compounds, immunomodulators and anti-angiogenesis agents. These studies are expanding our understanding of the biology of this disease and, although results from small phase I/II studies are encouraging, no advantage has yet been demonstrated in a randomised phase III setting. Immunotherapy using *Mycobacterium vaccae* has shown interesting activity in combination with chemotherapy in patients with advanced NSCLC (O'Brien *et al*. 2000).

Table 9.7 Randomised clinical trials of biological agents used as adjuvant therapy for NSCLC

Study	No. patients	Therapy	Outcome
Gail (1994)	473	Surgery ± intrapleural BCG	No significant difference
Holmes (1994)	141	Surgery ± intrapleural BCG	Better disease-free survival with CAP
Anthony *et al*. (1979)	318	Surgery + CAP or BCG/levamisole	Excess deaths in levamisole group
Amery (1978)	211	Surgery ± levamisole	No significant difference
(Ludwig 1985)	475	Intrapleural and intravenous *Corynebacterium parvum*	Adverse effect with biological therapy
Lee *et al*. (1994)	93	Surgery ± intrapleural Strep. pyogenes	No significant difference
Whyte *et al*. (1992)	63	Surgery/RT ± transfer factor	Non-significant survival benefit
Hollinshead *et al*. (1987)	234	Surgery ± adjuvant ± vaccine	Improved survival with vaccine
Takita *et al*. (1991)	85	Surgery ± specific immunotherapy	Improved survival with immunotherapy

BCG, Bacillus Calmette–Guérin; CAP, cyclophosphamide, doxorubicin, cisplatin; RT, radiotherapy.

The epidermal growth factor receptor (EGFR) pathway contributes to the aggressiveness of many tumour types, and is over-expressed in 40–80% of cases of NSCLC. A number of drugs have been developed that target the EGF receptor, including blocking antibodies (e.g. cetuximab) and EGFR tyrosine kinase inhibitors such as gefitinib and the more recently developed agent erlotinib which has been shown in a randomized trial to be capable of improving survival in relapsed NSCLC which have shown interesting results in early clinical studies (Raben *et al*. 2002; Van Zandwijk and Baas 2002; Cella 2003; Shepherd *et al*. 2004). Synergy exists between these compounds and standard chemotherapeutic agents in preclinical models, but the results from phase III trials in combination with chemotherapy for patients with advanced disease have not yet demonstrated advantage (Giaccone *et al*. 2002; Johnson *et al*. 2002).

Summary

Results to date suggest that the addition of systemic therapies to conventional surgery may improve survival rates. All of the reliable data so far use cisplatin-containing regimens and suggest a dose range of 20–30 mg/m^2/week for the cisplatin.

The optimal management of patients with stage III NSCLC remains controversial. Potential roles exist for surgery, radiotherapy and chemotherapy, but there are no standards of surgery or chemotherapy defined, compounded by uncertainty from difficulty establishing the nodal stage, where mediastinoscopy and/or positron emission tomography are not routinely available. Preoperative chemotherapy is being used in stage IIIA NSCLC in the absence of large randomised trials demonstrating survival benefit, in the hope of downsizing tumours to make them operable. The use of concurrent chemoradiation has been shown in several studies to be beneficial when compared with radiation alone, or sequential chemoradiation in patients with unresectable tumours, and may represent an alternative treatment to surgery for these patients.

Although the survival rates of patients who present with early stage NSCLC remain disappointingly low, much effort has been directed to improving this. There is no doubt that surgery offers the best hope of cure in patients with early stage disease, but the recurrence rates are high and, even among patients with stage IA disease, a third will relapse and die of their disease within 5 years. The majority of patients will develop intrathoracic or distant relapses and this has led to testing of systemic therapy in order to eradicate the residual disease left after surgery.

There is evidence of survival benefits from preoperative or postoperative chemotherapy, but a number of important questions remain, including: what is the optimal chemotherapy to use and how should it be sequenced with surgery or radiotherapy? Can we individualise the treatment based on molecular markers in the tumour? And fundamentally, can we extrapolate the experience in treating advanced disease into the management of patients with early disease? Further data are needed to evaluate whether these benefits are clinically significant or outweighed by increased toxicity.

The benefit and improvement in overall survival offered by adjuvant chemotherapy for NSCLC is comparable to that for other common cancers and yet it is not routinely offered to patients with lung cancer. The best advice to clinicians and patients is that the role and benefits of medical interventions in patients with early NSCLC should be discussed with patients, and that these approaches should continue to be evaluated in well designed clinical trials.

References

ALPI (Adjuvant Lung Project Italy) (2002). Final report of the Adjuvant Lung Project Italy (ALPI): an Italian/EORTC-LCG randomised trial of adjuvant chemotherapy in completely resected non-small cell lung cancer (NSCLC), on behalf of the ALPI/EORTC-LCG investigators. *Annals of Oncology* **13**(Suppl. 5), 9.

Amery, W. K. (1978). Final results of a multicenter placebo-controlled levamisole study of resectable lung cancer. *Cancer Treatment Reports* **62**(11), 1677–83.

Anon (2004). Uncertain future for Iressa. Scrip 21.12.04.

Anthony, H. M., Mearns, A. J. *et al.* (1979). Levamisol and surgery in bronchial carcinoma patients: increase in deaths from cardiorespiratory failure. *Thorax* **34**(1), 4–12.

Arriagada, R., Bergman, B. *et al.* (2004). Cisplatin-based adjuvant chemotherapy in patients with completely resected non-small-cell lung cancer. *New England Journal of Medicine.* **350**(4), 351–60.

Burkes, R. L., Shepherd, F. A. *et al.* (2005). Induction chemotherapy with mitomycin, vindesine and cisplatin for stage IIIA (T1–3, N2) unresectable non-small-cell lung cancer: final results of the Toronto phase II trial. *Lung Cancer* **47**(1), 103–9.

Cella, D. (2003). Impact of ZD1839 on non-small cell lung cancer-related symptoms as measured by the functional assessment of cancer therapy-lung scale. *Seminars in Oncology* **30**(1 Suppl. 1), 39–48.

Chen, Z. L., Perez, S. *et al.* (1993). Frequency and distribution of occult micrometastases in lymph nodes of patients with non-small-cell lung carcinoma. *Journal of the National Cancer Institute* **85**, 493–498.

Cullen, M. H., Billingham, L. J. *et al.* (1999). Mitomycin, ifosfamide, and cisplatin in unresectable non-small-cell lung cancer: effects on survival and quality of life. *Journal of Clinical Oncology* **17**, 3188–3194.

Dautzenberg, B., Chastang, C. *et al.* (1995). Adjuvant radiotherapy versus combined sequential chemotherapy followed by radiotherapy in the treatment of resected nonsmall cell lung carcinoma. A randomized trial of 267 patients. GETCB (Groupe d'Etude et de Traitement des Cancers Bronchiques). *Cancer* **76**, 779–786.

Depierre, A., Milleron, B. *et al.* (1999). Phase III trial of neoadjuvant chemotherapy in resectable stage I, II and III NSCLC: the French experience. *Proceedings of the American Society of Clinical Oncology* **18**, 465a (abstract 1792).

Elias, A., J. Herndorn, *et al.* (1997). A phase III comparison of best local-regionl therapy with or without chemotherapy (CT) for stage IIIA T1-3N2 non-small cell lung cancer (NSCLC): preliminary results. *Proceedings of the American Society of Clinical Oncology* **16**, 448a (abstract 1611).

Endo, S., Sato, Y. *et al.* (2004). Preoperative chemotherapy increases cytokine production after lung cancer surgery. *European Journal of Cardiothoracic Surgery* **26**(4), 787–91.

Feld, R., Rubinstein, L. *et al.* (1994). Adjuvant chemotherapy with cyclophosphamide, doxorubicin, and cisplatin in patients with completely resected stage I non-small cell lung cancer. An LCSG Trial. *Chest* **106**(Suppl. 6), 307S–309S.

Gail, M. H. (1994). A placebo-controlled randomized double-blind study of adjuvant intrapleural BCG in patients with resected T1NO, T1N1 or T2NO squamous cell carcinoma, adenocarcinoma, or large cell carcinoma of the lung. LCSG Protocol 771. *Chest* **106**(6 Suppl), 287S–292S.

Giaccone, G., Johnson, D. H. *et al.* (2002). A phase III clinical trial of ZD1839 (Iressa) in combination with gemcitabine and cisplatin in chemotherapy-naive patients with advanced non-small-cell lung cancer (INTACT 1). *Annals of Oncology* **13**(suppl. 5), 2.

Green, M. R., Ginsberg, R. *et al.* (1994). Induction therapy for stage III NSCLC: a consensus report. *Lung Cancer* **11**(Suppl. 3), S9–10.

Gregor, A., Thomson, C. S. *et al.* (2001). Management and survival of patients with lung cancer in Scotland diagnosed in 1995: results of a national population based study. *Thorax* **56**, 212–217.

Group, L. L. C. S. (1985). Adverse effect of intrapleural *Corynebacterium parvum* as adjuvant therapy in resected stage I and II non-small cell carcinoma of the lung. *Journal of Thoracic and Cardiovascular Surgery* **89**(6), 842–7.

Hirsch, F. R., Franklin, W. A. *et al.* (2001). Early detection of lung cancer: clinical perspectives of recent advances in biology and radiology. *Clinical Cancer Research* **7**, 5–22.

Hirsch, F. R., Merrick, D. T. *et al.* (2002). Role of biomarkers for early detection of lung cancer and chemoprevention. *European Respiratory Journal* **19**, 1151–1158.

Hollinshead, A., Stewart, T. H. *et al.* (1987). Adjuvant specific active lung cancer immunotherapy trials. Tumor-associated antigens. *Cancer* **60**(6), 1249–1262.

Holmes, E. C. (1994). Surgical adjuvant therapy for stage II and stage III adenocarcinoma and large cell undifferentiated carcinoma. *Chest* **106**(6 Suppl), 293S–296S.

Holmes, E. C., Hill, L. D. *et al.* (1985). A randomized comparison of the effects of adjuvant therapy on resected stages II and III non-small cell carcinoma of the lung. The Lung Cancer Study Group. *Annals of Surgery* **202**, 335–341.

Ichinose, Y., Tada, H. *et al.* (2001). A randomised phase III trial of post operative adjuvant chemotherapy in patients with completely resected stage IIIA-N2 NSCLC; Japan Clinical Oncology Group (JCOG 9304) Trial. *Proceedings of the American Society of Clinical Oncology* **20** (abstract 1241).

Italy, A. L. P. (2002). Final report of the Adjuvant Lung Project Italy (ALPI) – an Italian/EORTC-LCG randomised trial of adjuvant chemotherapy in completely resected non-small cell lung cancer (NSCLC), on behalf of the ALP/EORTC-LCG investigators. *Annals of Oncology* **13**(Suppl 5), 9.

Johnson, D. H., Herbst, R. *et al.* (2002). ZD1839 (Iressa) in combination with paclitaxel & carboplatin in chemotherapy-naive patients with advanced non-small-cell lung cancer (NSCLC): Results from a phase III clinical trial (INTACT 2). *Annals of Oncology* **13**(Suppl. 5), 127.

Kato, H., Ichinose, Y. *et al.* (2004). A randomized trial of adjuvant chemotherapy with uracil-tegafur for adenocarcinoma of the lung. *New England Journal of Medicine* **350**(17), 1713–1721.

Keller, S. M., Adak, S. *et al.* (2000). A randomized trial of postoperative adjuvant therapy in patients with completely resected stage II or IIIA non-small-cell lung cancer. Eastern Cooperative Oncology Group. *New England Journal of Medicine* **343**(17), 1217–1222.

Korst, R. J. & Ginsberg, R. J. (2001). Appropriate surgical treatment of resectable non-small-cell lung cancer. *World Journal of Surgery* **25**, 184–188.

Lad, T., Rubinstein, L. *et al.* (1988). The benefit of adjuvant treatment for resected locally advanced non-small-cell lung cancer. The Lung Cancer Study Group. *Journal of Clinical Oncology* **6**, 9–17.

Langer, C. J. (1999). The role of tegafur/uracil in pulmonary malignancy. *Drugs* **58**(Suppl. 3), 71–75.

Lee, Y. C., Luh, S. P. *et al.* (1994). Adjuvant immunotherapy with intrapleural *Streptococcus pyogenes* (OK–432) in lung cancer patients after resection. *Cancer Immunology and Immunotherapy* **39**(4), 269–274.

Ludwig Lung Cancer Study Group (1985). Adverse effect of intrapleural *Corynebacterium parvum* as adjuvant therapy in resected stage I and II non-small cell carcinoma of the lung. *Journal of Thoracic and Cardiovascular Surgery* **89**, 842–847.

Mattson, K. (2001). Neoadjuvant chemotherapy with docetaxel in non-small cell lung cancer. *Seminars in Oncology* **28**(3 suppl. 9), 33–36.

Mountain, C. F. (1997). Revisions in the international system for staging lung cancer. *Chest* **111**, 1710–1717.

Niiranen, A., Niitamo-Korhonen, S. *et al.* (1992). Adjuvant chemotherapy after radical surgery for non-small-cell lung cancer: a randomized study. *Journal of Clinical Oncology* **10**, 1927–1932.

Non-small Cell Lung Cancer Collaborative Group (1995). Chemotherapy in non-small cell lung cancer: a meta-analysis using updated data on individual patients from 52 randomised clinical trials. *British Medical Journal* **311**, 899–909.

O'Brien, M. E., Saini, A. *et al.* (2000). A randomized phase II study of SRL172 (*Mycobacterium vaccae*) combined with chemotherapy in patients with advanced inoperable non-small-cell lung cancer and mesothelioma. *British Journal of Cancer* **83**, 853–857.

Ohta, M., Tsuchiya, R. *et al.* (1993). Adjuvant chemotherapy for completely resected stage III non-small-cell lung cancer. Results of a randomized prospective study. The Japan Clinical Oncology Group. *Journal of Thoracic and Cardiovascular Surgery* **106**, 703–708.

Pantel, K., Izbicki, J. *et al.* (1996). Frequency and prognostic significance of isolated tumour cells in bone marrow of patients with non-small-cell lung cancer without overt metastases. *The Lancet* **347**, 649–653.

Pass, H. I., Pogrebniak, H. W. *et al.* (1992). Randomized trial of neoadjuvant therapy for lung cancer: interim analysis. *Annals of Thoracic Surgery* **53**, 992–998.

Pastorino, U. (1996). Benefits of neoadjuvant chemotherapy in NSCLC. *Chest* **109**(Suppl. 5), 96S–101S.

Pisters, K. M. (2000). The role of chemotherapy in early-stage (stage I and II) resectable non-small cell lung cancer. *Seminars in Radiation Oncology* **10**, 274–279.

Raben, D., Helfrich, B. A. *et al.* (2002). ZD1839, a selective epidermal growth factor receptor tyrosine kinase inhibitor, alone and in combination with radiation and chemotherapy as a new therapeutic strategy in non-small cell lung cancer. *Seminars in Oncology* **29**(1 Suppl. 4), 37–46.

Rosell, R. (1999). New approaches in the adjuvant and neoadjuvant therapy of non-small cell lung cancer, including docetaxel (Taxotere) combinations. *Seminars in Oncology* **26**(3 Suppl. 11), 32–37.

Rosell, R., Gomez-Codina, J. *et al.* (1994). A randomized trial comparing preoperative chemotherapy plus surgery with surgery alone in patients with non-small-cell lung cancer. *New England Journal of Medicine* **330**, 153–158.

Rosell, R., Font, A. *et al.* (1996). The role of induction (neoadjuvant) chemotherapy in stage IIIA NSCLC. *Chest* **109**(Suppl. 5), 102S–106S.

Rosell, R., Gomez-Codina, J. *et al.* (1999). Preresectional chemotherapy in stage IIIA non-small-cell lung cancer: a 7-year assessment of a randomized controlled trial. *Lung Cancer* **26**, 7–14.

Roth, J. A., Fossella, F. *et al.* (1994). A randomized trial comparing perioperative chemotherapy and surgery with surgery alone in resectable stage IIIA non-small-cell lung cancer. *Journal of the National Cancer Institute* **86**, 673–680.

Roth, J. A., Atkinson, E. N. *et al.* (1998). Long-term follow-up of patients enrolled in a randomized trial comparing perioperative chemotherapy and surgery with surgery alone in resectable stage IIIA non-small-cell lung cancer. *Lung Cancer* **21**, 1–6.

Scaglotti, G. V., Fossati, R. *et al.* (2003). Randomized study of adjuvant chemotherapy for completely resected stage I, II or IIIA non-small-cell lung cancer. *Journal of the National Cancer Institute* **95**(19), 1453–61.

Shepherd, F. A. (1997). Alternatives to chemotherapy and radiotherapy as adjuvant treatment for lung cancer. *Lung Cancer* **17**(Suppl. 1), S121–S136.

Shepherd, F. A., Johnston, M. R. *et al.* (1998). Randomized study of chemotherapy and surgery versus radiotherapy for stage IIIA non-small-cell lung cancer: a National Cancer Institute of Canada Clinical Trials Group Study. *British Journal of Cancer* **78**, 683–685.

Shepherd, F. A., Pereira, J., Ciuleanu, T. E., Tan, H. E., Hirsh, V., Thongprasert, S., Bezjak, A., Tu, D., Santabarbara, P., & Seymour, L. (2004). A randomized placebo-controlled trial of erlotinib in patients with advanced NSCLC following failure of first or second line chemotherapy. A National Cancer Institute of Canada Clinical Trials Group. *Journal of Clinical Oncology* **22**(145), 7022.

Shimizu, E., Kimura, K. *et al.* (1986). [A phase II study of UFT in non-small cell lung cancer]. *Gan To Kagaku Ryoho* **13**, 2970–2973.

Siegenthaler, M. P., Pisters, K. M. *et al.* (2001). Preoperative chemotherapy for lung cancer does not increase surgical morbidity. *Annals of Thoracic Surgery* **71**, 1105–1111; discussion 1111–1112.

Strauss, G. M., Herndon, J. *et al.* (2004). Randomized clinical trial of adjuvant chemotherapy with paclitaxel and carboplatin following resection in Stage IB non-small cell lung cancer (NSCLC): Report of Cancer and Leukemia Group B (CALGB) Protocol 9633. *Proceedings of the American Society of Clinical Oncology* **22**, Abst 7019.

Takita, H., Hollinshead, A. C. *et al.* (1991). Adjuvant, specific, active immunotherapy for resectable squamous cell lung carcinoma: a 5-year survival analysis. *Journal of Surgical Oncology* **46**(1): 9–14.

Van Zandwijk, N. and Baas, P. (2002). Second/third/fourth line therapy with tyrosine kinase inhibitors in NSCLC. *Tumori* 1(Suppl. 4), S37–38.

Wada, H., Hitomi, S. *et al.* (1996). Adjuvant chemotherapy after complete resection in non-small-cell lung cancer. West Japan Study Group for Lung Cancer Surgery. *Journal of Clinical Oncology* **14**, 1048–1054.

Waller, D., Peake, M. D. *et al.* (2004). Chemotherapy for patients with non-small cell lung cancer: the surgical setting of the Big Lung Trial. *European Journal of Cardiothoracic Surgery* **26**(1), 173–182.

Whyte, R. I., Schork, M. A. *et al.* (1992). Adjuvant treatment using transfer factor for bronchogenic carcinoma: long-term follow-up. *Annals of Thoracic Surgery* **53**(3), 391–396.

Winton, T. L., Livingstone, R. *et al.* (2004). A prospective randomized trial of adjuvant vinorelbine (VIN) and cisplatin (CIS) in completely resected stage IB and II non-small cell lung cancer (NSCLC) Intergroup JBR. 10. *Proceedngs of the American Society of Clinical Oncology* **22** Abstr. 7018.

Chapter 10

Advanced lung cancer: evidence and opinion for medical intervention

Marianne C. Nicolson

Introduction

The definition of 'medical intervention' here is taken to be treatment with chemotherapy. There is a peculiar resistance to accepting the data in support of chemotherapy for some types of advanced lung cancer. In the UK there are recent data to show that between 8 and 10% of patients with advanced non-small-cell lung cancer (NSCLC) receive chemotherapy (Non-small Cell Lung Cancer Collaborative Group 1995; Gregor *et al.* 2001). In the Scottish audit, it was reported that 43% of lung cancer patients received no treatment within 6 months of diagnosis. It can therefore be of little surprise that the survival rates for lung cancer are both static and lower than in countries where clinicians are rather more enthusiastic about trying to treat the disease. The treating clinician must balance enthusiasm to treat patients against their fitness for chemotherapy, so elderly patients and those of performance status 2 and greater are special groups who merit separate consideration. Development of managed clinical networks and discussion of patients at multidisciplinary meetings should increase the number of patients offered chemotherapy by committed lung cancer specialists. In this chapter, the evidence for chemotherapy will be presented in the hope that it will help to inform opinion and perhaps facilitate access for UK patients to this potentially effective therapy.

Chemotherapy or 'best supportive care' only?

The 'non-believers' claim that chemotherapy will adversely affect a patient's quality of life without giving significant gain in survival. This bias has been addressed in a meta-analysis and in several randomised trials, two of which are outlined below. The 52 randomised trials incorporating more than 9000 patients reported in the MRC meta-analysis showed a 10% absolute improvement in 1-year survival for those who received chemotherapy (Non-small Cell Lung Cancer Collaborative Group 1995). Prospective data are always more compelling, but in the mid-1990s, it would not have been possible in the US or many countries in mainland Europe to recruit to a trial where the randomisation was between single agent chemotherapy with best supportive care (BSC) and BSC alone. There was no such problem in the UK, and the first of these trials used gemcitabine. The patients' quality of life (QoL) was the primary endpoint, and the results showed an advantage for those in the chemotherapy arm (Anderson *et al*. 2000). There was no significant difference in survival (25% vs. 22% at 1 year) but in the subsequent trial of taxol and BSC versus BSC there was a statistically significant improvement in median survival (6.8 versus 4.8 months) and in time to disease progression (Ranson *et al*. 2000). Docetaxel with BSC versus BSC alone again demonstrated improved survival in favour of chemotherapy with 2-year survival in the docetaxel arm 12% whereas all of the BSC patients had died by 20 months (Roszkowski *et al.* 2000). For combination regimens, symptomatic benefit has been evaluated and even with one of the older regimens, mitomycin C, vinblastine and cisplatin (MVP), in 70% of patients there was improvement in tumour-related symptoms which was reported by the majority after only two cycles of treatment (Ellis *et al*. 1995).

How much treatment?

Having established that chemotherapy can be of benefit in advanced NSCLC, the aim is to deliver the appropriate amount of therapy. There is variation internationally on the number of chemotherapy cycles deemed necessary. In mainland Europe, some clinicians use the carcinoembryonic antigen (CEA) marker as a guide to when chemotherapy should stop. Their practice is to give more cycles than we do in the UK where six used to be the norm. This was challenged by a study in which MVP was given for three or six cycles in a randomised trial (Smith *et al.* 2001). There was no difference in response, time to progression or median survival for those patients who had six cycles while the trend was to improved QoL with fewer treatments. In addition to the benefits for the patient of reducing the number of hospital visits for chemotherapy, there are clear economic advantages to stopping therapy after three cycles when maximum palliation may have been achieved.

Old or new combinations?

There are various regimes in use and the choice depends on an individual clinician. In North America paclitaxel and carboplatin are frequently prescribed, whereas in France cisplatin and vinorelbine are more common. In the UK, the two most commonly used regimens are MVP (see above) and mitomycin, ifosfamide and carboplatin (MIC). The latter two employ 'older' drugs, which are felt by some to be less effective. In a recent abstract, MVP was compared with three other regimes incorporating cisplatin 100 mg/m^2 with either vinorelbine or gemcitabine. The response rate was lower for MVP (27% versus 27–48%) as was the median survival (6.4 months versus 9.0 to 9.6 months) (Melo *et al*. 2002). The conclusion of these authors was that MVP is no longer a therapeutic option. In addition, a comparison of four cycles of carboplatin and paclitaxel versus continuation of chemotherapy until progression showed that in 230 patients there was no benefit in survival, response rates or quality of life in continuing treatment beyond four cycles (Socinski *et al.* 2002). MIP, where cisplatin replaces carboplatin, has been compared with gemcitabine and carboplatin, the latter 'out patient' combination resulting in a 10% improvement in 1-year survival and 3.3 months longer median survival (Rudd *et al.* 2002).

Old versus new has also been addressed in a UK trial, now closed to recruitment, in which patients with advanced NSCLC were randomised to either MVP, MIC or carboplatin with docetaxel. In the Eastern Cooperative Oncology Group (ECOG) 1594 randomised study, 1155 patients with advanced NSCLC were treated with a combination of cisplatin or carboplatin and one of the 'newer' chemotherapy agents (Schiller *et al.* 2002). The treatments were cisplatin with paclitaxel, cisplatin and gemcitabine, cisplatin and docetaxel or carboplatin and paclitaxel. Differences in response rates, median survival and 1 and 2-year survivals were not statistically significant although there was a longer progression-free survival in favour of the cisplatin-gemcitabine arm. So old drugs may be slightly inferior, but there appears to be little to choose between the new ones.

Second-line chemotherapy?

In the UK the challenge is to increase the number of patients who receive any chemotherapy for NSCLC, but in the US, mainland Europe and those UK centres where patients do receive appropriate treatment there is an increasing number of patients who may be suitable for second-line chemotherapy for NSCLC. Docetaxel is the single agent of choice following the evidence published by Shepherd and colleagues, which demonstrated that, in 104 patients randomised to receive docetaxel 100 mg/m^2, 75 mg/m^2 or best supportive care (stratified by best response to cisplatin and performance status (PS)), the low response rate of 7.1% belied the benefit of median survival: 7.0 versus 4.6 months (Shepherd *et al.* 2000). In practice there are few patients who are fit for second-line chemotherapy and it may be that the new 'targeted' drugs such as the epidermal growth factor receptor (EGFR) inhibitors are effective and more tolerable. Initial phase II studies of the EGFR tyrosine kinase inhibitors gefitinib (Baselga *et al.* 2002) and erlotinib (Perez-Soler *et al.* 2001) indicated a survival benefit relative to BSC. This has subsequently been confirmed for erlotinib in a randomised, placebo-controlled study where it improved median survival by 42% from 4.7 months to 6.7 months as well as slowing symptomatic deterioration (Shepherd *et al.* 2004) but not demonstrated for gefitinib where preliminary analysis of a similarly designed study found that gefitinib did not significantly improve survival relative to BSC (Anon 2004).

So we treat everyone...?

Approximately 50% of patients with lung cancer will be aged 70 years or more and since 90% of lung cancers are diagnosed in current or previous smokers there is a high incidence of co-morbid disease. Cisplatin is a key drug in most regimens of combination chemotherapy for NSCLC but it can aggravate peripheral vascular disease and requires a fluid load that will be difficult to deliver in people with ischaemic heart disease and impaired left ventricular function. People over the age of 70 are also likely to have reduced renal and marrow reserve, therefore the risk of delivering to them potentially toxic chemotherapy must be weighed against the benefits of symptomatic improvement and enhanced survival.

Even enthusiasts will not claim that it is appropriate to treat with chemotherapy all patients diagnosed to have advanced NSCLC. In my own practice in 2000, 43% of NSCLC patients received chemotherapy but this is significantly above the national average, as seen from recent publications cited above. A critical evaluation of the age issue has shown that age alone is not an adverse factor for survival. It is also known that patients of 60 years and older are just as likely to accept chemotherapy when it is offered (Silvestri *et al.* 1998). It is incumbent on the treating clinician to inform patients that, although most patients have symptomatic improvement, by no means everyone will benefit and that average survival gain is around 2 months.

Some studies have investigated specifically the effects of chemotherapy in the elderly. Single agent vinorelbine was compared with BSC in a trial where all patients were aged over 70 and there was a clear benefit in survival in the chemotherapy arm (ELVIS 1999). However, combining vinorelbine with gemcitabine was not more effective than either agent alone (Gridelli *et al.* 2001).

In the ECOG 1594 trial, recruitment of patients of performance status 2 was stopped when they were found to be doing less well than fitter patients, and subgroup analysis revealed a response rate of only 14% with median survival 4.1 months (Sweeney *et al.* 2001). Such information has led to more trials being designed specifically for PS2+ patients. Here it is important to differentiate between those patients who have an acute deterioration in performance status because of the tumour and those whose co-morbidity limits what they can do and confers chronicity to their poor performance status. The former group may benefit more from chemotherapy. Equally, some clinicians who have witnessed patients improving on chemotherapy emphasise that the adherence to quoting *median* improvement in symptoms or survival misses the fact that some patients gain significant and durable benefit.

In small cell lung cancer (SCLC), the high response rate and improved survival with chemotherapy results in a recommendation that 67% of patients should receive it (SIGN Lung Cancer guideline no. 1995). Despite the enhanced chemosensitivity of the tumour, as in treatment of NSCLC, there is concern that patients who are elderly or of poor performance status may tolerate treatment less well and gain less benefit. Building on the study where combination chemotherapy with cyclophosphamide, adriamycin and vincristine (CAV) produced better survival and less toxicity than single agent oral etoposide in patients with extensive stage SCLC (Girling 1996), patients who had a less than 15% chance of surviving 1 year were randomised to either single agent carboplatin (AUC7) or CAV. There was improved response (38% versus 25%) and 1-year survival (12% versus 6%) in the CAV arm. It is important that more such trials are done so that we can establish properly the groups of patients who stand to gain – and more importantly lose – when treated with chemotherapy.

Conclusion

Lung cancer is the commonest cause of cancer death in the developed world. In all of our professional lifetimes we will continue to see many patients who are diagnosed with tumour at a stage where palliation is the only viable option. Chemotherapy can improve symptoms and life expectancy in many patients with lung cancer and should be made available to more of those who can benefit. We must continue to evaluate meaningful outcomes such as quality of life and 1-year survival, develop less toxic and targeted therapies but also aim to design trials for those elderly and poor performance status patients currently excluded from receiving chemotherapy as a palliative option. Adoption of the current evidence base by all clinicians involved in treating lung cancer patients should result in more people accessing chemotherapy. Let us hope that we will see in the next few years an improvement in the outlook for those diagnosed with this disease.

References

Anderson, H., Hopwood, P., Stephens, R. J. *et al.* (2000). Gemcitabine plus best supportive care (BSC) vs BSC in inoperable non-small cell lung cancer: a randomised trial with quality of life as the primary outcome. *British Journal of Cancer* **83**, 447–453.

Anon (2004). Uncertain future for Iressa. Scrip 21.12.04

Baselga, J., Kris, M., Yano, S. *et al.* (2002). Phase II trials (IDEAL 1 and IDEAL2) of ZD1839 (Iressa) in locally advanced or metastatic non-small cell lung cancer patients. *Annals of Oncology* **13**, 131 (abstract 481PD).

ELVIS (Elderly Lung Cancer Vinorelbine Italian Study) (1999). Effects of vinorelbine on quality of life and survival of elderly patients with advanced non-small cell lung cancer. *Journal of the National Cancer Institute* **91**, 66–72.

Ellis, P. A., Smith, I. E., Hardy, J. R. *et al.* (1995). Symptom relief with MVP (mitomycin C, vinblastine and cisplatin) chemotherapy in advanced non-small cell lung cancer. *British Journal of Cancer* **71**, 366–370.

Giaccone, G., Johnson, D. H., Menegold, C. *et al.* (2002). A phase III clinical trial of ZD1839 (Iressa) in combination with gemcitabine and cisplatin in chemotherapy-naïve patients with advanced non-small cell lung cancer (INTACT-1). *Annals of Oncology* **13**, 2 (abstract 40).

Girling, D. J. (1996). Comparison of oral etoposide and standard intravenous multidrug chemotherapy for small cell lung cancer: A stopped multicentre randomised trial; Medical Research Council Lung Cancer Working Party. *The Lancet* **348**, 563–566.

Gregor, A., Thomson, C. S., Brewster, D. H. *et al.* (2001). Management and survival of patients with lung cancer in Scotland diagnosed in 1995: results of a national population based study. *Thorax* **56**, 212–217.

Gridelli, C., Perrone, F., Cigolari, S. *et al.* (2001). The MILES (multicentre Italian lung cancer in the elderly study) phase III trial: Gemcitabine + vinorelbine vs. vinorelbine vs. gemcitabine in elderly advanced NSCLC patients. *Lung Cancer* **31**, 277–284.

Melo, M. J., Barradas, A., Costa, A. *et al.* (2002). Results of a randomised phase III trial comparing 4 cisplatin (P) based regimens in the treatment of locally advanced and metastatic non-small cell lung cancer: mitomycin/vinblastine/cisplatin (MVP) is no longer a therapeutic option. *Proceedings of the American Society for Clinical Oncology* 21, 302a.

Non-small Cell Lung Cancer Collaborative Group (1995) Chemotherapy in non-small cell lung cancer: A meta-analysis using updated data on individual patients from 52 randomised clinical trials. *British Medical Journal* 311, 899–909.

Perez-Soler, R., Chachoua, A., Huberman, M. *et al.* (2001). A phase II trial of the epidermal growth factor receptor (EGFR) tyrosine kinase inhibitor erlotinib following platinum-based chemotherapy in patients with advanced, EGFR-expressing, NSCLC. *Proceedings of the American Society for Clinical Oncology* 20, 310a (abstract 1235).

Ranson, M., Davidson, N., Nicolson, M. *et al.* (2000). Randomised trial of paclitaxel plus supportive care versus supportive care for patients with advanced non-small cell lung cancer. *Journal of the National Cancer Institute* 92, 1074–1080.

Roszkowski, K., Pluzanska, A., Krzakowski, M., Smith, A. P., Saigi, E., Aasebo, U., Parisi, A., Tran, N. P., Olivares, R. & Berille, J. (2000). A multicenter, randomised, phase III study of docetaxel plus best supportive care vrsus best supportive care in chemotherapy-naive patients with metastatic or non-resectable localised non-small cell lung cancer (NSCLC). *Lung Cancer* 27, 145–157.

Rudd, R. M., Gower, N. H., James, L. E. *et al.* (2002). Phase III randomised comparison of gemcitabine and carboplatin (GC) with mitomycin, ifosfamide and cisplatin (MIP) in advanced non-small cell lung cancer (NSCLC). *Proceedings of the American Society for Clinical Oncology* 21, 292a.

Schiller, J. H., Harrington, D., Belani, C. P. *et al.* (2002). Comparison of four chemotherapy regimens for advanced non-small cell lung cancer. *New England Journal of Medicine* 346, 92–98.

Shepherd, F. A., Pereira, J., Ciuleanu, T. E. *et al.* (2004). A randomized placebo-controlled trial of erlotinib in patients with advanced NSCLC following failure of first or second line chemotherapy. A National Cancer Institute of Canada Clinical Trials Group trial. *Journal of Clinical Oncology* 22, 145 (abstract 7022).

Shepherd, F. A., Dancey, J., Ramlau, R. *et al.* (2000). Prospective randomised trial of docetaxel versus best supportive care in patients with non-small cell lung cancer previously treated with platinum-based chemotherapy. *Journal of Clinical Oncology* 18, 2095–2103.

Silvestri, G., Pritchard, R. & Welch, H. G. (1998). Preferences for chemotherapy in patients with advanced non-small cell lung cancer: Descriptive study based on scripted interviews. *British Medical Journal* 317, 771–775.

Smith, I. E., O'Brien, M. E., Talbot, D. *et al.* (2001). Duration of chemotherapy in advanced non-small cell lung cancer: A randomised trial of three versus six courses of mitomycin, vinblastine and cisplatin. *Journal of Clinical Oncology* 19, 1336–1343.

Socinski, M. A., Schell, M. J., Peterman, A., Bakri, K., Yates, S., Gitten, S., Unger, P., Lee, J., Lee, J.-H., Tynan, M., Moore, M. & Kies, M. S. (2002). Phase III trial comparing a defined duration of therapy versus continuous therapy followed by second line therapy in advanced-stage IIIB/IV non-small cell lung cancer. *Journal of Clinical Oncology* 20, 1335–1343.

Sweeney, C. J., Zhu, J., Sandler, A. B. *et al.* (2001). Outcome of patients with performance status of 2 in Eastern Cooperative Oncology Group Study E1594: A phase II trial in patients with metastatic non-small cell lung carcinoma. *Cancer* 92, 2639–2647.

Chapter 11

Current science and opinion in the management of mesothelioma

Dean A. Fennell and Robin Rudd

Aetiology and epidemiology

Malignant mesothelioma is a tumour which arises from mesothelial or possibly more primitive sub-mesothelial cells. It occurs most commonly in the pleura but also in the peritoneum and rarely can arise in the pericardium or tunica vaginalis testis. Most cases of mesothelioma are caused by asbestos exposure. The causal relation is just as well established for peritoneal mesothelioma as for pleural mesothelioma (Doll and Peto 1985). The relation to asbestos exposure is less clearly established for pericardial and testicular mesothelioma because these conditions are rare and systematic study is difficult.

Mesothelioma has been increasing in incidence throughout Western Europe for several decades and is expected to continue do so until a peak is reached between 2010 and 2020 (Peto *et al.* 1999). There are currently around 1600 new cases annually in the UK and the incidence is expected to at least double over the next 15 years. This reflects the increasing use of asbestos in industrialised countries until the mid-1970s and the long latent period, around 40 years on average, between exposure and disease.

Diagnosis and staging

The diagnosis is often confidently anticipated from the clinical history of asbestos exposure, presentation with breathlessness or chest pain, and characteristic radiological features of pleural effusion with or without pleural thickening. Computed tomography (CT) typically shows pleural thickening which may be grossly lobulated, slightly irregular or uniform (Patz *et al.* 1992). Extension of the pleural thickening onto the mediastinal aspect of the pleura and loss of the fat plane between pleural thickening and the pericardium are features in favour of malignancy rather than benign asbestos-related pleural thickening.

Diffuse malignant mesothelioma falls into three main histological types: epithelioid, which is most common, sarcomatoid and mixed or biphasic. The epithelioid variety displays several patterns including tubulopapillary and glandular. Histochemical and immunohistochemical stains assist in differentiating epithelioid mesothelioma from adenocarcinoma, the most common and difficult differential diagnosis (Cury *et al.* 2000). The pathological type is of prognostic significance and histological diagnosis is important if any specific treatment is contemplated. Cytology of effusions and blind percutaneous biopsy with an Abrams needle each achieve a diagnosis in only about a quarter of cases (Boutin and Rey 1993). If pleural thickening or mass lesions are evident ultrasound or CT guided cutting needle biopsy gives much better results than blind biopsy. In one series of 70 patients with pleural disease, including 52 with mesothelioma, the sensitivity of this technique was 77%, specificity 88%, accuracy 80%, positive predictive value 100% and negative predictive value 57% (Heilo *et al.* 1999). Another series found that a correct histologic diagnosis of malignant mesothelioma was made by cutting needle biopsy in 18 of 21 patients (86% sensitivity and 100% specificity) (Adams *et al.* 2001).

Thoracoscopic biopsy under direct vision will yield a diagnosis in most cases and is the investigation of choice if the CT scan does not show any lesions suitable for guided percutaneous biopsy, or if this technique has failed to yield a diagnosis. In a series of 188 patients with mesothelioma, thoracoscopy provided the diagnosis in 98% of cases (Boutin and Rey 1993). Open biopsy is occasionally necessary when a percutaneous biopsy has failed to give the diagnosis and the pleural space is obliterated so that thoracoscopy is not possible. Even open biopsy occasionally fails to give a definitive diagnosis, particularly when sparse malignant cells are set in a profuse fibrous stroma as in the desmoplastic variant.

Several staging systems have been used. The most widely used nowadays is that devised by the International Mesothelioma Interest Group (IMIG) based upon a TNM (tumour, node, metastasis) system (Rusch 1995). Magnetic resonance imaging offers little advantage over the CT scan unless radical surgery is under consideration when it may help to delineate the extent of involvement of the diaphragm, mediastinum and chest wall (Patz *et al.* 1992). Positron emission tomography (PET) can identify and stage mesothelioma and help to differentiate it from benign pleural thickening, which usually has low uptake of 2-fluoro-2-deoxy-D-glucose (FDG) (Benard *et al.* 1998).

The relation between clinical stage according to the IMIG system and survival has not been clearly established. A prognostic model based upon age, sex, histological type and leucocyte count devised from EORTC trial data was reported to predict survival (Curran *et al.* 1998) and this has recently been validated on a different dataset (Fennell *et al.* 2003b). This model can be used to stratify patients entering clinical trials.

Treatment

Old retrospective studies found no survival advantage from any mode of treatment and until recently it was widely felt that mesothelioma is an untreatable disease for which only palliative measures are appropriate. Many still hold this view but there has been increasing interest in the possibilities for specific anti-tumour therapy. On the basis of recent data it appears that a small minority of patients is suitable for potentially curative therapy including radical surgery and many others may be considered for anti-tumour chemotherapy, immunotherapy or other biological agents, which may modify the course of the disease. There is also increasing understanding of the importance of active symptom control which can improve quality of life in a significant proportion of patients (Muers *et al.* 2004).

Symptom control

The most important aspects of active symptom control involve prevention of recurrence of pleural effusions and pain control. The usual analgesic ladder culminating in opiates or transdermal fentanyl is often effective but, if not, intercostal nerve blocks, radiotherapy and cordotomy may be helpful. Other symptoms that commonly require treatment are excessive sweating, for which cimetidine, thioridazine or thalidomide may be helpful, and anorexia, which may respond to steroid therapy with prednisolone or medroxyprogesterone acetate.

Management of pleural effusion

For most patients with tumours unsuitable for radical surgery it is important for quality of life to obtain effective pleurodesis at an early stage. Repeated ineffective attempts at pleural drainage often lead to a loculated effusion, often infected, which cannot be drained effectively, and a rind of tumour on the visceral pleura rendering it impossible to obtain re-expansion of the lung. Thoracoscopic talc poudrage is regarded as the most effective method and should be used first if readily available, although medical bedside pleurodesis using talc in suspension according to a defined protocol is probably of comparable efficacy (Yim *et al.* 1996). Some surgeons advocate so-called cytoreductive surgery, that is, removal of as much as possible of the tumour, usually by means of video-assisted thoracoscopy (Grossebner *et al.* 1999). It has not been demonstrated in a randomised trial that there are quality of life or survival advantages from partial resection and pleurodesis compared with pleurodesis alone.

For the situation where the lung is bound down by visceral pleural tumour so that pleurodesis cannot be achieved, there are advocates of insertion of a pleuro-peritoneal shunt (e.g. Denver shunt) to transfer fluid from the pleural space to the abdominal cavity from where it is reabsorbed (Tsang *et al.* 1990). A subcutaneous catheter is implanted incorporating a pumping chamber located beneath the skin, which the patient is supposed to operate by pressing on it repeatedly many times each day. Common problems are blockage of the shunt or, if it remains patent, spread of tumour to the peritoneum leading to worse symptoms and poorer quality of life. Repeated aspiration as required or an in-dwelling pleural catheter for continuous bag drainage are alternative approaches which many patients find acceptable in this situation.

Radiotherapy

Mesotheliomas are commonly stated to be radio-resistant but this is not necessarily the case as marked tumour shrinkage may be observed after radiotherapy to subcutaneous tumours. However, radiotherapy seldom produces a partial response of intra-thoracic disease, as assessed by radiological criteria, and it has not been found to improve survival. The lack of response of intra-thoracic disease is probably related at least partly to the difficulty in administering a sufficient dose to disease spread over a large area. Radiotherapy may be helpful for reducing the size of chest wall masses and alleviating localised pain in more than half the patients treated but symptom relief usually lasts only 3 months or less (Bissett *et al.* 1991). The dose of radiotherapy does not appear to influence response (Davis *et al.* 1994).

Prophylactic irradiation of biopsy tracks substantially reduces the frequency of tumour seeding, from 40% to 0% in one randomised trial, which used a dose of 7 Gy daily for 3 days (Boutin *et al.* 1995). Ideally prophylactic radiotherapy should be administered within 4 weeks of the biopsy or drainage procedure and all sites that have been used should be irradiated.

Chemotherapy

A number of recent phase II studies of various chemotherapy regimes have demonstrated objective response rates comparable to those seen in advanced non-small cell lung cancer and worthwhile palliation of symptoms in half or more of the patients treated, even among those who have not shown objective radiological responses as defined by conventional criteria. A study of the combination of mitomycin, vinblastine and cisplatin (MVP) administered 3 weekly, a regime which has been widely used for non-small cell lung cancer for many years, reported partial response on radiological criteria in 8 of 39 (20%) patients and 24 (62%) reported symptom relief (Middleton *et al.* 1998). Median survival was disappointing at 6 months. In an extended series of 150 patients the partial response rate was lower at 15% with a similar median survival of 7 months (Andreopoulou *et al.* 2003).

A study of single agent vinorelbine administered on an out-patient basis in cycles of an injection each week for 6 weeks reported seven partial responses among 29 patients (24%) with symptomatic benefit as assessed by symptom checklist in around half the patients (Steele *et al.* 2000b). The regime was generally well tolerated with no treatment-related deaths. Median survival was 10.6 months. In an extended series of 65 patients the partial response rate was 21% with a median survival of 13 months (Steele *et al.* 2000a).

A study of 21 patients treated with gemcitabine and cisplatin reported a high partial response rate of 47.6% and median survival of 9.5 months (Byrne *et al.* 1999). Patient questionnaire quality of life data were not included but patients were reported to have benefited symptomatically. However, further studies of this regime have shown lower response rates between 16 and 33% with median survivals between 9.6 and 13 months (Nowak *et al.* 2002; van Haarst *et al.* 2002; Castagneto *et al.* 2003). Carboplatin is apparently as effective as cisplatin in combination with gemcitabine with a partial response rate of 26% and median survival of 15 months (Favaretto *et al.*

2003). Gemcitabine alone has minimal activity with reported single agent response rates of 0% of 17 patients (Kindler *et al.* 2001) and 7% of 27 patients (van Meerbeeck *et al.* 1999). Paclitaxel has little activity in mesothelioma (van Meerbeeck *et al.* 1996; Vogelzang *et al.* 1999). Irinotecan in combination with cisplatin and mitomycin has conferred a response rate of 35% in previously untreated patients and 30% in patients who had previously received chemotherapy, mostly with vinorelbine alone or in combination with oxaliplatin (Fennell *et al.* 2003a, c).

Pemetrexed (Alimta®), a multi-targeted anti-folate agent, has excited considerable interest. As a single agent the response rate reported among performance status (PS) 0–1 patients was 18% with a median survival of 10.7 months (Scagliotti *et al.* 2003). Activity is higher in combination with a platinum agent, either cisplatin or carboplatin (Hughes *et al.* 2002). Only one large-scale randomised trial of chemotherapy has been completed. This compared pemetrexed in combination with cisplatin with single agent cisplatin (Vogelzang *et al.* 2003). The design was altered part way through recruitment because of a high rate (7%) of toxic deaths in the pemetrexed arm. Vitamin supplementation with B12 and folate, shown in other studies to reduce toxicity, was introduced for all patients in both arms of the study and the recruitment target was increased from 280 to 456. Median survival with the combination was 12.1 months compared with 9.3 months in the control arm ($p = 0.02$) and in the fully vitamin supplemented groups the median survivals were 13.3 months vs. 10.0 months ($p = 0.051$). There were symptomatic and quality of life advantages for the combination but these were partly accounted for by progressive deterioration during chemotherapy in the control patients.

There are several reasons for caution in interpretation of this study. Eight randomised patients were excluded from the survival analysis because they did not receive chemotherapy so it was not an intention-to-treat analysis. Vitamin supplementation increased survival in both arms of the study and the survival advantage in the fully vitamin supplemented patients was not statistically significant. Most importantly, the control arm, that is, moderately high dose single agent cisplatin, is not standard therapy for mesothelioma and few clinicians would consider this regime with low efficacy and substantial toxicity to be a worthwhile treatment option outside a clinical trial. On present evidence pemetrexed appears to be an agent with useful activity in mesothelioma, which certainly merits further study but is not clearly superior to other agents with activity in mesothelioma.

The important questions of whether chemotherapy confers clinically significant survival and quality of life advantages compared with active supportive care are being addressed in a randomised study known as MSO-1, organised by the British Thoracic Society with the Medical Research Council Lung Cancer Study Group, funded by Cancer Research UK. The full study, which aims to recruit 840 patients, is in progress following a feasibility study which showed that around 20% of patients were willing to be randomised between three arms comprising two types of chemotherapy, each of which has been shown to produce objective responses and symptom relief: vinorelbine and the combination of mitomycin, vinblastine and cisplatin (MVP), and an active supportive care (ASC) arm. The feasibility study showed that ASC alone is capable of producing substantial symptom relief, confirming the importance of this trial (Muers *et al.* 2004).

Extra-pleural pneumonectomy (EPP) and trimodality therapy

Radical surgery is the only treatment that may have any realistic chance of achieving long-term survival. Pleural mesothelioma can be radically excised by extra-pleural pneumonectomy, that is, removal of the whole lung and both layers of pleura, taking also any involved pericardium and diaphragm, which are then reconstituted with synthetic materials. An impermeable material is used for the diaphragm to prevent filling of the chest cavity with peritoneal fluid but the pericardial patch must be fenestrated to avoid tamponade. Sites of previous pleural biopsy or drainage are also excised in case there has been seeding with tumour. Intra-pleural and extra-pleural lymph nodes are sampled for accurate pathological staging. Following surgery radiotherapy to the thorax and chemotherapy are commonly used, referred to as trimodality therapy (Sugarbaker *et al.* 1999). Typically total doses of 30 Gy to the hemithorax and 40 Gy to the mediastinum are used. Various chemotherapy regimes have been used at different times. The treatment is empirical as there have been no randomised trials to determine what additional benefit, if any, is conferred by the addition of these modalities to surgery.

Sugarbaker's group (Sugarbaker *et al.* 1999) described results in 183 patients treated in this way. There were seven peri-operative deaths (3.8%). For the other patients the median survival was 19 months, with 38% surviving 2 years and 15% surviving 5 years. These rather disappointing figures for the whole group reflect a broad spectrum of outcomes according to different prognostic variables. The important variables predicting a better outcome were epithelioid tumour type, lack of extra-pleural lymph node involvement and negative resection margins. Among a subset of 31 patients with all these features the median survival was 51 months, with 68% surviving 2 years and 46% surviving 5 years. The poor outcome in patients with extra-pleural node involvement means that it is important to exclude these patients from radical surgery as far as possible. The sensitivity of contrast enhanced magnetic resonance imaging (MRI) for node involvement is low and it has been suggested that preoperative node staging by mediastinoscopy should be performed (Pilling *et al.* 2003). However, the negative predictive value of mediastinoscopy is also low and not significantly better than that of CT (de Perrot *et al.* 2003). PET scanning may be worthwhile but the optimal means of preoperative staging remains to be defined.

Similar results from extra-pleural pneumonectomy have been reported by Rusch's group (Rusch *et al.* 2003). The procedure was performed in 150 patients. Various adjuvant therapies with radiotherapy and cisplatin-based chemotherapies were used in sequential phase II trials. Higher tumour T and N status, higher stage and non-epithelioid histology had expected adverse effects on survival, while adjuvant therapy had a significant beneficial impact on survival. The site of relapse differs according to the type of surgery. Following extra-pleural pneumonectomy, distant relapse, particularly in the contralateral pleura and abdomen, is more common than local relapse whereas local relapse is more common after more limited resection by pleurectomy (Rusch and Venkatraman 1996).

On the basis of these data it is reasonable to consider radical surgery for highly selected patients with early stage disease, that is, IMIG stages I and perhaps II without extra-pleural node involvement, with epithelioid histology and good performance status. It is inevitable that some patients believed to have node negative epithelioid tumours on the basis of small biopsy samples will prove to have biphasic tumours or node involvement when more extensive tissue is available for examination after resection. However, the outcome in patients with sarcomatoid and biphasic tumours, or with extra-pleural node involvement is very poor and radical surgery should probably not be offered outside a clinical trial to patients known in advance to have these characteristics. There is reasonably good evidence from retrospective studies that hemithorax irradiation reduces local recurrence rates but the effect on survival is uncertain. The role of adjuvant chemotherapy is also uncertain, particularly as ineffective regimes have often been used in reported surgical series. By analogy with other cancers, neoadjuvant chemotherapy may be more promising. A phase II study has demonstrated the feasibility of this approach (Stahel *et al.* 2003). EPP was performed in 22 of 30 patients (73%) who received neoadjuvant chemotherapy with gemcitabine and cisplatin and median survival was 20 months. A randomised trial of EPP (MARS) is being planned in Europe, beginning with a feasibility study to discover whether patients will be willing to consent to randomisation between such radically different treatment options.

Other modalities

Immunotherapy

Various methods of immunotherapy have been attempted (Stahel *et al.* 2003). *In vitro* asbestos fibres reduce the ability of natural killer (NK) cells to destroy mesothelioma cells, and the activity of the NK cells can be restored by interleukin-2 (IL-2) (Upham *et al.* 1995). Systemic IL-2 therapy has been demonstrated to have low activity against mesothelioma although it is of interest that, occasionally, tumour regression occurs (Mulatero *et al.* 2001). Intra-pleural IL-2 is more active; 11/22 partial responses and 1/22 complete response were reported in one study, although the median survival of 18 months for this group comprising nearly all stage I and II epithelioid tumours was disappointing (Astoul *et al.* 1998). Complications including empyema and difficulty in maintaining access to the pleural space reduce the practicality of this form of treatment.

Recombinant human interferon gamma can control cell cycle progression *in vitro* (Vivo *et al.* 2001). However, interferon has conferred little clinical benefit when used as a single agent for the treatment of mesothelioma. One study found one partial response out of 13 evaluable patients (Ardizzoni *et al.* 1994). Interferon has also been used in combination with chemotherapy but with little evidence of additional benefit to balance the increased toxicity (Parra *et al.* 2001).

Gene therapy

There has been considerable interest in the possibility of gene therapy for mesothelioma but work is at an early stage and it is not yet a practical treatment option. A phase I clinical trial put recombinant adenovirus (rAd) containing herpes simplex virus thymidine kinase (HSV*tk*) gene into the pleural space of patients with mesothelioma. The gene should render the tumour cells susceptible to attack by the antiviral drug ganciclovir, which was administered for 14 days. Therapy was well tolerated, with evidence of significant gene transfer in 11 of 20 patients (Sterman *et al.* 1998).

Disruption of the 9p21 locus is common in mesothelioma and leads to loss of both the p16INK4a and p14ARF gene products. Re-expression of p16INK4a using an adenovirus gene therapy results in cell cycle arrest, apoptosis and tumour regression in xenografts models (Frizelle *et al.* 1998). Because of concern regarding adenoviral vector safety, alternative methods of gene transfer are under investigation. Re-expression of p16INK4a by means of a recombinant peptide has been achieved *in vitro* and *in vivo* in xenograft models. Other modes of gene therapy including suicide gene therapy and immunostimulant gene therapy are under investigation (Frizelle *et al.* 2003).

New targets for therapy
Cell death pathways

Mesothelioma cells exhibit significant resistance to programmed cell death or *apoptosis*, a physiological process that underlies the efficacy of all conventional cytotoxic cancer therapies (Narasimhan *et al.* 1998). The recent increase in understanding of the fundamental mechanisms that lead to apoptosis now provides a framework for understanding why mesothelioma is such an unresponsive cancer. Furthermore, important new molecular targets have recently been identified, with potential for the development of novel effective therapy.

Apoptosis is characterised by cell shrinkage, plasma membrane blebbing, nuclear condensation and internucleosomal fragmentation (Kerr *et al.* 1972). These phenomena are mediated by activation of a group of aspartate specific proteases that exist in all nucleated cells as inactive zymogens, termed caspases. Caspase zymogens are rapidly activated during apoptosis. This event follows physiological permeabilisation of mitochondrial membranes, and is accompanied by release of apoptosis inducing proteins. A major caspase activator, cytochrome C, assembles a caspase inducing complex or *apoptosome*, with apoptosis protease activating factor-1 (APAF-1). The first caspase to be activated, caspase 9 then activates downstream executioner caspases. Prevention of caspase activation results in resistance to apoptosis inducers including chemotherapy. Mesothelioma cells express proteins that prevent apoptosis, via direct inhibition of caspase 9. The inhibitor of apoptosis protein (IAP) family is a group of proteins that structurally resemble baculovirus proteins. The IAP members termed *survivin* and *IAP-1* have been validated as functionally relevant regulators of apoptosis threshold in mesothelioma cells (Gordon *et al.* 2002; Xia *et al.* 2002).

Downregulation of survivin expression by antisense oligonucleotides in mesothelioma cell lines enhances spontaneous apoptosis and mediates chemosensitisation (Xia *et al.* 2002). This effect is seen in the survivin expressing cells but not in the non-survivin expressing cells. The level of expression of IAP-1 correlates with sensitivity to cisplatin-induced apoptosis, implicating a role for IAP-1 in regulating apoptosis threshold in the mesothelioma cell. Stable disruption of IAP-1 gene expression increases not only spontaneous apoptosis, but enhances susceptibility to cisplatin-induced apoptosis by approximately 20-fold (Gordon *et al.* 2002). As such, these findings suggest that redundant IAP expression plays an important role in regulating cellular apoptosis threshold, and validates both IAP-1 and survivin as novel targets for experimental drug development. Survivin is not expressed in normal adult tissue, but is re-expressed in malignant cells (Ambrosini *et al.* 1997). This suggests that survivin could be a highly specific target for therapy.

Natural inhibitors of survivin and IAP-1 exist, and can be exploited for therapy. Two proteins released from mitochondria during apoptosis, second derived mitochondrial activator of caspases (SMAC) and OMI/HtrA2, bind IAPs, suppressing their caspase inhibitory activity. Thus, SMAC peptides have been shown to be efficient chemosensitisers *in vivo* (Yang *et al.* 2003). The interaction between SMAC and the baculovirus internal repeat (BIR) domain of IAPs has been characterised. SMAC can be mimicked by small molecules, which are currently an active area of development and have potential for therapy of mesothelioma.

Mitochondrial permeabilisation, a critical event during apoptosis, is prevented by the inhibitor protein $BCL\text{-}X_L$ which is highly expressed in mesothelioma. Downregulation of $BCL\text{-}X_L$ by antisense oligonucleotides increases sensitivity of mesothelioma cells to chemotherapy (Mohiuddin *et al.* 2001). The physical interaction between $BCL\text{-}X_L$ and pro-apoptotic homologue BAK is well characterised and resembles the docking of a ligand to its receptor. This has enabled the development of small molecule $BCL\text{-}X_L$ inhibitors currently in early development and entering early clinical evaluation.

Survival pathways

Mesothelioma cells express the epidermal growth factor receptor (EGFR), a member of the erbB family of growth factor receptors. Inhibition of EGFR signalling mediates apoptosis of mesothelioma cells (Janne *et al.* 2002), and has potential as a novel therapeutic modality in this disease. EGFR promotes cell survival by activating a series of downstream proteins within the phosphotidylinositol-3-kinase (PI3K) pathway, which ultimately inhibits apoptosis. AKT (protein kinase B), a protein downstream of EGFR/PI3K is activated by phosphorylation and suppresses the natural BCL-X_L inhibitor, BAD, following its phosphorylation and sequestration to scaffold protein. AKT also promotes glycolysis by enhancing the function of hexokinase II, which antagonises mitochondrial permeabilisation.

EGFR can be inhibited by small molecules that block the intrinsic tryrosine kinase activity, such as ZD1839 (gefitinib), OSI774 (erlotinib) or monoclonal antibody such as cetuximab. A recent study in non-small cell lung cancer has demonstrated synergy between cisplatin, vinorelbine and cetuximab in a randomised phase II trial comparing cisplatin and vinorelbine with or without cetuximab (Rosell *et al.* 2003). Response rate was increased significantly in the triplet arm.

EGFR antagonism may be limited by constitutive downstream activation of the PI3K pathway. Current evidence suggests that autocrine stimulation of EGFR underlies activity. Furthermore, despite the comparable EGFR expression in mesothelioma and normal mesothelial cells, the sensitivity to EGFR inhibition is higher in mesothelioma suggesting greater dependence on this pathway and potential for tumour selectivity.

Hypoxia

Low oxygen tension (hypoxia) is a common property of solid tumours. We have recently shown that mesothelioma cells express hypoxia inducible transcription factor subunit 1 alpha or HIF-1α (Fennell *et al.* 2003a). The expression of HIF-1α was validated as a marker of hypoxia, and is found in over 80% of mesothelioma specimens. This hypoxia inducible subunit dimerises with the constitutively activated beta subunit, translocates to the nucleus and induces transcription of proteins involved in glycolysis, anti-apoptosis, angiogenesis and metastasis. Glucose transporter-1 (GLUT-1) is a hypoxia inducible protein that is expressed in approximately one-fifth of cases studied. Hypoxia is a significant target for a novel family of drugs capable of selectively targeting hypoxic regions, so-called bioreductive agents. These include tirapazemine, which has been to shown to exhibit activity in mesothelioma when combined with cisplatin in a phase I clinical trial in solid tumours (Johnson *et al.* 1997). HIF-1α itself is a potential target for therapy, and selective inhibitors are currently being sought (Semenza 2003). Such agents could provide important new strategies for treating mesothelioma, in combination with either a biological agent or chemotherapy.

References

Adams, R. F., Gray, W., Davies, R. J. & Gleeson, F. V. (2001). Percutaneous image-guided cutting needle biopsy of the pleura in the diagnosis of malignant mesothelioma. *Chest* **120**, 1798–1802.

Ambrosini, G., Adida, C. & Altieri, D. C. (1997). A novel anti-apoptosis gene, survivin, expressed in cancer and lymphoma. *Nature Medicine* **3**, 917–921.

Andreopoulou, E., Ross, P., O'Brien, M. *et al.* (2003). Chemotherapy in patients with malignant mesothelioma: outcome and predictive factors. *Lung Cancer* **41**(Suppl. 2), 12.

Ardizzoni, A., Pennucci, M. C., Castagneto, B., Mariani, G. L., Cinquegrana, A., Magri, D., Verna, A., Salvati, F. & Rosso, R. (1994). Recombinant interferon alpha-2b in the treatment of diffuse malignant pleural mesothelioma. *American Journal of Clinical Oncology* **17**, 80–82.

Astoul, P., Picat-Joossen, D., Viallat, J. R. & Boutin, C. (1998). Intrapleural administration of interleukin-2 for the treatment of patients with malignant pleural mesothelioma: a Phase II study. *Cancer* **83**, 2099–2104.

Benard, F., Sterman, D., Smith, R. J., Kaiser, L. R., Albelda, S. M. & Alavi, A. (1998). Metabolic imaging of malignant pleural mesothelioma with fluorodeoxyglucose positron emission tomography. *Chest* **114**, 713–722.

Bissett, D., Macbeth, F. R. & Cram, I. (1991). The role of palliative radiotherapy in malignant mesothelioma. *Clinical Oncology* **3**, 315–317.

Boutin, C. & Rey, F. (1993). Thoracoscopy in pleural malignant mesothelioma: a prospective study of 188 consecutive patients. Part 1: Diagnosis. *Cancer* **72**, 389–393.

Boutin, C., Rey, F. & Viallat, J. R. (1995). Prevention of malignant seeding after invasive diagnostic procedures in patients with pleural mesothelioma. A randomized trial of local radiotherapy. *Chest* **108**, 754–758.

Byrne, M. J., Davidson, J. A., Musk, A. W., Dewar, J., van Hazel, G., Buck, M., de Klerk, N. H. & Robinson, B. W. (1999). Cisplatin and gemcitabine treatment for malignant mesothelioma: a phase II study. *Journal of Clinical Oncology* **17**, 25–30.

Castagneto, B., Zai, S., Dongiovanni, E., Manzin, E., Clerico, M. & Botta, M. (2003). Cisplatin and gemcitabine in malignant pleural mesothelioma: A phase II study. *Proceedings of the American Society of Clinical Oncology* **22**, 656.

Curran, D., Sahmoud, T., Therasse, P., van Meerbeeck, J., Postmus, P. E. & Giaccone, G. (1998). Prognostic factors in patients with pleural mesothelioma: the European Organization for Research and Treatment of Cancer experience. *Journal of Clinical Oncology* **16**, 145–152.

Cury, P. M., Butcher, D. N., Fisher, C., Corrin, B. & Nicholson, A. G. (2000). Value of the mesothelium-associated antibodies thrombomodulin, cytokeratin 5/6, calretinin, and CD44H in distinguishing epithelioid pleural mesothelioma from adenocarcinoma metastatic to the pleura. *Modern Pathology* **13**, 107–112.

Davis, S. R., Tan, L. & Ball, D. L. (1994). Radiotherapy in the treatment of malignant mesothelioma of the pleura, with special reference to its use in palliation. *Australasian Radiology* **38**, 212–214.

de Perrot, M., Shargall, Y., Wadell, T. K. *et al.* (2003). Importance of nodal status and impact of mediastinoscopy in preoperative staging of patients with malignant pleural mesothelioma. *Lung Cancer* **41**(Suppl. 2), 272.

Doll, R. & Peto, J. (1985). *Effects on Health of Exposure to Asbestos*. London: HMSO.

Favaretto, A., Aversa, S., Paccagnella, A. *et al.* (2003). Gemcitabine combined to carboplatin in malignant pleural mesothelioma: a multicentric phase II study. *Lung Cancer* **41**(Suppl. 2), 218.

Fennell, D., Klabatsa, A., Sheaff, M., Evans, M. T., Shamash, J., Steele, J. & Rudd, R. (2003a). Expression and prognostic significance of Hypoxia-inducible factor 1 alpha in malignant pleural mesothelioma. *Lung Cancer* **42**(Suppl. 2).

Fennell, D., Parmar, A., Shamash, J., Evans, M. T., Steele, J. & Rudd, R. M. (2003b). Statistical validation of the EORTC prognostic model for malignant pleural mesothelioma based on three consecutive phase II trials. *Lung Cancer* **41**(Suppl. 2), S12 (abstract O-30).

Fennell, D., Steele, J., Shamash, J., Evans, M. T., Sheaff, M. & Rudd, R. M. (2003c). Second line therapy of malignant pleural mesothelioma with irinotecan, cisplatin, and mitomycin C (IPM): a phase II study. *Lung Cancer* **41**(Suppl.), S221 (abstract P-518).

Frizelle, S. P., Grim, J., Zhou, J., Gupta, P., Curiel, D. T., Geradts, J. & Kratzke, R. A. (1998). Re-expression of p16INK4a in mesothelioma cells results in cell cycle arrest, cell death, tumor suppression and tumor regression. *Oncogene* **16**, 3087–3095.

Frizelle, S., Tricker, E., Kratzke, M., Niehans, G. & Kratzke, R. (2003). Gene therapy of mesothelioma with p16 peptide therapy. *Lung Cancer* **41**(Suppl. 2), 220.

Gordon, G. J., Appasani, K., Parcells, J. P., Mukhopadhyay, N. K., Jaklitsch, M. T., Richards, W. G., Sugarbaker, D. J. & Bueno, R. (2002). Inhibitor of apoptosis protein-1 promotes tumor cell survival in mesothelioma. *Carcinogenesis* **23**, 1017–1024.

Grossebner, M. W., Arifi, A. A., Goddard, M. & Ritchie, A. J. (1999). Mesothelioma: VATS biopsy and lung mobilization improves diagnosis and palliation. *European Journal of Cardiothoracic Surgery* **16**, 619–623.

Heilo, A., Stenwig, A. E. & Solheim, O. P. (1999). Malignant pleural mesothelioma: US-guided histologic core-needle biopsy. *Radiology* **211**(3), 657–659.

Hughes, A., Calvert, P., Azzabi, A., Plummer, R., Johnson, R., Rusthoven, J., Griffin, M., Fishwick, K., Boddy, A. V., Verrill, M. & Calvert, H. (2002). Phase I clinical and pharmacokinetic study of pemetrexed and carboplatin in patients with malignant pleural mesothelioma. *Journal of Clinical Oncology* **20**, 3533–3544.

Janne, P. A., Taffaro, M. L., Salgia, R. & Johnson, B. E. (2002). Inhibition of epidermal growth factor receptor signaling in malignant pleural mesothelioma. *Cancer Research* **62**, 5242–5247.

Johnson, C. A., Kilpatrick, D., von Roemeling, R., Langer, C., Graham, M. A., Greenslade, D., Kennedy, G., Keenan, E. & O'Dwyer, P. J. (1997). Phase I trial of tirapazamine in combination with cisplatin in a single dose every 3 weeks in patients with solid tumors. *Journal of Clinical Oncology* **15**, 773–780.

Kerr, J. F., Wyllie, A. H. & Currie, A. R. (1972). Apoptosis: a basic biological phenomenon with wide-ranging implications in tissue kinetics. *British Journal of Cancer* **26**, 239–257.

Kindler, H. L., Millard, F., Herndon, J. E. 2nd, Vogelzang, N. J., Suzuki, Y. & Green, M. R. (2001). Gemcitabine for malignant mesothelioma: A phase II trial by the Cancer and Leukemia Group B. *Lung Cancer* **31**, 311–317.

Middleton, G. W., Smith, I. E., O'Brien, M. E., Norton, A., Hickish, T., Priest, K., Spencer, L. & Ashley, S. (1998). Good symptom relief with palliative MVP (mitomycin-C, vinblastine and cisplatin) chemotherapy in malignant mesothelioma. *Annals of Oncology* **9**, 269–273.

Mohiuddin, I., Cao, X., Fang, B., Nishizaki, M. & Smythe, W. R. (2001). Significant augmentation of pro-apoptotic gene therapy by pharmacologic bcl-xl down-regulation in mesothelioma. *Cancer Gene Therapy* **8**, 547–554.

Muers, M. F., Rudd, R. M., O'Brien, M. E. R., Qian, W., Hodson, A., Parmar, M. K. B. & Girling, D. J. (2004). British Thoracic Society (BTS) randomised feasibility study of active symptom control with or without chemotherapy in malignant pleural mesothelioma: ISRCTN 54469112. *Thorax* **59**, 144–148.

Mulatero, C. W., Penson, R. T., Papamichael, D., Gower, N. H., Evans, M. & Rudd, R. M. (2001). A phase II study of combined intravenous and subcutaneous interleukin-2 in malignant pleural mesothelioma. *Lung Cancer* **31**, 67–72.

Narasimhan, S. R., Yang, L., Gerwin, B. I. & Broaddus, V. C. (1998). Resistance of pleural mesothelioma cell lines to apoptosis: relation to expression of Bcl-2 and Bax. *American Journal of Physiology* **275**(1 Part 1), L165–L171.

Nowak, A. K., Byrne, M. J., Williamson, R., Ryan, G., Segal, A., Fielding, D., Mitchell, P., Musk, A. W. & Robinson, B. W. (2002). A multicentre phase II study of cisplatin and gemcitabine for malignant mesothelioma. *British Journal of Cancer* **87**, 491–496.

Parra, H. S., Tixi, L., Latteri, F., Bretti, S., Alloisio, M., Gravina, A., Lionetto, R., Bruzzi, P., Dani, C., Rosso, R., Cosso, M., Balzarini, L., Santoro, A. & Ardizzoni, A. (2001). Combined regimen of cisplatin, doxorubicin, and alpha-2b interferon in the treatment of advanced malignant pleural mesothelioma: a Phase II multicenter trial of the Italian Group on Rare Tumors (GITR) and the Italian Lung Cancer Task Force (FONICAP). *Cancer* **92**, 650–656.

Patz, E. F. Jr, Shaffer, K., Piwnica-Worms, D. R., Jochelson, M., Sarin, M., Sugarbaker, D. J. & Pugatch, R. D. (1992). Malignant pleural mesothelioma: value of CT and MR imaging in predicting resectability. *American Journal of Roentgenology* **159**, 961–966.

Peto, J., Decarli, A., La Vecchia, C., Levi, F. & Negri, E. (1999). The European mesothelioma epidemic. *British Journal of Cancer* **79**, 666–672.

Pilling, J., Stewart, D., Muller, S. & Waller, D. (2003). The case for routine mediastinoscopy prior to radical resection of malignant pleural mesothelioma. *Lung Cancer* **41**(Suppl. 2), 272.

Rosell, R., Ramlau, R. & Szczesna, A. *et al.* (2003). Randomized phase II clinical trial of cetuximab in combination with cisplatin (C) and vinorelbine (V) or CV alone in patients with advanced Epidermal Growth Factor Receptor (EGFR)-expressing non-small-cell lung cancer (NSCLC). ECCO12, Copenhagen, conference proceedings.

Rusch, V. W. (1995). A proposed new international TNM staging system for malignant pleural mesothelioma. From the International Mesothelioma Interest Group. *Chest* **108**, 1122–1128.

Rusch, V. W. & Venkatraman, E. (1996). The importance of surgical staging in the treatment of malignant pleural mesothelioma. *Journal of Thoracic and Cardiovascular Surgery* **111**, 815–825 (discussion 825–826).

Rusch, V., Venkatraman, E., Rosenzweig, K. & Krug, L. M. (2003). Adjuvant therapy, stage and tumor histology impact prognosis after resection of malignant pleural mesothelioma. *Lung Cancer* **41**(Suppl. 2), 59.

Scagliotti, G. V., Shin, D. M., Kindler, H. L., Vasconcelles, M. J., Keppler, U., Manegold, C., Burris, H., Gatzemeier, U., Blatter, J., Symanowski, J. T. & Rusthoven, J. J. (2003). Phase II study of pemetrexed with and without folic acid and vitamin B12 as front-line therapy in malignant pleural mesothelioma. *Journal of Clinical Oncology* **21**, 1556–1561.

Semenza, G. L. (2003). Targeting HIF-1 for cancer therapy. *Nature Reviews. Cancer* **3**, 721–732.

Stahel, R., Weder, W. & Ballabeni, P. *et al.* (2003). Neoadjuvant chemotherapy followed by pleuropneumonectomy for pleural mesothelioma: a multicenter phase II trial of the SAKK. *Lung Cancer* **41**(Suppl. 2), 59.

Steele, J., Shamash, J., Gower, N., Evans, M., Tischkowitz, M. & Rudd, R. (2000a). Vinorelbine (navelbine) given as a single agent for malignant pleural mesothelioma. Results from 65 patients at a single centre. *Lung Cancer* **29**(Suppl. 1), 18.

Steele, J. P., Shamash, J., Evans, M. T., Gower, N. H., Tischkowitz, M. D. & Rudd, R. M. (2000b). Phase II study of vinorelbine in patients with malignant pleural mesothelioma. *Journal of Clinical Oncology* **18**(23), 3912–3917.

Sterman, D. H., Kaiser, L. M. & Albelda, S. M. (1998). Gene therapy for malignant pleural mesothelioma. *Hematology/Oncology Clinics of North America* **12**, 553–568.

Sugarbaker, D. J., Flores, R. M., Jaklitsch, M. T., Richards, W. G., Strauss, G. M., Corson, J. M., DeCamp, M. M. Jr, Swanson, S. J., Bueno, R., Lukanich, J. M. *et al.* (1999). Resection margins, extrapleural nodal status, and cell type determine postoperative long-term survival in trimodality therapy of malignant pleural mesothelioma: results in 183 patients. *Journal of Thoracic and Cardiovascular Surgery* **117**, 54–63 (discussion 63–65).

Tsang, V., Fernando, H. C. & Goldstraw, P. (1990). Pleuroperitoneal shunt for recurrent malignant pleural effusions. *Thorax* **45**, 369–372.

Upham, J. W., Garlepp, M. J., Musk, A. W. & Robinson, B. W. (1995). Malignant mesothelioma: new insights into tumour biology and immunology as a basis for new treatment approaches. *Thorax* **50**, 887–893.

van Haarst, J. M., Baas, P., Manegold, C., Schouwink, J. H., Burgers, J. A., de Bruin, H. G., Mooi, W. J., van Klaveren, R. J., de Jonge, M. J. & van Meerbeeck, J. P. (2002). Multicentre phase II study of gemcitabine and cisplatin in malignant pleural mesothelioma. *British Journal of Cancer* **86**, 342–345.

van Meerbeeck, J., Debruyne, C., van Zandwijk, N., Postmus, P. E., Pennucci, M. C., van Breukelen, F., Galdermans, D., Groen, H., Pinson, P., van Glabbeke, M. *et al.* (1996). Paclitaxel for malignant pleural mesothelioma: a phase II study of the EORTC Lung Cancer Cooperative Group. *British Journal of Cancer* **74**, 961–963.

van Meerbeeck, J. P., Baas, P., Debruyne, C., Groen, H. J., Manegold, C., Ardizzoni, A., Gridelli, C., van Marck, E. A., Lentz, M. & Giaccone, G. (1999). A Phase II study of gemcitabine in patients with malignant pleural mesothelioma. European Organization for Research and Treatment of Cancer Lung Cancer Cooperative Group. *Cancer* **85**, 2577–2582.

Vivo, C., Levy, F., Pilatte, Y., Fleury-Feith, J., Chretien, P., Monnet, I., Kheuang, L. & Jaurand, M. C. (2001). Control of cell cycle progression in human mesothelioma cells treated with gamma interferon. *Oncogene* **20**, 1085–1093.

Vogelzang, N. J., Herndon, J. E. 2nd, Miller, A., Strauss, G., Clamon, G., Stewart, F. M., Aisner, J., Lyss, A., Cooper, M. R., Suzuki, Y. *et al.* (1999). High-dose paclitaxel plus G-CSF for malignant mesothelioma: CALGB phase II study 9234. *Annals of Oncology* **10**(5), 597–600.

Vogelzang, N. J., Rusthoven, J. J., Symanowski, J., Denham, C., Kaukel, E., Ruffie, P., Gatzemeier, U., Boyer, M., Emri, S., Manegold, C. *et al.* (2003). Phase III study of pemetrexed in combination with cisplatin versus cisplatin alone in patients with malignant pleural mesothelioma. *Journal of Clinical Oncology* **21**, 2636–2644.

Xia, C., Xu, Z., Yuan, X., Uematsu, K., You, L., Li, K., Li, L., McCormick, F. & Jablons, D. M. (2002). Induction of apoptosis in mesothelioma cells by antisurvivin oligonucleotides. *Molecular Cancer Therapeutics* **1**, 687–694.

Yang, L., Mashima, T., Sato, S., Mochizuki, M., Sakamoto, H., Yamori, T., Oh-Hara, T. & Tsuruo, T. (2003). Predominant suppression of apoptosome by inhibitor of apoptosis protein in non-small cell lung cancer H460 cells: therapeutic effect of a novel polyarginine-conjugated Smac peptide. *Cancer Research* **63**, 831–837.

Yim, A. P., Chan, A. T., Lee, T. W., Wan, I. Y. & Ho, J. K. (1996). Thoracoscopic talc insufflation versus talc slurry for symptomatic malignant pleural effusion. *Annals of Thoracic Surgery* **62**, 1655–1658.

Chapter 12

New biological approaches for effective therapy of non-small-cell lung cancer

Dean A. Fennell

Introduction

Non-small-cell lung cancer (NSCLC) is a massive health burden worldwide. In the UK it accounts for over a quarter of all cancer deaths, and is the fifth most common all-cause mortality. Eighty per cent of all NSCLC cases present with either locally advanced or metastatic disease (stages III_B and IV). Systemic therapy is the mainstay of treatment in this population, employing conventional cytotoxic drugs in the form of either doublet or triplet combinations. Overall, survival from NSCLC has not improved significantly during the past 25 years. This has led to the perception that therapy of NSCLC may now have reached a therapeutic plateau (Shepherd 1999). The proportion of patients exhibiting objective tumour responses is typically below 50%, reflecting inherent resistance to chemotherapy. New therapeutic strategies are urgently required to improve patient survival, and are likely to come from a better understanding of underlying biology and how this relates to failure of therapy.

Conventional cytotoxic therapies for cancer, in general, rely on the efficient induction of programmed cell death or *apoptosis* (Kerr *et al.* 1972; Mow *et al.* 2001). This process is phylogenetically conserved (observed in species as diverse as yeast to humans), and biochemically stereotyped. Apoptosis plays a fundamental role during development, and is required for immune system ontogeny. The factors that determine response to chemotherapy are multifactorial and include DNA repair capacity, cell cycle distribution and proliferation potential (Joseph *et al.* 2000). However, cancers that respond to chemotherapy are typically apoptosis sensitive, and exhibit objective tumour responses that can often lead to complete remission. This is commonly observed in germ cell cancers and leukaemia. Historically, complete remission has been a prerequisite for cure. Conversely, incurable solid tumours including advanced NSCLC, recurrent small cell lung cancer and mesothelioma, exhibit apoptosis resistance *in vitro* and *in vivo* (Joseph *et al.* 2000).

Failure of conventional therapy in most solid cancers involves either *de novo* or acquired apoptosis resistance. The potential for therapeutic chemosensitisation to improve long-term outcome in cancer is an emerging therapeutic objective in oncology that is stimulating new strategies for therapy. The last decade has seen an enormous growth in knowledge of the basic mechanisms that underlie cancer apoptosis resistance, with potential to yield tumour selective and effective pharmacological approaches to reversing this phenotype. These advances, as they relate specifically to NSCLC are discussed in this chapter.

Apoptosis: understanding treatment failure in NSCLC

Apoptosis was first described in 1972 as a morphological phenomenon involving cell shrinkage, plasma membrane blebbing, nuclear condensation and fragmentation (Kerr *et al.* 1972). In the early 1990s, it emerged that chemotherapeutic drugs were effective inducers of apoptosis (Kaufmann 1989; Kaufmann 1996). NSCLC exhibits cross-resistance to a diverse range of apoptosis inducers, and *in vitro* short-term tests for resistance predict survival following chemotherapy (Volm *et al.* 1985).

Apoptosis is mediated by a highly conserved family of aspartate specific serine proteases, which reside in the cytoplasm of all nucleated cells, termed *caspases*. These proteins are constitutively inactive, until initiation of apoptosis, when they target several intracellular proteins for demolition. It is emerging that NSCLC cells exhibit several molecular 'lesions', which prevent engagement of the apoptosis machinery. These processes are likely to account for the underlying chemoresistant NSCLC phenotype (Shivapurkar *et al.* 2003). Emerging opportunities for selective targeting of apoptosis pathways are stimulating development of new drugs, capable of improving both objective tumour response and possibly overall survival in patients with NSCLC.

The core apoptosis machinery incorporates the essential molecular apparatus through which a diverse range of cytotoxic stimuli, including radiotherapy as well as conventional cytotoxic drugs, act. Mitochondria play a central role in apoptosis signalling. Between their inner and outer mitochondrial membranes, several pro-apoptotic (apoptogenic) proteins are harboured. Following an apoptotic stimulus, the outer membrane undergoes permeabilisation, leading to release of the apoptogenic proteins, and activation of caspases. Cytochrome C, a major apoptogenic protein, is constitutively involved in respiratory chain electron transport on the inner mitochondrial membrane. Upon its release, it forms a heterotrimeric complex or *apoptosome* in the presence of dATP in association with apoptosis protease activating factor 1 (APAF-1) and pro-caspase 9 (Li *et al.* 1997; Zou *et al.* 1999). This results in the autocatalytic activation of caspase 9, and downstream activation of caspases including caspase 3 (Li *et al.* 1997; Zou *et al.* 1999). Other proteins are released from mitochondria and include second mitochondria derived activator of caspases (SMAC) (MacKenzie and LaCasse 2000), apoptosis inducing factor (AIF) (Lorenzo *et al.* 1999; Susin *et al.* 1999) and OMI/HtrA2 (Suzuki *et al.* 2001; Hegde *et al.* 2002).

Caspase 3 expression is upregulated in NSCLC, showing strong positive correlation with survival, and inverse correlation with lymph node metastasis (Koomagi and Volm 2000; Takata *et al.* 2001; Wei *et al.* 2001). In stage I NSCLC however, an inverse correlation with survival has been documented in one study (Takata *et al.* 2001). The translocation of caspase 3 from the cytosol to the nucleus, which occurs following assembly of the apoptosome, has been shown to be defective in NSCLC, accounting in part for chemoresistance (Joseph *et al.* 2001).

The inner mitochondrial membrane also undergoes permeabilisation during apoptosis. This critical event is essential for cell death, and directly causes cessation of respiration. Flow of hydrogen ions through complex V of the respiratory chain yields energy that is used to synthesise ATP from ADP during oxidative phosphorylation. This flow is generated by an electrochemical gradient, established across the inner mitochondrial membrane. Electron transport yields energy that is used to pump protons out of the mitochondrial matrix into the intermembrane space. Once the inner membrane is permeabilised, this gradient collapses resulting in failure of oxidative phosphorylation and cell death. Opening of a large pore structure is thought to underlie mitochondrial inner membrane permeabilisation or permeability transition (PT) (Hirsch *et al.* 1998). This structure, termed the permeability transition pore complex (PTPC), is a major regulator of apoptosis and spans both the inner and the outer mitochondrial membranes (Lemasters *et al.* 1998). PT is a prerequisite for the killing of NSCLC cells (Joseph *et al.* 2002).

The inner membrane component of the PTPC comprises the adenine nucleotide translocator (ANT), which normally exchanges pyridine nucleotides (ADP, ATP) across the inner membrane, as part of the normal process of exporting newly synthesised ATP into the cell cytoplasm. During apoptosis, the ANT undergoes a conformational change resulting in formation of a non-specific pore with a size cut-off < 1500 Da. The ANT binds several other proteins within the PTPC, including in the outer membrane, the voltage dependent anion channel (VDAC), hexokinase II, the peripheral benzodiazepine receptor. In the intermembrane space, ANT binds creatine kinase, and in the inner membrane, cyclophillin D, a molecular target of binding of cyclosporin A.

Specific proteins cause mitochondrial permeabilisation. BAX and BAK are pro-apoptotic, multi-domain members of the BCL-2 protein family. Their activation has been described as an essential gateway for apoptosis (Wei *et al.* 2001). Normally, they reside as inactive proteins in the cytoplasm but, during a cytotoxic stimulus, undergo a conformational change resulting in exposure of one terminal, which results in their movement to the mitochondrial membrane (Wolter *et al.* 1997; Nechushtan *et al.* 1999). The PTPC directs the translocation of BAX, BAK (De Giorgi *et al.* 2002). At the outer mitochondrial membrane, BAX, BAK undergo homo-oligomerisation and formation of large clusters, which appear to be required for permeabilisation. The outer membrane component of the PTPC, VDAC, may be important in mediating outer membrane permeabilisation, at least to cytochrome C. This protein normally conducts anions but, during apoptosis, undergoes a conformational change resulting in release of cytochrome C (Shimizu *et al.* 2001). The release of other proteins has been shown to be under differential control (Pardo *et al.* 2003), and other mechanisms may include outer membrane rupture, or formation of a novel outer mitochondrial membrane conductance (Shimizu *et al.* 2000; Guo *et al.* 2003).

BAX, BAK are physiologically antagonised by direct physical interaction with the anti-apoptotic homologues that include BCL-2, and BCL-X_L. Heterodimerisation results in stoichiometric inhibition of pro-apoptotic function. The balance of pro-apoptotic to anti-apoptotic BCL-2 family members has been likened to a rheostat or *apostat* that tunes the cellular apoptosis threshold. The structural basis of this physical interaction has been elucidated, and reveals a receptor–ligand type interaction, in which the BH3 domain of BAX,BAK docks within the cleft formed from the BH1, BH2 and BH3 domains (Sattler *et al.* 1997).

Homologues of BAX,BAK, which possess only one BCL-2 homology (BH) domain, termed BH3, include BID. This class of BH3 proteins allosterically modify BAX,BAK resulting in its activation (Eskes *et al.* 2000). BID is directly activated following ligation of cell surface death receptors, resulting in its truncation and translocation to mediate mitochondrial permeabilisation in a BAX,BAK dependent manner. A second class of BH3-only proteins, including BAD, is constitutively inactivated by phosphorylation on serines 112, 136 or 155. This results in its inactivation via sequestration to membrane scaffold proteins such as 14-3-3. Cell survival pathways, which signal from cell surface growth factor receptors via phosphoinositide-3-kinase/AKT, or the mitogen activated protein kinase (MAPK), mediate this inactivation. Upon dephosphorylation, activated BAD dissociates from 14-3-3 and interacts directly with the BCL-2 protein family member, BCL-X_L. BAD therefore represents a crossroads between cell survival regulation and apoptosis.

The tumour suppressor, p53, plays a major role in apoptosis, acting as a sensor for DNA damage, and mediates mitochondrial permeabilisation in part (not exclusively) via BH3-only proteins PUMA and NOXA (Gu *et al.* 2003). NOXA has been shown not to be mutated in lung cancer (S.H. Lee *et al.* 2003).

p53 is mutated in at least 50% of specimens. Mutation frequency of p53 correlates with smoking history (Esposito *et al.* 1997), and is associated with its upregulation (Brattstrom *et al.* 1998). Normal p53 genotype has been shown to be highly predictive for good response to cisplatin-based treatment and survival in patients with advanced NSCLC (Kandioler-Eckersberger *et al.* 1999). There has been some discrepancy regarding its significance in early stage disease (Fujino *et al.* 1995; Lee *et al.* 1995; Dalquen *et al.* 1996; Fukuyama *et al.* 1997; Schiller *et al.* 2001). This may be because the prognostic significance of normal/mutated p53 is dependent on histology and choice of antibody used (Nishio *et al.* 1996; Apolinario *et al.* 1997).

Caspases can be activated directly via an extrinsic signal transduction pathway involving death receptors of the tumour necrosis factor (TNF) family. These include CD95 (FAS, Apo-1, TNF-R, and TRAIL receptors DR1, DR2, DR3, DR4). Death receptors interact with a death adaptor protein such as FADD, which recruits caspase 8 and 10 to a death inducing signalling complex or DISC. Caspases 8/10 are cleaved and activate downstream effector caspases including caspase 3 and 7. Caspases 8/10 cleave the BH3 only protein, BID, resulting a truncated form that allosterically activates BAX, BAK.

Pro-caspase 8 is expressed in NSCLC, but less frequently expressed in small cell lung cancer (Joseph *et al*. 1999); caspase 10 has been shown to be under-expressed in some NSCLC cell lines (Shivapurkar *et al*. 2002). Other components of the DISC have been shown to be lost in some lung cancer cell lines but this is more common in small cell lung cancer compared with NSCLC (Shivapurkar *et al*. 2002; Hopkins-Donaldson *et al*. 2003).

Apoptosome dysregulation in NSCLC

Caspase activation is an essential step during apoptosis. Chemotherapy is a potent activator of caspases, which can be blocked by specific peptide inhibitors *in vitro* and *in vivo*. It has recently been shown that caspase activation is suppressed in NSCLC because of expression of physiological caspase repressors, termed inhibitor of apoptosis proteins or IAPs. This family of proteins is related to baculovirus anti-apoptosis protein, and possesses baculoviral inhibitor repeat (BIR) domains. IAPs act by binding caspase 9 to inhibit the apoptosome and downstream caspases. Molecular pathological studies have confirmed that IAPs are expressed *in vivo*, and exhibit prognostic significance.

IAP expression: valid targets in NSCLC?

In vitro, gemcitabine (2',2'-difluorodeoxycytidine) induces cell cycle arrest in S phase resulting in secondary apoptosis, which has been shown to be associated with increased expression of the nuclear transcription factor and anti-apoptosis protein Nfkappa beta (NFkB). The increase in NFkB activity occurs secondary to decreased expression of IkappaB-alpha, and is also associated with an increase in IAP-1 (Bandala *et al*. 2001). Expression of a dominant negative IkappaB-alpha results in failure of IAP upregulation and sensitisation to gemcitabine. Conversely, overexpression of IAP-1 abrogates the effects of dominant negative IkappaB-alpha. This suggests that, *in vitro* at least, IAP-1 plays a significant role in regulating sensitivity to deoxynucleotide analogues in NSCLC (Bandala *et al*. 2001).

Survivin, an IAP discovered in 1997, is an embryonic protein that is re-expressed in cancer but not normal adult tissues, where it regulates apoptosis and mitotic spindle checkpoint (Ambrosini *et al*. 1997; Li *et al*. 1998). Survivin is expressed in most human malignancies including NSCLC (Monzo *et al*. 1999). Levels of survivin mRNA have been measured in patients with stages IA and IB NSCLC using real-time quantitative RT-PCR. The level of expression was increased in 96% of tumour specimens, with expression most prominent in squamous cell carcinoma (Falleni *et al*. 2003). Expression does not correlate with patient survival. A role in tumorigenesis is implicated by the level of expression in early stage NSCLC, as well as dysplastic bronchial squamous metaplasia.

X-linked inhibitor of apoptosis (XIAP) is the most potent inhibitor of caspases and apoptosis in the IAP family, and is expressed in NSCLC *in vivo* (Ferreira *et al*.

2001b). Decreased apoptosome activity in NSCLC has been correlated with the level of XIAP, as opposed to reduction in the level of one or more apoptosome subunits (Yang *et al.* 2003). Giaccone's group has investigated the expression of XIAP *in vivo* using immunohistochemistry in a series of radically resected NSCLC patients, and reported relatively specific expression of XIAP in tumour, compared with normal tissue (Ferreira *et al.* 2001a). Paradoxically, the high expression of XIAP was correlated with increased survival, verified by multivariate analysis, suggesting a more complex role for this protein *in vivo* than suggested by *in vitro* studies. Furthermore, no correlation with objective tumour response has been reported (Ferreira *et al.* 2001b).

Expression of c-IAP1 and c-IAP2 has been observed in NSCLC specimens in addition to XIAP; however, their expression does not predict objective tumour response (Ferreira *et al.* 2001a). The expression of IAP-2 mRNA has been shown not to be specifically elevated in NSCLC compared with control samples, in contrast to XIAP (Hofmann *et al.* 2002). Expression of IAP1 was particularly elevated in low stage adenocarcinoma (289% increase in stage I, compared with only 44% increase in stages III and IV).

Despite the reported lack of correlation of IAPs with either clinical response or survival, the prevalent expression of IAPs in NSCLC suggests a functional, and perhaps cooperative, or redundant role in regulating cellular apoptotic threshold. New pharmacological strategies are emerging for their inhibition, and have therapeutic potential. *In vitro* down-regulation of XIAP by antisense oligonucleotides induces apoptosis and enhances chemotherapeutic activity against human lung cancer cells (Hu *et al.* 2003). This effect has also been observed *in vivo*, with 15 mg/kg XIAP antisense oligonucleotide in combination with 5 mg/kg vinorelbine, significantly delaying tumour establishment more than either agent alone. As such, XIAP is likely to be functional in NSCLC cells, and clinical studies to target this IAP are warranted.

The novel anti-apoptosis protein, AAC-1, has been shown to be expressed in a minority of NSCLC tumour samples (12%), and positive expression is strongly associated with poor survival compared with tumours negative for AAC-1 (Sasaki *et al.* 2001).

IAP-caspase 9 antagonism as a therapeutic approach in NSCLC

The mitochondrial pro-apoptotic protein, SMAC, disrupts the interaction between caspase 9 and IAP proteins, and therefore de-represses apoptosome function to activate caspases. Restoration of apoptosome activity can be achieved pharmacologically, by treating NSCLC with cell permeable SMAC N7 heptapeptide (SMAC-N7), to disrupt the interaction between caspase 9 and XIAP (Yang *et al.* 2003). SMAC peptide reverses apoptosis resistance of lung cancer cells *in vitro*, and mediates tumour shrinkage *in vivo*, in combination with chemotherapy (Yang *et al.* 2003). The SMAC/IAP interaction may also be disrupted by small molecules, an area of active research (Glover *et al.* 2003). This suggests that approaches to block endogenous apoptosome inhibition in NSCLC may present an important strategy for enhancing chemotherapeutic efficacy.

Exploiting the extrinsic death receptor pathway in NSCLC

The death receptors provide a physiological input into the core death pathway, by both directly activating pro-caspases 8 and 10, and activating the BH3 domain only protein, BID. Exploitation of this pathway presents a novel opportunity to either induce apoptosis or potentiate cytotoxic therapy. CD95 (Fas) receptor is only mutated in less than 10% of cases (Lee *et al.* 1999), and its ligand has been shown to be too toxic for therapeutic exploitation. However, tumour necrosis factor-related apoptosis inducing ligand (TRAIL) receptor targeting is currently being explored in the clinic, and is associated with potent antitumour activity with minimal side-effects *in vivo*.

Lung cancers frequently exhibit allelic loss of chromosome 8p21-22, a region that contains TRAIL receptors 1 and 2. Gadzar's group sequenced TRAIL R1 in 21 primary NSCLC samples and 31 lung cancer cell lines. Two missense alterations in the ectodomain were identified which cosegregated in 96% of samples, as determined by DNA sequencing and restriction fragment length polymorphism analysis (Fisher *et al.* 2001). Frequency of homozygosity for the altered alleles was 35% (Fisher *et al.* 2001). The mutations are localised near the ligand binding site of TRAIL-R1 and are likely to affect ligand interaction, based on the crystal structure of TRAIL-R1 and homology of TRAIL-R1 and TRAIL-R2.

TRAIL-R2 expression has been shown in one study to be expressed in 100 out of 100 primary NSCLC specimens. Furthermore, analysis of the death domain by DNA sequencing failed to identify mutations (Wu *et al.* 2000). This suggests that TRAIL-R2 is likely to be functional in NSCLC and therefore a target for therapeutic intervention. The synthetic retinoid CD437 up-regulates TRAIL receptors in NSCLC cells, and synergistically interacts with TRAIL to induce apoptosis (Sun *et al.* 2000); this is not observed in normal lung epithelial cells.

TRAIL enhances apoptosis induced by chemotherapy in NSCLC cells, and is not constitutively inhibited by the caspase 8 inhibitory protein, FLIP (Frese *et al.* 2002). Based on the observed synergy, it has been suggested that combined TRAIL and chemotherapy may be a promising treatment modality. Caspase 8 appears to be important for chemotherapy induced apoptosis suggesting that enhancement of extrinsic signalling in NSCLC by TRAIL should be synergistic (Ferreira *et al.* 2000).

Recent evidence suggests that in NSCLC cells the apoptosis inhibitor AKT inhibits TRAIL induced apoptosis by a mechanism that involves inhibition of BID cleavage (Kandasamy and Srivastava 2002). This interaction between the survival pathway and extrinsic death pathway could, in theory, limit efficacy of TRAIL *in vivo*.

Survival pathway targeting for NSCLC therapy

NSCLC cells express epidermal growth factor receptors (EGFR), a target for therapy that is currently the subject of active exploration in several clinical studies across solid tumour oncology. EGFR is a member of the erbB family of transmembrane growth factor receptors. Other members of this protein family include erbB2 (HER2), erbB3 (HER3) and erbB4 (HER4). The erbB family of growth receptors is characterised by an extra-cellular ligand binding domain, a transmembrane domain and an intracellular domain with intrinsic tyrosine kinase activity that is involved in intracellular signal transduction. EGFR is activated upon binding of epidermal growth factor (EGF), transforming growth factor alpha (TGF-α) or amphoregulin, and results in homo- or heterodimerisation of an EGFR monomer with another receptor of the erbB family. Receptor dimerisation leads to tyrosine kinase activation and receptor autophosphorylation, recruiting intracellular substrates, which are then phosphorylated, resulting in anti-apoptotic or mitogenic signalling.

Early *in vitro* studies demonstrated correlation of EGFR expression with chemosensitivity (Lei *et al.* 1999), and *in vivo* correlation with survival, warranting investigation as a novel therapeutic target. EGFR can be antagonised either by inhibition of intrinsic receptor tyrosine kinase activity (e.g. erlotinib, gefitinib), or by blocking the ligand–receptor interaction via antibodies (cetuximab). Monotherapy studies with gefitinib employed doses of 250 mg od po and 500 mg od po in patients who had received prior courses of therapy (Fukuoka *et al.* 2003). The response rates were 15% overall and were associated with improvement in quality of life. However, survival was not significantly improved. A number of randomised clinical trials have now been reported that have failed to show significant potentiation of chemotherapy in NSCLC. However, one recent randomised study comparing vinorelbine and cisplatin with or without the EGFR-specific monoclonal antibody, cetuximab, has demonstrated significant levels of synergy, suggesting the importance of the choice of drug combination (Gatzemeier *et al.* 2003). The utility of the EGF receptor as a target in NSCLC has been verified in a recent randomized comparison of the small molecule EGFR tyrosine kinase inhibitor erlotinib with best supportive care alone in patients relapsing after one or two lines of conventional cytotoxic chemotherapy. Erlotinib increased median survival by 42% from 4.7 to 6.7 months as well as significantly slowing symptomatic deterioration (Shepherd *et al.* 2004). Interestingly, gefitinib – another drug in the same class – failed significantly to improve survival in a similarly designed study (Anon 2004), suggesting important differences between members of this drug family. Other factors including drug sequencing may be very important in achieving clinical synergy.

The pharmacodynamics of EGFR antagonists are complex. There is considerable crosstalk between the phosphoinositide-3-kinase (PI3K) and MAPK pathways, which cooperate to increase NSCLC survival (H. Y. Lee *et al.* 2003). Because EGFR inhibition relies on inhibition of phosphorylation of downstream proteins, any mechanisms that ensure constitutive activation (phosphorylation) of these downstream targets may be sufficient to antagonise EGFR blockade and enforce survival signalling. One important anti-apoptosis pathway involved in downstream signalling from the EGFR is the phosphoinositide-3-kinase pathway (Crowell and Steele 2003). Following dimerisation and autophosphorylation of the EGFR, the PI3K heterodimer is recruited to the plasma membrane where it becomes activated. PI3K metabolises phosphotidylinositol 3,4,5 trisphosphate (PtdIns(3,4,5)P_3) to yield PtdIns(4,5)P_2, which binds AKT (protein kinase B) via its pleckstrin homology domain, resulting in its phosphorylation to AKT and activation.

AKT is an important anti-apoptotic protein and directly regulates the core apoptosis pathway; it lies at the intersection of glycolytic metabolism, survival signalling and apoptosis regulation. AKT has been shown to be constitutively active in NSCLC (Brognard *et al.* 2001), and phosphorylates the pro-apoptotic BCL-2 family member, BAD, on serine 136 (Zha *et al.* 1996). This results in the sequestration of the BH3-only domain protein to 14-3-3 scaffold protein, rendering it inactive (Datta *et al.* 1997). During apoptosis, BAD is de-phosphorylated, allowing it to heterodimerise with, and antagonise, BCL-X_L. This function de-represses BAX/BAK enabling more efficient mitochondrial permeabilisation. AKT also directly antagonises BAX translocation by a mechanism that requires glycolysis; AKT promotes recruitment of the glycolytic enzyme hexokinase II to the outer mitochondrial membrane, which is sufficient to inhibit BAX action (Gottlob *et al.* 2001; Tsuruta *et al.* 2002).

Evidence suggests that constitutive activation of AKT in NSCLC predicts response in NSCLC in contrast to receptor density (Janmaat *et al.* 2003). This may be critically important with regard to the clinical efficacy achievable by EGFR inhibitors in NSCLC. This may also explain why the level of expression of EGFR does not predict response to specific inhibitors. Efficacy of EGFR inhibition by gefitinib is highly dependent upon the phosphorylation status of BAD at serine 136 (Gilmore *et al.* 2002). Constitutive activation of AKT could therefore prevent core apoptosis signalling by preventing activation and translocation of this BH3-only protein. New approaches to obviating blocks downstream of EGFR are in development. The compound SRI13368 is an AKT inhibitor that has been adopted by the NCI's rapid access to preventive intervention development (RAPID) programme for accelerated clinical development. Other groups are actively engaged in the development of novel AKT inhibitors.

BAD binds BCL-X_L, preventing its interaction with BAX, BAK. The structural basis of this interaction has been elucidated, enabling small molecules to be identified that can mimic this action. Such agents have potential as novel BCL-X_L and BCL-2 antagonists, exhibit high (nanomolar) binding affinity and are entering clinical investigations. Further developments in high throughput screening will enable rapid selection of highly selective small molecules and should accelerate the development of effective agents for NSCLC.

References

Ambrosini, G., Adida, C. & Altieri, D. C. (1997). A novel anti-apoptosis gene, survivin, expressed in cancer and lymphoma. *Nature Medicine* **3**, 917–921.

Anon (2004). Uncertain future for Iressa. Scrip 21.12.04.

Apolinario, R. M., van der Valk, P., de Jong, J. S., Deville, W., van Ark-Otte, J., Dingemans, A. M., van Mourik, J. C., Postmus, P. E., Pinedo, H. M. & Giaccone, G. (1997). Prognostic value of the expression of p53, bcl-2, and bax oncoproteins, and neovascularization in patients with radically resected non-small-cell lung cancer. *Journal of Clinical Oncology* **15**, 2456–2466.

Bandala, E., Espinosa, M., Maldonado, V. & Melendez-Zajgla, J. (2001). Inhibitor of apoptosis-1 (IAP-1) expression and apoptosis in non-small-cell lung cancer cells exposed to gemcitabine. *Biochemical Pharmacology* **62**, 13–19.

Brattstrom, D., Bergqvist, M., Lamberg, K., Kraaz, W., Scheibenflug, L., Gustafsson, G., Inganas, M., Wagenius, G. & Brodin, O. (1998). Complete sequence of p53 gene in 20 patients with lung cancer: comparison with chemosensitivity and immunohistochemistry. *Medical Oncology* **15**, 255–261.

Brognard, J., Clark, A. S., Ni, Y. & Dennis, P. A. (2001). Akt/protein kinase B is constitutively active in non-small cell lung cancer cells and promotes cellular survival and resistance to chemotherapy and radiation. *Cancer Research* **61**, 3986–3997.

Crowell, J. A. & Steele, V. E. (2003). AKT and the phosphatidylinositol 3-kinase/AKT pathway: important molecular targets for lung cancer prevention and treatment. *Journal of the National Cancer Institute* **95**, 252–253.

Dalquen, P., Sauter, G., Torhorst, J., Schultheiss, E., Jordan, P., Lehmann, S., Soler, M., Stulz, P., Mihatsch, M. J. & Gudat, F. (1996). Nuclear p53 overexpression is an independent prognostic parameter in node-negative non-small cell lung carcinoma. *Journal of Pathology* **178**, 53–58.

Datta, S. R., Dudek, H., Tao, X., Masters, S., Fu, H., Gotoh, Y. & Greenberg, M. E. (1997). Akt phosphorylation of BAD couples survival signals to the cell- intrinsic death machinery. *Cell* **91**(2), 231–241.

De Giorgi, F., Lartigue, L., Bauer, M. K., Schubert, A., Grimm, S., Hanson, G. T., Remington, S. J., Youle, R. J. & Ichas, F. (2002). The permeability transition pore signals apoptosis by directing Bax translocation and multimerization. *FASEB Journal* **16**, 607–609.

Eskes, R., Desagher, S., Antonsson, B. & Martinou, J. C. (2000). Bid induces the oligomerization and insertion of Bax into the outer mitochondrial membrane. *Molecular and Cellular Biology* **20**, 929–935.

Esposito, V., Baldi, A., De Luca, A., Micheli, P., Mazzarella, G., Baldi, F., Caputi, M. & Giordano, A. (1997). Prognostic value of p53 in non-small cell lung cancer: relationship with proliferating cell nuclear antigen and cigarette smoking. *Human Pathology* **28**, 233–237.

Falleni, M., Pellegrini, C., Marchetti, A., Oprandi, B., Buttitta, F., Barassi, F., Santambrogio, L., Coggi, G. & Bosari, S. (2003). Survivin gene expression in early-stage non-small cell lung cancer. *Journal of Pathology* **200**, 620–626.

Ferreira, C. G., Span, S. W., Peters, G. J., Kruyt, F. A. & Giaccone, G. (2000). Chemotherapy triggers apoptosis in a caspase-8-dependent and mitochondria-controlled manner in the non-small cell lung cancer cell line NCI-H460. *Cancer Research* **60**, 7133–7141.

Ferreira, C. G., van der Valk, P., Span, S. W., Jonker, J. M., Postmus, P. E., Kruyt, F. A. & Giaccone, G. (2001a). Assessment of IAP (inhibitor of apoptosis) proteins as predictors of response to chemotherapy in advanced non-small-cell lung cancer patients. *Annals of Oncology* **12**, 799–805.

Ferreira, C. G., van der Valk, P., Span, S. W., Ludwig, I., Smit, E. F., Kruyt, F. A., Pinedo, H. M., van Tinteren, H. & Giaccone, G. (2001b). Expression of X-linked inhibitor of apoptosis as a novel prognostic marker in radically resected non-small cell lung cancer patients. *Clinical Cancer Research* **7**, 2468–2474.

Fisher, M. J., Virmani, A. K., Wu, L., Aplenc, R., Harper, J. C., Powell, S. M., Rebbeck, T. R., Sidransky, D., Gazdar, A. F. & El-Deiry, W. S. (2001). Nucleotide substitution in the ectodomain of trail receptor DR4 is associated with lung cancer and head and neck cancer. *Clinical Cancer Research* **7**, 1688–1697.

Frese, S., Brunner, T., Gugger, M., Uduehi, A. & Schmid, R. A. (2002). Enhancement of Apo2L/TRAIL (tumor necrosis factor-related apoptosis-inducing ligand)-induced apoptosis in non-small cell lung cancer cell lines by chemotherapeutic agents without correlation to the expression level of cellular protease caspase-8 inhibitory protein. *Journal of Thoracic and Cardiovascular Surgery* **123**(1), 168–174.

Fujino, M., Dosaka-Akita, H., Harada, M., Hiroumi, H., Kinoshita, I., Akie, K. & Kawakami, Y. (1995). Prognostic significance of p53 and ras p21 expression in nonsmall cell lung cancer. *Cancer* **76**, 2457–2463.

Fukuoka, M., Yano, S., Giaccone, G., Tamura, T., Nakagawa, K., Douillard, J. Y., Nishiwaki, Y., Vansteenkiste, J., Kudoh, S., Rischin, D. *et al.* (2003). Multi-institutional randomized phase II trial of gefitinib for previously treated patients with advanced non-small-cell lung cancer. *Journal of Clinical Oncology* **21**, 2237–2246.

Fukuyama, Y., Mitsudomi, T., Sugio, K., Ishida, T., Akazawa, K. & Sugimachi, K. (1997). K-ras and p53 mutations are an independent unfavourable prognostic indicator in patients with non-small-cell lung cancer. *British Journal of Cancer* **75**, 1125–1130.

Gatzemeier, U., Rosell, R., Ramlau, R., Robinet, G., Szczesna, A., Quoix, E., Font, A., Jimenez, E., Mueser, M. & Harstrick, A. (2003). Cetuximab (C225) in combination with cisplatin/vinorelbine vs. cisplatin/vinorelbine alone in the first-line treatment of patients (pts) with epidermal growth factor receptor (EGFR) positive advanced non-small-cell lung cancer (NSCLC). *Proceedings of the American Society of Clinical Oncology* **22**, 642, abstract 2582.

Gilmore, A. P., Valentijn, A. J., Wang, P., Ranger, A. M., Bundred, N., O'Hare, M. J., Wakeling, A., Korsmeyer, S. J. & Streuli, C. H. (2002). Activation of BAD by therapeutic inhibition of epidermal growth factor receptor and transactivation by insulin-like growth factor receptor. *Journal of Biological Chemistry* **277**, 27643–27650.

Glover, C. J., Hite, K., DeLosh, R., Scudiero, D. A., Fivash, M. J., Smith, L. R., Fisher, R. J., Wu, J. W., Shi, Y., Kipp, R. A. *et al.* (2003). A high-throughput screen for identification of molecular mimics of Smac/DIABLO utilizing a fluorescence polarization assay. *Analytical Biochemistry* **320**, 157–169.

Gottlob, K., Majewski, N., Kennedy, S., Kandel, E., Robey, R. B. & Hay, N. (2001). Inhibition of early apoptotic events by Akt/PKB is dependent on the first committed step of glycolysis and mitochondrial hexokinase. *Genes and Development* **15**, 1406–1418.

Gu, J., Zhang, L., Swisher, S. G., Liu, J., Roth, J. A. & Fang, B. (2003). Induction of p53-regulated genes in lung cancer cells: implications of the mechanism for adenoviral p53-mediated apoptosis. *Oncogene* **23**(6), 1300–1307.

Guo, L., Pietkiewicz, D., Pavlov, E. V., Grigoriev, S. M., Kasianowicz, J. J., Dejean, L. M., Korsmeyer, S. J., Antonsson, B. & Kinnally, K. W. (2003). The effects of cytochrome c on the mitochondrial apoptosis-induced channel MAC. *American Journal of Physiology* **286**, C1109–C1117.

Hegde, R., Srinivasula, S. M., Zhang, Z., Wassell, R., Mukattash, R., Cilenti, L., DuBois, G., Lazebnik, Y., Zervos, A. S., Fernandes-Alnemri, T. *et al.* (2002). Identification of

Omi/HtrA2 as a mitochondrial apoptotic serine protease that disrupts inhibitor of apoptosis protein-caspase interaction. *Journal of Biological Chemistry* **277**, 432–438.

Hirsch, T., Susin, S. A., Marzo, I., Marchetti, P., Zamzami, N. & Kroemer, G. (1998). Mitochondrial permeability transition in apoptosis and necrosis. *Cell Biology and Toxicology* **14**, 141–145.

Hofmann, H. S., Simm, A., Hammer, A., Silber, R. E. & Bartling, B. (2002). Expression of inhibitors of apoptosis (IAP) proteins in non-small cell human lung cancer. *Journal of Cancer Research and Clinical Oncology* **128**, 554–560.

Hopkins-Donaldson, S., Ziegler, A., Kurtz, S., Bigosch, C., Kandioler, D., Ludwig, C., Zangemeister-Wittke, U. & Stahel, R. (2003). Silencing of death receptor and caspase-8 expression in small cell lung carcinoma cell lines and tumors by DNA methylation. *Cell Death and Differentiation* **10**, 356–364.

Hu, Y., Cherton-Horvat, G., Dragowska, V., Baird, S., Korneluk, R. G., Durkin, J. P., Mayer, L. D. & LaCasse, E. C. (2003). Antisense oligonucleotides targeting XIAP induce apoptosis and enhance chemotherapeutic activity against human lung cancer cells in vitro and in vivo. *Clinical Cancer Research* **9**, 2826–2836.

Janmaat, M. L., Kruyt, F. A., Rodriguez, J. A. & Giaccone, G. (2003). Response to epidermal growth factor receptor inhibitors in non-small cell lung cancer cells: limited antiproliferative effects and absence of apoptosis associated with persistent activity of extracellular signal-regulated kinase or Akt kinase pathways. *Clinical Cancer Research* **9**, 2316–2326.

Joseph, B., Ekedahl, J., Sirzen, F., Lewensohn, R. & Zhivotovsky, B. (1999). Differences in expression of pro-caspases in small cell and non-small cell lung carcinoma. *Biochemical and Biophysical Research Communications* **262**, 381–387.

Joseph, B., Lewensohn, R. & Zhivotovsky, B. (2000). Role of apoptosis in the response of lung carcinomas to anti-cancer treatment. *Annals of the New York Academy of Sciences* **926**, 204–216.

Joseph, B., Ekedahl, J., Lewensohn, R., Marchetti, P., Formstecher, P. & Zhivotovsky, B. (2001). Defective caspase-3 relocalization in non-small cell lung carcinoma. *Oncogene* **20**, 2877–2888.

Joseph, B., Marchetti, P., Formstecher, P., Kroemer, G., Lewensohn, R. & Zhivotovsky, B. (2002). Mitochondrial dysfunction is an essential step for killing of non-small cell lung carcinomas resistant to conventional treatment. *Oncogene* **21**, 65–77.

Kandasamy, K. & Srivastava, R. K. (2002). Role of the phosphatidylinositol 3'-kinase/PTEN/Akt kinase pathway in tumor necrosis factor-related apoptosis-inducing ligand-induced apoptosis in non-small cell lung cancer cells. *Cancer Research* **62**, 4929–4937.

Kandioler-Eckersberger, D., Kappel, S., Mittlbock, M., Dekan, G., Ludwig, C., Janschek, E., Pirker, R., Wolner, E. & Eckersberger, F. (1999). The TP53 genotype but not immunohistochemical result is predictive of response to cisplatin-based neoadjuvant therapy in stage III non-small cell lung cancer. *Journal of Thoracic and Cardiovascular Surgery* **117**, 744–750.

Kaufmann, S. H. (1989). Induction of endonucleolytic DNA cleavage in human acute myelogenous leukemia cells by etoposide, camptothecin, and other cytotoxic anticancer drugs: a cautionary note. *Cancer Research* **49**, 5870–5878.

Kaufmann, S. H. (1996). Proteolytic cleavage during chemotherapy-induced apoptosis. *Molecular Medicine Today* **2**, 298–303.

Kerr, J. F., Wyllie, A. H. & Currie, A. R. (1972). Apoptosis: a basic biological phenomenon with wide-ranging implications in tissue kinetics. *British Journal of Cancer* **26**, 239–257.

Koomagi, R. & Volm, M. (2000). Relationship between the expression of caspase-3 and the clinical outcome of patients with non-small cell lung cancer. *Anticancer Research* **20**(1B), 493–496.

Lee, H. Y., Srinivas, H., Xia, D., Lu, Y., Superty, R., LaPushin, R., Gomez-Manzano, C., Gal, A. M., Walsh, G. L., Force, T. *et al.* (2003). Evidence that phosphatidylinositol 3-kinase- and mitogen-activated protein kinase kinase-4/c-Jun NH2-terminal kinase-dependent Pathways cooperate to maintain lung cancer cell survival. *Journal of Biological Chemistry* **278**(26), 23630–23638.

Lee, J. S., Yoon, A., Kalapurakal, S. K., Ro, J. Y., Lee, J. J., Tu, N., Hittelman, W. N. & Hong, W. K. (1995). Expression of p53 oncoprotein in non-small-cell lung cancer: a favorable prognostic factor. *Journal of Clinical Oncology* **13**, 1893–1903.

Lee, S. H., Shin, M. S., Park, W. S., Kim, S. Y., Kim, H. S., Han, J. Y., Park, G. S., Dong, S. M., Pi, J. H., Kim, C. S. *et al.* (1999). Alterations of Fas (Apo-1/CD95) gene in non-small cell lung cancer. *Oncogene* **18**, 3754–3760.

Lee, S. H., Soung, Y. H., Lee, J. W., Kim, H. S., Lee, J. H., Park, J. Y., Cho, Y. G., Kim, C. J., Kim, S. Y., Park, W. S. *et al.* (2003). Mutational analysis of Noxa gene in human cancers. *Acta Pathologica, Microbiologica et Immunologica Scandinavica* **111**, 599–604.

Lei, W., Mayotte, J. E. & Levitt, M. L. (1999). Enhancement of chemosensitivity and programmed cell death by tyrosine kinase inhibitors correlates with EGFR expression in non-small cell lung cancer cells. *Anticancer Research* **19**(1A), 221–228.

Lemasters, J. J., Nieminen, A. L., Qian, T., Trost, L. C., Elmore, S. P., Nishimura, Y., Crowe, R. A., Cascio, W. E., Bradham, C. A., Brenner, D. A. *et al.* (1998). The mitochondrial permeability transition in cell death: A common mechanism in necrosis, apoptosis and autophagy. *Biochimica et Biophysica Acta Bioenergetics* **2**, 177–196.

Li, F., Ambrosini, G., Chu, E. Y., Plescia, J., Tognin, S., Marchisio, P. C. & Altieri, D. C. (1998). Control of apoptosis and mitotic spindle checkpoint by survivin. *Nature* **396**, 580–584.

Li, P., Nijhawan, D., Budihardjo, I., Srinivasula, S. M., Ahmad, M., Alnemri, E. S. & Wang, X. (1997). Cytochrome c and dATP-dependent formation of Apaf-1/caspase-9 complex initiates an apoptotic protease cascade. *Cell* **91**, 479–489.

Lorenzo, H. K., Susin, S. A., Penninger, J. & Kroemer, G. (1999). Apoptosis inducing factor (AIF): a phylogenetically old, caspase-independent effector of cell death. *Cell Death and Differentiation* **6**, 516–524.

MacKenzie, A. & LaCasse, E. (2000). Inhibition of IAP's protection by Diablo/Smac: new therapeutic opportunities? *Cell Death and Differentiation* **7**(10), 866–867.

Monzo, M., Rosell, R., Felip, E., Astudillo, J., Sanchez, J. J., Maestre, J., Martin, C., Font, A., Barnadas, A. & Abad, A. (1999). A novel anti-apoptosis gene: Re-expression of survivin messenger RNA as a prognosis marker in non-small-cell lung cancers. *Journal of Clinical Oncology* **17**, 2100–2104.

Mow, B. M., Blajeski, A. L., Chandra, J. & Kaufmann, S. H. (2001). Apoptosis and the response to anticancer therapy. *Current Opinion in Oncology* **13**(6), 453–462.

Nechushtan, A., Smith, C. L., Hsu, Y. T. & Youle, R. J. (1999). Conformation of the Bax C-terminus regulates subcellular location and cell death. *EMBO Journal* **18**, 2330–2341.

Nishio, M., Koshikawa, T., Kuroishi, T., Suyama, M., Uchida, K., Takagi, Y., Washimi, O., Sugiura, T., Ariyoshi, Y., Takahashi, T. *et al.* (1996). Prognostic significance of abnormal p53 accumulation in primary, resected non-small-cell lung cancers. *Journal of Clinical Oncology* **14**, 497–502.

Pardo, O. E., Lesay, A., Arcaro, A., Lopes, R., Ng, B. L., Warne, P. H., McNeish, I. A., Tetley, T. D., Lemoine, N. R., Mehmet, H. *et al.* (2003). Fibroblast growth factor 2-mediated translational control of IAPs blocks mitochondrial release of Smac/DIABLO and apoptosis in small cell lung cancer cells. *Molecular and Cellular Biology* **23**, 7600–7610.

Sasaki, H., Moriyama, S., Yukiue, H., Kobayashi, Y., Nakashima, Y., Kaji, M., Fukai, I., Kiriyama, M., Yamakawa, Y. & Fujii, Y. (2001). Expression of the antiapoptosis gene, AAC-11, as a prognosis marker in non-small cell lung cancer. *Lung Cancer* **34**, 53–57.

Sattler, M., Liang, H., Nettesheim, D., Meadows, R. P., Harlan, J. E., Eberstadt, M., Yoon, H. S., Shuker, S. B., Chang, B. S., Minn, A. J. *et al.* (1997). Structure of Bcl-xL-Bak peptide complex: recognition between regulators of apoptosis. *Science* **275**, 983–986.

Schiller, J. H., Adak, S., Feins, R. H., Keller, S. M., Fry, W. A., Livingston, R. B., Hammond, M. E., Wolf, B., Sabatini, L., Jett, J. *et al.* (2001). Lack of prognostic significance of p53 and K-ras mutations in primary resected non-small-cell lung cancer on E4592: a Laboratory Ancillary Study on an Eastern Cooperative Oncology Group Prospective Randomized Trial of Postoperative Adjuvant Therapy. *Journal of Clinical Oncology* **19**, 448–457.

Shepherd, F. A. (1999). Chemotherapy for non-small cell lung cancer: have we reached a new plateau? *Seminars in Oncology* **26**(1 Suppl. 4), 3–11.

Shepherd, F. A., Pereira, J., Ciuleanu, T. E. *et al.* (2004). A randomised placebo-controlled trial of erlotinib in patients with advanced NSCLC following failure of first or second line chemotherapy. A National Cancer Institute of Canada Clinical Trials Group trial *Journal of Clinical Oncology* **22**, 145 (abstract 7022).

Shimizu, S., Ide, T., Yanagida, T. & Tsujimoto, Y. (2000). Electrophysiological study of a novel large pore formed by Bax and the voltage-dependent anion channel that is permeable to cytochrome c. *Journal of Biological Chemistry* **275**, 12,321–12,325.

Shimizu, S., Matsuoka, Y., Shinohara, Y., Yoneda, Y. & Tsujimoto, Y. (2001). Essential role of voltage-dependent anion channel in various forms of apoptosis in mammalian cells. *Journal of Cell Biology* **152**, 237–250.

Shivapurkar, N., Reddy, J., Matta, H., Sathyanarayana, U. G., Huang, C. X., Toyooka, S., Minna, J. D., Chaudhary, P. M. & Gazdar, A. F. (2002). Loss of expression of death-inducing signaling complex (DISC) components in lung cancer cell lines and the influence of MYC amplification. *Oncogene* **21**, 8510–8514.

Shivapurkar, N., Reddy, J., Chaudhary, P. M. & Gazdar, A. F. (2003). Apoptosis and lung cancer: a review. *Journal of Cellular Biochemistry* **88**, 885–898.

Sun, S. Y., Yue, P., Hong, W. K. & Lotan, R. (2000). Augmentation of tumor necrosis factor-related apoptosis-inducing ligand (TRAIL)-induced apoptosis by the synthetic retinoid 6-[3-(1-adamantyl)-4-hydroxyphenyl]-2-naphthalene carboxylic acid (CD437) through up-regulation of TRAIL receptors in human lung cancer cells. *Cancer Research* **60**, 7149–7155.

Susin, S. A., Lorenzo, H. K., Zamzami, N., Marzo, I., Snow, B. E., Brothers, G. M., Mangion, J., Jacotot, E., Costantini, P., Loeffler, M. *et al.* (1999). Molecular characterization of mitochondrial apoptosis-inducing factor. *Nature* **397**, 441–446.

Suzuki, Y., Imai, Y., Nakayama, H., Takahashi, K., Takio, K. & Takahashi, R. (2001). A serine protease, HtrA2, is released from the mitochondria and interacts with XIAP, inducing cell death. *Molecular Cell* **8**, 613–621.

Takata, T., Tanaka, F., Yamada, T., Yanagihara, K., Otake, Y., Kawano, Y., Nakagawa, T., Miyahara, R., Oyanagi, H., Inui, K. *et al.* (2001). Clinical significance of caspase-3 expression in pathologic-stage I, nonsmall-cell lung cancer. *International Journal of Cancer* **96**(Suppl.), 54–60.

Tsuruta, F., Masuyama, N. & Gotoh, Y. (2002). The phosphatidylinositol-3-kinase (PI3K)-Akt pathway suppresses Bax translocation to mitochondria. *Journal of Biological Chemistry* **277**, 14040–14047.

Volm, M., Drings, P., Mattern, J., Sonka, J., Vogt-Moykopf, I. & Wayss, K. (1985). Prognostic significance of DNA patterns and resistance-predictive tests in non-small cell lung carcinoma. *Cancer* **56**, 1396–1403.

Wei, M. C., Zong, W. X., Cheng, E. H., Lindsten, T., Panoutsakopoulou, V., Ross, A. J., Roth, K. A., MacGregor, G. R., Thompson, C. B. & Korsmeyer, S. J. (2001). Proapoptotic BAX and BAK: a requisite gateway to mitochondrial dysfunction and death. *Science* **292**, 727–730.

Wolter, K. G., Hsu, Y. T., Smith, C. L., Nechushtan, A., Xi, X. G. & Youle, R. J. (1997). Movement of Bax from the cytosol to mitochondria during apoptosis. *Journal of Cell Biology* **139**, 1281–1292.

Wu, W. G., Soria, J. C., Wang, L., Kemp, B. L. & Mao, L. (2000). TRAIL-R2 is not correlated with p53 status and is rarely mutated in non-small cell lung cancer. *Anticancer Research* **20**(6B), 4525–4529.

Yang, L., Mashima, T., Sato, S., Mochizuki, M., Sakamoto, H., Yamori, T., Oh-Hara, T. & Tsuruo, T. (2003). Predominant suppression of apoptosome by inhibitor of apoptosis protein in non-small cell lung cancer H460 cells: therapeutic effect of a novel polyarginine-conjugated Smac peptide. *Cancer Research* **63**, 831–837.

Zha, J., Harada, H., Yang, E., Jockel, J. & Korsmeyer, S. J. (1996). Serine phosphorylation of death agonist BAD in response to survival factor results in binding to 14-3-3 not BCL-X(L). *Cell* **87**, 619–628.

Zou, H., Li, Y., Liu, X. & Wang, X. (1999). An APAF-1.cytochrome c multimeric complex is a functional apoptosome that activates procaspase-9. *Journal of Biological Chemistry* **274**, 11,549–11,556.

PART 4

Clinical governance

Chapter 13

Lung cancer and the National Cancer Plan

Michael D. Peake

Introduction

The National Cancer Plan (NCP) was published in 2001 (DoH 2001) as an attempt to define problems, targets and, in some instances, solutions, relating to cancer services in England. One of the major stimuli behind the initiative was data from European (Berrino *et al.* 1999), US (SEER 2002) and UK (NHS Executive 2000a) sources demonstrating the poorer survival of cancer patients in the UK compared with most other countries in the Western world.

It is also clear from the NHS National Performance Indicators (NHS Executive 2000a) that there are wide variations in the rate of long-term survival in cancer patients between different areas in England. With respect to lung cancer, the 5-year survival in the UK in patients diagnosed in the late 1980s (Berrino *et al.* 1999) was around 7% in males compared with an average for Europe of 9% (10 and 12% in Finland and Iceland, respectively) and 13% in the USA (SEER 2002). All of these data, however, relate to a period before the publication of the Calman–Hine report (Calman & Hine 1995), which proposed major changes in the way cancer services were to be organised.

Lung cancer services before Calman–Hine

Before the reorganisation of NHS cancer services that began with the Calman–Hine report, there were many problems, some of which can be summarised as follows:

- poorly co-ordinated, fragmented services
- hardly any multidisciplinary team-working
- huge variations in access to specialist care (both diagnostic and therapeutic)
- huge variations in radical treatment and 5-year survival rates (across the districts of England, 5-year survival rates varied from around 2% to 8% in patients diagnosed between 1991 and 1993 (NHS Executive 2000a))
- very low professional and public profile of the disease
- very patchy interest in key professional groups (e.g. respiratory physicians and oncologists)
- very few specialist nurses
- clinical trial entry very low
- lack of any explicit standards of care.

Undertreatment

There is evidence of undertreatment of various aspects of lung cancer in the recent past from a variety of sources. In a large study of cancer registry data from the Northern and Yorkshire Region (NYCRIS 1999), over 25% of patients never saw a lung cancer specialist and there was a clear relationship between the overall level of active treatment and survival, especially in patients with non-small cell lung cancer (NSCLC) (Cartman *et al.* 2002). Looking at cancer registry data over the early to mid-1990s, surgical resection rates varied, region by region, from around 2% to over 15% (e.g. Wells 2001); in the Royal College of Physicians Lung Cancer Audit of practice in 1997/98, resection rates varied from 0% to nearly 30% (RCP 1999), although this was not a population-based study. A study of lung cancer practice in Scotland in 1995 revealed that only 49.7% of patients with small cell lung cancer received combination chemotherapy, well below international rates (Gregor *et al.* 2001). No precise data are available with regard to the more detailed management of NSCLC, but a variety of smaller audits suggest that no more than 10% of such patients receive chemotherapy.

CHART (continuous hyperfractionated accelerated radiotherapy), despite being devised and studied in the UK (Saunders *et al.* 1997) and hailed as the biggest advance in the management of NSCLC in recent years, is currently only available (for logistic and resource-related reasons) in a minority of centres in the country. We also know from the study of the 'standard' radiotherapy arms of the CHART study and various MRC studies, that there are very wide variations in both palliative and radical radiotherapy doses. Maguire has recently demonstrated (Maguire & Kelly 2002) that in locally advanced (stage III) disease, combination chemoradiotherapy, the international standard applied in most other European and US centres, is being under-used in the UK. In terms of research, the UK entry of lung cancer patients into clinical trials is low, probably around 5–6% nationally. All these elements contribute, probably to a varying extent in different areas of the UK, to our poor outcomes.

Delays in diagnosis and treatment

The other key element that makes for a good health service is the provision of timely services for referrals, diagnosis and treatment. Extended waiting times have long been a feature of the NHS in many areas, but the first clear evidence of the problems as they relate specifically to lung cancer came with an audit carried out in 1993 in Cambridge (Billing & Wells 1996). Some key features of the delays that were demonstrated are shown in Table 13.1. It is clear that the overall and totally unacceptable delay (mean 109 days) from referral to surgery is made up of a series of smaller delays at every step of the way on the care pathway.

Table 13.1 Delays in stages of diagnosis and treatment of lung cancer patients (Billing & Wells 1996)

Delays from:	Mean (days)	95% CI (days)
Presentation to surgery	109	92 to 127
Presentation to chest physician referral	32	21 to 42
Presentation to chest radiograph	26	14 to 38
Chest radiograph to chest physician referral	15	8 to 21
Chest physician referral to surgical referral	58	45 to 71
Chest physician referral to consultation	15	11 to 19
Fibreoptic bronchoscopy	14	6 to 21
CT scanning	18	13 to 23
Percutaneous needle biopsy	15	10 to 20
Surgical referral to operation	24	19 to 30
Surgical referral to consultation	10	4 to 16
Staging by mediastinoscopy	20	11 to 29

Government initiatives

The Calman–Hine report was the first of what has turned out to be a series of government initiatives with the aim of improving both the experience and the outcomes of care for cancer patients. The major initiatives are as follows:

- Calman–Hine Report: 1995
- establishment of cancer networks: 1997
- regional and national accreditation (peer review): 1997 onwards
- 2-week urgent referral initiative: 2000
- Cancer Services Collaborative project: 2000 onwards
- National Cancer Plan: 2001
- additional (theoretically 'earmarked') cancer funding: 2001 onwards
- NICE guidelines for chemotherapy in NSCLC: 2001
- National Cancer Research Network: 2001 onwards
- National Cancer Data Set: 2002
- National Comparative Audit of Lung Cancer Services – the LUCADA project: 2003 onwards
- National Cancer Patients' Survey: 2002.

The National Cancer Plan

The NCP was, in many ways, an aspirational plan, which had four key elements:

- to save more lives ('…by 2010 our survival rates will compare with the best in Europe')
- to ensure best professional support and treatment for all patients

- to tackle inequalities in cancer care and outcomes
- to build for the future (workforce development, research, etc.) ('…so that the NHS never falls behind in cancer care again').

The NCP has been criticised for being essentially a political statement and, clearly, there is within it a significant political element. It is, however, much more than that. Firstly, it was clearly professionally driven from the outset; the Calman–Hine initiative was a process led by many experienced clinicians and much of the concern expressed about standards of care before and since then has come from a wide range of professional groups. Secondly, It was the result of a process of wide professional consultation with large numbers of clinical and lay 'stakeholders'. Finally, the NCP was a response to genuine and growing public concern about standards of cancer care in the UK. It takes as its aim the achievement of standards of care that one would wish for one's own loved ones.

The NCP was heralded as being backed by a serious injection of ring-fenced cash: an additional £570 million per annum by 2003–2004. This was clearly welcome, but there have been many instances where funds have not got through to the 'front line' as a result of differing local priorities. The publication of the NICE guidance on the use of newer chemotherapeutic agents in NSCLC (National Institute for Clinical Excellence 2001) is one instance, however, where additional funds have been evident for the use of these agents in appropriate patients. Another important area is the provision of new and replacement computed tomography (CT) and magnetic resonance imaging (MRI) scanners and linear accelerators. When surveyed in 2000 there were wide regional variations in the availability of these important pieces of equipment and many existing scanners were very old. This situation has been reversed with monies from the National Opportunities Fund derived from the National Lottery.

Prevention was a key element of the NCP and initiatives on smoking cessation and diet are of relevance for lung cancer. The network of smoking cessation services that was established between 2000 and 2001 has, to date (DoH personal communication), resulted in around 250,000 people quitting the habit. The recent banning of tobacco advertising is also a positive step. The 'Five-a-day' initiative to try to increase the intake of fruit, particularly by children and disadvantaged communities, is widely seen as being a success; almost 100 community initiatives and children in nearly 8000 schools receive one free piece of fruit a day.

There are still clearly significant problems with the shortage of skilled manpower in many key areas. With particular relevance to lung cancer, these include the clinical specialities of thoracic surgery, clinical oncology, pathology and radiology, plus the allied professions of therapy and general radiography. A creative use of changes in the skill mix within radiology departments has had some impact on waiting times for imaging and there is a significant increase in the numbers of oncologists and pathologists by all projections. Thoracic surgery is still a major shortage speciality and overseas recruitment together with the small planned increase in specialist registrar numbers seems highly unlikely to solve the problem.

Waiting times

From April 2000 the DoH mandated a maximum 2-week wait from first referral from primary care to being seen in a specialist unit for patients suspected of having lung cancer. This was supported by the publication of referral guidelines for suspected cancer (NHS Executive 2000b). These were based on a systematic review of the literature (such as it is) on symptoms and symptom patterns as predictors of a diagnosis of lung cancer in a primary care setting. This target has largely been achieved by most units (around 95% nationally in 2002), but sometimes at the expense of other, non-cancer patients. Several audits have revealed that the percentage of patients referred via this route that turn out to have lung cancer is around the 40–50% mark. From December 2002 monitoring of the 2005 NCP interim targets of 31 days from referral to diagnosis, 31 days from diagnosis to first definitive treatment and 62 days from first referral to treatment, has been in place for lung cancer patients. These are challenging targets for many units and yet are still a great deal longer than we would all like to be able to achieve.

The Cancer Services Collaborative programme

During 1999 a programme of service improvement using process re-engineering methodology was adopted by the DoH. It was based on methods developed by Don Berwick and colleagues (Berwick 1998) at the Institute for Healthcare Improvement in Boston, USA. This was introduced as the Cancer Services Collaborative (CSC) programme into nine pilot cancer networks in 2000 and is currently being rolled out across all 34 English Cancer Networks as the Service Improvement Programme. The aim of the initiative is: 'To improve the *experience* and *outcome* of care for patients with cancer' using the tool of *process re-engineering*. This is a concept that has been unknown or alien to clinicians until recently, but there is no doubt that in many areas where it has been applied it has had a major positive impact on the standards of care.

The starting point for most of these initiatives has been 'process mapping'. This is a technique that should involve all members of a team from the lead clinician to the porter who transports the biopsy specimens. By taking the time out to map the patients' pathway through the maze of the referral, diagnostic, staging and management elements of their care, many problems and obstacles to the smooth and efficient running of the process emerge. The whole team takes ownership of the problems and each individual in the team gets to understand the importance of what he or she is doing from the patients' perspective. A few major areas for concern are then chosen for early action and smaller project groups established to develop ideas and plans for change. These are then implemented piecemeal and carefully monitored for their effect on the process using a 'plan', 'do', 'study', 'act' (PDSA) cycle (see

Figure 13.1). Each one of these cycles may only tackle a small part of the pathway, but by incremental implementation and monitoring of change, over time, major improvements can be achieved. An example of how the process, when applied to referral for specialist palliative care in West London, improved referral rates, is shown in Figure 13.2.

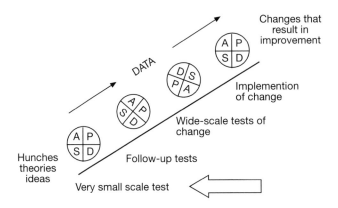

Figure 13.1 Schematic representation of 'plan', 'do', study', 'act' (PDSA) cycles.

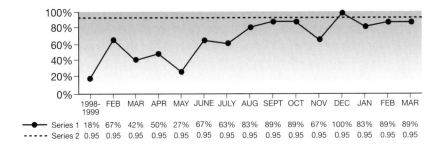

Figure 13.2 Percentage of patients referred over time in the West London Cancer Network with the application of several 'PDSA' cycles.

The CSC has been particularly effective in improving referral and diagnostic processes, multidisciplinary team-working, improving links (and communication) with primary care and in providing better choice, certainty and information for patients along their care pathway. To date, the impact in the major therapeutic areas such as surgery, radiotherapy and chemotherapy has been less marked. Currently (2003) it is estimated that around 30% of cancer patients in England are being managed by teams that have undergone some degree of process re-engineering, and the data that are coming through suggest that the impact on waiting times, at least, has been impressive. 'Phase III' of the CSC involves trying to establish this approach universally into the mainstream of clinical care within the English Cancer Networks. This is a challenging target but one that could reap major rewards for cancer patients.

Multidisciplinary teams

One of the most important developments in the organisation of cancer care in England over the last 6 or 7 years has been the gradual establishment of specialist multidisciplinary teams (MDTs) as the unit of cancer care. This arrangement serves many functions including: (a) the provision of a single focus point for referrals; (b) the opportunity for patients to receive a multi-professional opinion on their care, in theory at least, unfettered by the gatekeeper role that various professional groups have espoused in the past; (c) the cementing of the identity of the specialist team, including nursing and administrative personnel; and (d) the provision of a focal point for the collection of high-quality data for audit purposes. There is emerging audit evidence of the impact of these teams on a variety of indicators of performance. These include:

• increased histological confirmation rates
• increased resection rates
• increased use of chemotherapy (especially in NSCLC)
• increased use of combination therapy
• increased clinical trial entry.

It is also likely that the standard of staging is improved by this method of working, although I am not aware of any formal evidence to support this contention to date. Effective MDT working clearly needs the involvement of the full range of specialities, particularly thoracic surgeons and oncologists, both of which, as has been alluded to above, are in short supply. Video-conferencing is emerging as a very useful technique in several areas and it is likely that some smaller teams will have to pool their resources to achieve the benefits of scale. It is no longer acceptable for individual clinicians to work in fields such as this in isolation.

Audit, appraisal and patient satisfaction

High-quality audit of activity, performance and outcomes is an essential tool in our attempt to improve standards and to target scarce resources effectively. Many local attempts have been made at the audit of lung cancer services, and the cancer registries (NYCRIS 1999) and Royal College of Physicians (Peake *et al.* 2003) have carried out larger-scale studies. Following on from the publication of the RCP's data set for lung cancer (Thompson *et al.* 1999), the DoH has now published a National Cancer Data Set (NHSIA 2002) which is to form the basis of the forthcoming national comparative audit of lung cancer services: the LUng CAncer DAta (LUCADA) project. This will begin in 2004 and will start to produce national, risk adjusted, comparative data in 2004. Complementary to this is the Cancer Accreditation process, or Peer Review, the first round of which was completed in 2001. This gave a series of snapshots of the process and manpower resource issues in every English Cancer Network. It is intended to be an ongoing process and has proved as useful to assessors, in picking up ideas for their own units, as it has for the units being assessed. When put together in the future with high-quality audit data and data on the patient and carer perspective on the standards of local services from national patient surveys, it should be possible to compile a much more 'holistic' view of the strengths and weaknesses of local services and to identify the most appropriate way to target resources to achieve improvements.

Research

The establishment of the National Cancer Research Institute (NCRI) and the National Cancer Research Network provides, for the first time in the UK, the possibility of a real increase in the number of patients being entered into high-quality multi-centre trials. Lung cancer has been the poor relation in cancer research for many years, a situation that is made only too clear in the report of the NCRI funding partners (NCRI 2002), which has shown that only 3.5% of the cancer partnership funding is spent on lung cancer, despite the fact that around 22% of cancer deaths are from this cause. This is in stark contrast to breast cancer, on which 17.7% of partnership funding is spent, despite the fact that it accounts for only 8% of cancer deaths, and leukaemia where the figures are 17.7% and 3%, respectively. There is clearly a great deal of work to be done to reverse this trend.

Summary

It is clear that lung cancer services in the UK in general and in England in particular have improved a great deal in the last 6 or 7 years. The National Cancer Plan, for all its political elements is, I believe, a serious and aspirational attempt to improve the standards and outcomes of NHS cancer care up to the best international standards. It behoves all of us involved in the clinical care of these patients and the associated research to make the most of the opportunities that are now presenting themselves.

References

Berrino, F., Capocaccia, J., Estève, J., Gatta, G., Hakulinen, T., Micheli, A., Sant, M. & Verdecchia, A. (1999). Survival of cancer patients in Europe: the Eurocare-2 Study. *IARC Scientific Publications* No. 151.

Berwick, D. M. (1998). Developing and testing change in delivery of care. *Annals of Internal Medicine* **128**, 651–656.

Billing, J. S. & Wells, F. C. (1996). Delays in the diagnosis and surgical treatment of lung cancer. *Thorax* **51**, 903–906.

Calman, K. & Hine, D. (1995). *A Policy Framework for Commissioning Cancer Services. A Report by the Expert Advisory Group on Cancer to the Chief Medical Officers of England and Wales*. London: Department of Health.

Cartman, M. L., Hatfield, A. C., Muers, M. F., Peake, M. D., Haward, R. A. & Forman, D. on behalf of the Yorkshire Cancer Management Study Group, Northern and Yorkshire Cancer Registry and Information Service (2002). Lung cancer: district active treatment rates affect survival. *Journal of Epidemiology and Community Health* **56**, 424–429.

DoH (Department of Health) (2001). *The NHS National Cancer Plan*. London: Department of Health.

Gregor, A., Thompson, C. S., Brewster, D. H., Stroner, P. L., Davidson, J., Fergusson, R. J. & Milroy, R. on behalf of the Scottish Lung Cancer Trial Group and the Scottish Cancer Therapy Network (2001). Management and survival of lung cancer patients diagnosed in 1995 in Scotland: results of a national, population based study. *Thorax* **56**, 212–217.

Maguire, J. & Kelly, V. (2002). Sub-optimal treatment is a contributory factor to poor UK survival rates in non-small cell lung cancer. *Proceedings of the American Society of Clinical Oncology* **21**, 1197 (p300a).

NCRI (National Cancer Research Institute) (2002). *Strategic Analysis 2002*. London (www.ncri.org.uk).

National Institute for Clinical Excellence (2001). *Guidance on the Use of Docetaxel, Paclitaxel, Gemcitabine and Vinorelbine for the Treatment of Non-Small Cell Lung Cancer*. London: NICE.

NHS Executive (2000a). *National Performance Indicators for the NHS*. London: Department of Health.

NHS Executive (2000b). *Referral Guidelines for Suspected Cancer*. London: Department of Health.

NHSIA (NHS Information Authority) (2002). *The National Cancer Data Set*. Available online at: www.nhsia.nhs.uk/cancer.

NYCRIS (Northern and Yorkshire Cancer Registry and Information Service) (1999). Cancer Treatment Policies and their Effects on Survival: Lung Cancer. *NYCRIS Key Sites Report no. 2*. Northern and Yorkshire Cancer Registry and Information Service, Leeds, UK

Peake, M. D., Thompson, S., Lowe, D. & Pearson, M. G. (2003). Ageism in the management of lung cancer. *Age and Ageing* **32**, 171–177.

RCP (Royal College of Physicians) (1999). Lung Cancer: A national comparative audit. Internal report. London: Royal College of Physicians.

Saunders, M., Dische, S., Barrett, A., Harvey, A., Gibson, D. & Parmar, N. (1997). Continuous hyperfractionated accelerated radiotherapy (CHART) versus conventional radiotherapy in non-small cell lung cancer; a randomised multicentre trial. *The Lancet* **350**, 161–166.

SEER (2002). *Cancer Statistics Review 1973–1999*. National Cancer Institute, USA (http://seer.cancer.gov/csr/1973_1999).

Thompson, S., Peake, M. D., Macbeth, F. & Pearson, M. G. (eds) (1999). *Lung Cancer: A Core Data Set*. London: Royal College of Physicians.

Wells, F. (2001). Variations in the surgical resection rate for lung cancer. In *The Effective Management of Lung Cancer* (Muers, M., Macbeth, F., Wells, F. and Miles, A., eds). pp. 25–30. London: Aesculapius Medical Press.

Chapter 14

Impact of lung cancer patient groups on the delivery of the clinical service: accumulated experience

Jesme Baird

Introduction

This chapter provides an update to the chapter, 'The impact of lung cancer patient groups on the delivery of the clinical service', within the textbook, *The Effective Management of Lung Cancer* (Muers *et al.* 2001). The original chapter examined the emerging role of lung cancer patients in influencing and improving the quality of lung cancer service provision. Breast cancer and HIV patient groups, in particular, have shown that patients can be successful in raising awareness, improving disease profile, increasing funding and altering clinical services. Historically, there has been little mobilisation of lung cancer patients in this respect. Undoubtedly, there are, inherent in this disease, a number of barriers to such patient involvement:

- poor survival
- few lung cancer patient organisations to champion the cause (only two in the world)
- a general negativity surrounding the disease, both within the professional community and in the general public. This is mirrored in an under-reporting of lung cancer in the media and perpetuated by the 'own fault' stigma associated with smoking.

In general, patients can have an impact on clinical service provision both by *direct involvement* in the process itself (so-called 'user involvement') and by *exerting external pressure* for service change and improvement, through media campaigning and political lobbying.

In lung cancer, there is an obvious need to overcome barriers and create a structure within which lung cancer patient representatives can contribute: from inside the health system and by exerting pressure for improvement from outside the system. During 2001/2002, the Roy Castle Lung Cancer Foundation and others undertook a number of initiatives in this area and continue to work energetically in implementing new developments through 2004, the current year.

User involvement

User involvement in the NHS

In recent years, major health service policy documents, for example *The NHS Plan* (Department of Health 2000a), have expressed the intent for the NHS to become more patient focused. However, it is only in the past year that central strategies have been published, setting a framework to achieve this requirement. As responsibility for health is devolved within the UK, individual strategies have been produced. In England, the relevant document is *Involving Patients and the Public in Healthcare* (Department of Health 2001). In Scotland, it is *Patient Focus and Public Involvement: Working Together for a Healthy Caring Scotland* (Scottish Executive Health Department 2001b) and in Wales, *Signposts: A Practical Guide to Public and Patient Involvement in Wales* (National Assembly for Wales 2001). Though quite different, each strategy underlines the benefits of user involvement in improving outcomes of health care, increasing patient satisfaction and in strengthening public confidence in the NHS. Each strategy sets out a framework for patients and the public to be involved both at a collective/strategic level and on an individual basis.

Such involvement in service provision broadly takes two forms, namely:

- patient consultation through surveys and questionnaires or through patient focus groups
- active partnership with user representatives as members of committees or working groups.

At all levels throughout the NHS, including within cancer services, the views of patients, carers and the public are being pursued in this way. What is unclear, however, is the actual impact that such involvement is having on service provision.

- Are those involved, either on committees or through surveys, able or adequately trained to provide a collective and representative view?
- Do the views of lay representatives affect services or, in reality, are they given much less weighting than those of health professionals and managers?

To date, as concluded in a relatively recent systematic review (Crawford *et al.* 2002), there is evidence to support the notion that involving patients has contributed to changes in services in a number of settings. There is, however, no evidence of such involvement directly improving the quality of care or the outcome for patients. The challenge, therefore, as lay involvement continues to be embedded within health services, is to ensure that it is appropriate, representative and its impact monitored.

User involvement in cancer services

With the publication by the Department of Health (1995) of *A Policy Framework for Commissioning Cancer Services* and the recommendation that services be 'patient centred', the way was paved for cancer patient involvement in service provision. Since then, user involvement has been highlighted in many subsequent Department of Health planning publications relating to cancer throughout the UK: *National Cancer Plan: A Plan for Investment: A Plan for Reform* (Department of Health 2000b), *Cancer Information Strategy* (Department of Health 2000c), *Cancer in Scotland: Action for Change* (Scottish Executive Health Department 2001a).

During 2001/2002 and throughout the current year 2004, there has been increased statutory and voluntary sector involvement in seeking and implementing the views of cancer patients.

Cancer service patient survey

In July 2002, a survey of more than 65,000 patients (74% of those approached) was published, giving their views of cancer services. The survey showed that, in most cases, patients were receiving high levels of care: for example, 86% had complete confidence in their doctors; 79% felt they were treated with respect and dignity at all times. However, the survey highlighted variations between trusts.

The patients surveyed came from 172 NHS trusts in England, and the questions related to care between July 1999 and June 2000. As the *National Cancer Plan* (Department of Health 2000b) was published after the survey was carried out, the findings will act as a baseline, upon which improvements can be measured at the individual trust level. Of the 65,000 views, only 4000 (6%) were from lung cancer patients.

Cancer Services Collaborative patient experience projects

In England, as part of the Cancer Services Collaborative, a number of projects have measured how patients rate their care and have monitored the impact of system changes. A key area has been to improve communication between patients and their clinical team. This has been achieved in a variety of ways, such as written patient information booklets, patient held records and taped consultations. The Service Improvement Manuals (produced by the NHS Modernisation Agency), including the Lung Cancer Manual, give details of individual projects and how changes have resulted in improvement.

CancerVOICES Project

Macmillan Cancer Relief/Cancerlink's CancerVOICES project aims to empower people living with cancer to have their voices heard, and use their experiences to help shape the future of cancer services and research in the UK. Crucially, the project provides support and training for such user representatives. Through the work of facilitators in each of the 34 cancer networks, people with cancer will be listened to wherever policy and strategy are being developed.

In addition to the above, there are many individual examples of surveys of patient views. Also, cancer user representatives continue to be involved with a myriad of health strategy setting bodies and committees. Their combined impact is difficult to assess.

The review of *NHS Cancer Care in England and Wales* (Commission for Health Improvement and the Audit Commission 2001) concluded that cancer services still have a long way to go before they are truly 'patient focused'. This review, however, only addressed the progress in implementing recommendations of the 1995 Calman–Hine report, *A Policy Framework for Commissioning Cancer Services*. It did not take into account the multiple policy changes and initiatives that have taken place in the intervening years.

Lung cancer and user representation

During 2002, lung cancer patients and carers were involved in the generic cancer work outlined above; that is, within the Cancer Patient Survey, the Cancer Services Collaborative and the CancerVOICES project. More specifically, the Roy Castle Lung Cancer Foundation's Lung Cancer Patient Support Network has facilitated the placing of user representatives on a variety of key cancer and lung cancer committees and policy making bodies: NICE Guideline Development Group for Lung Cancer Treatment and Diagnosis, SIGN Lung Cancer Guideline Group, Scottish Cancer Group, National Cancer Research Network, Clinical Standards Board Scotland, Cancer Network Lung Cancer Groups in the South-east and the west of Scotland. User representatives have attended and presented at a number of national and international meetings, on issues of relevance to them.

The Foundation's lung cancer user representatives are a combination of Foundation employees, who have regular contact with lung cancer patients, and patients/carers themselves, who are members of the Lung Cancer Patient Support Network. The Foundation currently has 21 monthly groups in its Patient Network. These groups ensure that patients/carers are supported through their cancer experience and, for those who express an interest, the Foundation is able to train and offer support in campaigning, in media work and in user involvement on a variety of NHS strategy-setting bodies. The groups also act as 'focus groups', providing consensus patient/carer opinion, on a wide range of issues associated with lung cancer.

From 2003, the Foundation has employed a Lung Cancer Patient Involvement Co-ordinator. The function of this post is to motivate more patients/carers to be involved, to establish training programmes in association with other agencies and to ensure that such user representatives are supported.

Exerting external pressure

External influences, such as public pressure and political pressure, can have a positive impact on service delivery. We have seen this in such diseases as breast cancer and HIV/AIDS, where a mobilisation of patients and a high media profile have resulted in positive outcomes for sufferers. Historically, there has been little for lung cancer.

The general public seem unaware of the massive scale of the lung cancer problem. Indeed, in a survey carried out by NOP World for the Roy Castle Lung Cancer Foundation, publicised in November 2001, most people surveyed did not know that lung cancer was the biggest cancer killer in the UK. The challenge is, therefore to mobilise lung cancer patients, to raise the public and media profile of this disease and, through contact with health funders and politicians, to campaign for improvement.

Raising lung cancer awareness and campaigning for change

During 2002, Macmillan Cancer Relief and the Roy Castle Lung Cancer Foundation came together in planning a UK-wide campaign as part of Global Lung Cancer Awareness Month – November. There were several facets to the campaign:

1. Media: there were 14 regional launches of the campaign, across the UK, designed to engage local media and so disseminate messages about lung cancer, in particular, the importance of early diagnosis in improving outcomes for this disease and where to find help if lung cancer is diagnosed.
2. General public information: through a variety of distribution routes, disseminate over 1 million leaflets (*Early Diagnosis of Lung Cancer Could Save Your Life*) and over 1 million beer mats (*Check 'em Out*).
3. Stage events to mark Lung Cancer Awareness Month: over 100 lung cancer nurses volunteered to do this in a variety of locations such as hospitals, GP surgeries and shopping centres.
4. Lung cancer case histories: newspapers and magazines responded to real life personal accounts of disease. Over 60 lung cancer patients and carers have volunteered to 'tell their individual story' as part of the awareness raising campaign.
5. In targeting politicians, the key message was the desperate shortage of thoracic surgeons and the need for a dramatic increase to bring the UK in line with European average standards. This was explained within the report of the joint working group of the British Thoracic Society and the Society of Cardiothoracic Surgeons of Great Britain and Ireland, *The Critical Under Provision of Thoracic Surgery in the UK*, published in January 2002.

At the end of November 2002, the impact of this campaign was assessed and its results have been employed in subsequent strategy in 2003 and 2004.

International dimension

Internationally, lung cancer patient advocates developed a collective 'voice' during 2001/2002. The Global Lung Cancer Coalition (GLCC) of patient organisations currently has members in nine countries. The GLCC aims both to motivate public support and to motivate researchers and health policy groups to improve patient access to quality treatment and care. It does this through international press releases, representative attendance at key meetings and support of Global Lung Cancer Awareness Month.

In recent years, the involvement of patient representatives in key meetings and on key committees has been encouraged by many international professional societies and bodies. Patient organisations representing many diseases have embraced this. Currently, opportunities are emerging for lung cancer patient advocates. In particular, the recurring World Conference on Lung Cancer which typically includes a science-based patient advocate symposium. This has been the first international professional meeting to dedicate a session to lung cancer patient representatives.

Conclusions

Health professionals, service planners, charities and patients are all committed to best practice. Patients can be a powerful voice in helping to achieve this and their involvement should be viewed as constructive.

The year 2004 has seen a dramatic increase in lung cancer patient group involvement in service planning and delivery. In particular, the number of lung cancer user representatives has increased. As with all patient involvement, we do not yet know what impact such patients will have.

The Macmillan Cancer Relief/Roy Castle Lung Cancer Foundation campaign for Lung Cancer Awareness Month marked the first extensive lung cancer campaign in the UK, bringing together patients and professionals with the media, general public and politicians.

Future statutory and voluntary sector initiatives will continue to increase the media profile of lung cancer, raise public awareness and encourage patient representatives to be involved in local services and national bodies. Ultimately, their impact should improve lung cancer services and outcomes.

To date, lung cancer patient involvement is in its infancy. This is only the start; we have a long way to go.

References

British Thoracic Society and the Society of Cardiothoracic Surgeons of Great Britain and Ireland (2002). *The Critical Under-Provision of Thoracic Surgery in the UK.* Report of a joint Working Group.

Commission for Health Improvement and The Audit Commission (2001). *National Service Framework Assessments No.1: NHS Cancer Care in England and Wales.*

Crawford, M. J. *et al.* (2002). Systematic review of involving patients in the planning and development of health care. *British Medical Journal* **325**, 1263–1265.

Department of Health (1995). *Policy Framework for Commissioning Cancer Services: a Report by the Expert Advisory Group on Cancer to the Chief Medical Officers of England and Wales.* London: HM Stationery Office.

Department of Health (2000a). *The NHS Plan: A Plan for Investment: A Plan for Reform.* London: HM Stationery Office.

Department of Health (2000b). *National Cancer Plan: A Plan for Investment: A Plan for Reform.* London: HM Stationery Office.

Department of Health (2000c). *Cancer Information Strategy.* London: HM Stationery Office.

Department of Health (2001). *Involving Patients and the Public in Healthcare.* London: HM Stationery Office.

Department of Health (2002). 28173/*National Surveys of NHS Patients: Cancer. National Overview 1999/2000.* London: HM Stationery Office.

Muers, F. M., Macbeth, F., Wells, F. C. & Miles, A. (2001). *The Effective Management of Lung Cancer.* London: Aesculapius Medical Press.

National Assembly for Wales (2001). *Signposts: A Practical Guide to Public and Patient Involvement in Wales.* Cardiff: National Assembly for Wales.

Scottish Executive Health Department (2001a). *Cancer in Scotland: Action for Change.* Edinburgh: Stationery Office.

Scottish Executive Health Department (2001b). *Patient Focus and Public Involvement: Working Together for a Healthy Caring Scotland.* Edinburgh: Stationery Office.

Chapter 15

Defining the role of the lung cancer nurse specialist and the multidisciplinary team in increasing the effectiveness of service delivery

Tessa Fitzpatrick and Tess Craig

Introduction

Lung cancer service delivery is an extremely complicated process with numerous different components. Patients follow a variety of routes through the health care system. The majority of patients present to their general practitioners (GPs) with symptoms such as cough, haemoptysis, breathlessness, poor appetite, weight loss, chest pain and tiredness. Patients with unexplained or persistent symptoms should then be investigated in accordance with national guidelines (NHSE 2000a) and, if appropriate, urgent referral made to a chest physician under the 2-week rule. However, it is important to note that up to 5% of patients may present with a normal chest radiograph (CXR) (Laroche and Lowry 2001), which may delay eventual access to specialist services. There are also a significant number of patients who first present to secondary care as acute emergencies.

Whichever route is followed, patients then embark on a process of investigation involving a chest physician, radiologist and histopathologist, and possibly also a surgeon. These investigations necessitate visits to hospital, with possible admission for overnight stay or longer in the event of complications. Having reached a diagnosis, and if surgery is not an option, referral may then be made to an oncologist for treatment. Subsequent hospital admissions may also be necessary for reasons such as facilitating control of symptoms that are difficult to manage at home. Referral to a specialist palliative care service may also be required at some stage. Lung cancer service delivery is therefore complex, with patients under the care of different clinicians at different stages of the process. There is, consequently, a need for effective communication and co-ordination to prevent the service from becoming fragmented.

This complex nature of cancer can result in patients seeing many health professionals throughout their illness (CHI/Audit Commission 2001a). Smith *et al.* (1999) carried out a study into the total number of doctors encountered by 50 patients during their cancer care. This period ranged from 4 months to 26 years with a median time of 2 years and 4 months. Diagnoses included breast, lung and gastrointestinal cancers. Those identified included GPs and doctors encountered during inpatient stays, outpatient clinics and at a hospice. Data were collected using semi-structured interviews and a retrospective review of hospital medical notes. Results demonstrated that the minimum number of doctors encountered by patients was 13, the maximum was 97 and the median was 32. Patients with a history of less than 1 year met 28 doctors on average.

Whilst these numbers are a cause for concern, it is likely that the problem is underestimated. This study only looked at doctors who had signed entries in hospital medical notes and GPs whom patients recollected seeing. Patients may have seen other GPs during their care but no retrospective review of GP records was undertaken. In addition, it does not take into account those doctors who met patients informally; for example as part of a wider team on a ward round. Furthermore, doctors are only one element of the multidisciplinary team and patients come into contact with many other health professionals during their cancer care. When one considers the numbers of nursing, allied health professional and ancillary staff that patients also meet over this time it is unsurprising that patients often find the system confusing.

The multidisciplinary team

The importance of a multidisciplinary approach to the management of lung cancer was highlighted in the Standing Medical Advisory Committee report of 1994. This concept was reinforced in the white paper, *A First Class Service: Quality in the New NHS* (DoH 1998), which strongly recommended enhanced teamwork between professionals. *The NHS Cancer Plan* (DoH 2000) recognises the challenge of cancer and the importance of collaboration and partnership in providing high-quality, patient-centred care. The potential advantage of effective multidisciplinary working is in facilitating co-ordinated care, enhancing communication and promoting a seamless service (NHSE 1998). Although this idea initially presented some operational challenges to lung cancer teams, the model has since gained momentum and is now central to the delivery of patient care.

The core members of a lung cancer multidisciplinary team include a chest physician, an oncologist, a radiologist, a specialist nurse, a histopathologist, a palliative care specialist and a thoracic surgeon (NHSE 1998). Some lung cancer teams may have a much wider membership, whereas others may be smaller but no less effective. Whilst the ideal situation would involve all professionals meeting together on a weekly basis, in reality this may not always be possible and arrangements have to reflect local resources. Cancer units have local multidisciplinary team meetings followed by a wider network meeting at the cancer centre. All cases of lung cancer should be reviewed prospectively with multidisciplinary decisions being reached regarding all aspects of diagnosis, treatment and care of individual patients. In accordance with guidelines developed within the network site-specific groups, the multidisciplinary teams across the network participate in data collection and audit, and consider the entry of eligible patients into clinical trials. This process of multidisciplinary team working is supported in the *Manual of Cancer Services Standards* (NHSE 2000b), which provides a framework against which local cancer networks in England can measure the quality of services that they provide.

The lung cancer nurse specialist

Lung cancer nurse specialists are a relatively new concept in the care of patients with lung cancer; there were only a handful of nurses working in this capacity before 1995. Postholders are usually senior Registered General Nurses who have had several years' experience in a relevant field such as respiratory medicine, cancer or palliative care, depending on the nature of the post, and either have completed or are prepared to undertake study at degree level.

The number of specialist nurses in lung cancer has increased significantly following the Calman–Hine Report (DoH 1995), which emphasised the potential value of site-specific nurses in improving care for cancer patients. This concept was further endorsed in the Department of Health guidance, *Improving Outcomes in Lung Cancer* (NHSE 1998), in which the specialist nurse was identified as a core member of the lung cancer multidisciplinary team. The contribution of specialist cancer nurses to improving care is further acknowledged in subsequent reports (DoH 2000, NHSE 2000c), as part of the drive to ensure that patients and carers receive better support and information, and to facilitate the patients' understanding of their illness. A further influence on the growth of specialist nurse roles has been the advent of government investment in lung cancer. This funding has enabled trusts to create specialist nurse posts to enhance existing lung cancer services.

In response to the rising numbers of lung cancer nurse specialists, the National Lung Cancer Forum for Nurses was launched in 1999 with an aim of improving care for lung cancer patients by providing members with peer support, education and opportunities for networking and sharing best practice.

The role of the lung cancer nurse specialist is now acknowledged, with recognition of its strengths in terms of providing information, emotional support and improving symptom control to patients (NHSE 1998). One of the aims stated in *The NHS Cancer Plan* (DoH 2000) is to ensure that cancer patients get appropriate professional support and care in addition to the best treatments. Patients themselves assert that good communication, support, information and symptom control are high priorities (DoH 2000). In lung cancer, health professionals have a duty to address these needs for the benefit of patients, and the lung cancer nurse specialist is well placed to contribute significantly to this process. A diagnosis of lung cancer has a devastating impact on the lives of patients and carers. Patients often present with advanced disease in which the median survival is less than 4 months (NHSE 1998). There is therefore only a short opportunity to address the complex needs of both the patient and the carers and it is essential that this is done as effectively as possible.

As the focus of care is centred on the patient it is important to examine the way in which patients view the role of the lung cancer nurse specialist. In the current political climate the issue of quality is high on the agenda, with the development of many initiatives to enhance patient care (DoH 1998, 2000). Frameworks are in place to monitor progress and facilitate improvements through agencies such as the Healthcare Commission (CHAI), the Cancer Services Collaborative Improvement Partnership and peer review bodies. In a review of cancer services by the then Commission for Health Improvement and the Audit Commission (CHI/Audit Commission 2001a), the views of patients regarding their recent experience of cancer care were elicited through focus groups (CHI/Audit Commission 2001b). A sample of 85 patients with colorectal, ovarian and lung cancer was drawn from 15 trusts in England and Wales. The study provides some evidence of improvement in different areas of cancer care, with positive feedback regarding specialist nurses. It would appear that patients perceive the specialist nurses as being particularly useful in terms of providing support and information. Patients valued the involvement of specialist nurses at the time of diagnosis and felt that they had more time to listen to their concerns and to guide them through the system. Some of the problems highlighted by patients included poor co-ordination of services and the fragmentation of care due to inadequate communication and planning between professionals (CHI/Audit Commission 2001a). Effective multidisciplinary working can address these issues for the benefit of patients, thus improving service delivery.

The role of the lung cancer nurse specialist is diverse and governed not only by local need, but also by the phase of the illness in which the specialist nurse meets the patient. Specialist nurses work in the diagnostic, treatment and palliative stages; some are involved with lung cancer patients in more than one phase and others are involved throughout the illness. Moore (2002) carried out a questionnaire-based study to investigate the profile of lung cancer nurse specialists in the United Kingdom and to identify the nature of their practice. The sample consisted of 110 specialist nurses who were members of the National Lung Cancer Forum for Nurses in 2000. Previous studies carried out into the role of the specialist nurse have looked at samples drawn from outside the sphere of lung oncology, giving the study by Moore particular relevance. Moore found that the main elements of the role undertaken were: providing emotional and social support to patients and carers, providing continuity for patients, facilitating improved communication both with patients and between health care teams, working across boundaries and guiding patients through the system.

In addition, it is important to recognise that, whilst lung cancer nurse specialists are committed to their role in improving care for patients, there are some issues which must be addressed in order to enhance lung cancer service delivery. In her investigation of the challenging aspects of the role, Moore identified three themes: high clinical workload, lack of support and the emotional burden of lung cancer. These findings reflect those of Bousfield (1997) who undertook a phenomenological investigation into the role of the clinical nurse specialist. Bousfield emphasises the potential of the clinical nurse specialist as both a change agent and a leader, and advocates the importance of a clearly defined role for clinical nurse specialists, as lack of clarity inhibits role development. Loftus and McDowell (2000) acknowledge that having a sense of one's personal and professional boundaries is important in helping nurses to remain emotionally intact. These findings in the study by Moore are extremely important when looking to the future and considering the retention of this group of highly skilled and knowledgeable professionals.

The lung cancer nurse specialist, the multidisciplinary team and the increased effectiveness of service delivery

Many cancer patients want information on their diagnosis, prognosis, treatment options and side-effects (Fallowfield *et al.* 1990; Meredith *et al.* 1996). The Calman–Hine Report (DoH 1995) recommended that there should be high-quality communication at all stages of the disease and that clear information about treatment options should be given to patients and carers in a way that they can understand. This has been reinforced in *The NHS Cancer Plan* (DoH 2000), which links good communication with a quality service and emphasises the need for health professionals to listen to patients and to involve them at every level in their care. It acknowledges that effective communication is central in empowering patients to take an active role in making decisions about their care. The NHS Cancer Plan also asserts that failures in communication account for many complaints. Furthermore, poor communication can result in patients and carers losing confidence in the health professionals involved in their care (Bennett & Alison 1996) thus hindering any effective therapeutic relationship. Faulkner & Maguire (1994) maintain that effective communication between health professionals, patients and carers is essential to help with the process of adjusting to a diagnosis of cancer.

The lung cancer nurse specialist is ideally placed to take an active role in facilitating successful communication with patients and carers, thus enhancing the effectiveness of service delivery. Consideration is given to physical, spiritual and psychosocial needs throughout this process. Some specialist nurses meet patients in the investigative phase whereas others meet patients at diagnosis or in the palliative stage. The success of this initial meeting between the lung cancer nurse specialist and the patient and carer is central to establishing an effective and trusting relationship at a time of high anxiety. Lung cancer nurse specialists prefer to be present when a patient is given significant news, in particular that of the diagnosis. This enables them to gain a valuable insight into the discussion between the respiratory physician and patient about the extent of the disease and the management plan. Following this discussion patients are usually offered a chance to speak further with the specialist nurse. This may take place either in the hospital setting or at home depending on the remit of the specialist nurse. This provides an opportunity to reinforce and clarify information regarding the extent of the disease and treatment given in the clinic.

Many clinicians inform GPs of the involvement of the lung cancer nurse specialist in clinic letters, thus enhancing the process of communication between the two health care teams.

Specialist nurses have made a major contribution to the development of written information to improve patient understanding, in line with the national standards (NHSE 2000b). Some lung cancer teams utilise patient held records as a means of enhancing the quality of information and communication for patients (Hayward 1998), an initiative to which specialist nurses have demonstrated commitment. McCann (1998) acknowledges the importance of patient held records, but cautions that their success is dependent on the co-operation of the many health professionals involved in caring for patients with cancer.

Lung cancer nurse specialists who visit in the community often arrange to see the patient at home 2 or 3 days following diagnosis, allowing time for the initial news to sink in. Many patients have family members or a friend present at this visit and, as the specialist nurse is there as a guest, the patient is in control and is likely to be more at ease than in the hospital setting. It is therefore easier to have a full discussion about concerns raised by the patient such as fears and worries in relation to the illness, the treatment or what the future may hold.

Another area that the lung cancer nurse specialist considers is whether the patient wishes to be referred to other health professionals such as the occupational therapist or physiotherapist. The nurse has an ideal opportunity to assess the needs of the patient in relation to the environment with regard to activities such as climbing stairs or bathing, and is skilled at addressing these issues in a sensitive manner and at a pace appropriate to the individual. Some patients may be keen to accept help immediately, whereas others may need more time to adjust to the diagnosis and to become more accepting of the physical limitations of their illness.

With the permission of the patient, the lung cancer nurse specialist can refer the patient to the community nurse, thus reinforcing links with the primary health care team. Other issues that can be considered include referral to other agencies for help with applying for benefits and assessing whether an application needs to be made for a charitable grant to help with financial problems such as the cost of heating or stair lift rental.

The lung cancer nurse specialist continues to support the patient through the treatment phase either by telephone or by visiting at home, advising on symptom control and liaising regularly with the respiratory physician, the oncologist and GP as appropriate. Once the patient is more stable, the nurse steps back, enabling the patient to feel more in control. Patients are always aware that they can contact their nurse if they develop any new problems or have any concerns. Services are flexible and meet the changing needs of patients at varying stages throughout the disease, providing continuity of care and enhancing service delivery.

Lung cancer nurse specialists work closely with respiratory physicians, oncologists and palliative care teams and facilitate a smooth pathway through the service for patients. This is done in a variety of ways such as initiating investigations, ensuring that appropriate arrangements are in place for follow-up and organising admission if a patient's condition warrants this. There is a constant awareness of the need to ensure that primary care teams are kept informed of such developments. All these initiatives are central to providing an efficient and effective service to lung cancer patients.

The results of the study by Smith *et al.* (1999) into the numbers of doctors encountered by patients during their cancer care serve to illustrate the importance of the specialist nurse in providing continuity of care for patients. Patients and carers need to have the security of knowing that they have access to a nurse who is aware of their situation and who can advise them and refer them on to other professionals as necessary, ensuring that patients do not become lost in the system.

The need for effective liaison between hospital and primary care teams is paramount. As part of the review of cancer services by the then Commission for Health Improvement and the Audit Commission (CHI/Audit Commission 2001a), the views of GPs and community nurses were sought (CHI/Audit Commission 2001c). This was undertaken in a series of focus groups with a total of 57 GPs and 67 community nurses. One of the recurring themes from both GPs and community nurses was that their roles were being discounted in the process of patient care following diagnosis. Both groups felt that they lacked relevant information from medical and nursing colleagues based within hospital settings. GPs emphasised the need for detailed and timely information at diagnosis, during treatment and on discharge. Community nurses also highlighted the advantage of early introduction to cancer patients to enable them to work proficiently (CHI/Audit Commission 2001c). These problems can be addressed by effective multidisciplinary working to improve the service to patients.

It would appear that the majority of lung cancer nurse specialists are hospital-based (Moore 2002) with a minority working across the boundary between hospital and community. However, specialist nurses endeavour to liaise with community colleagues in a number of ways. They are often involved in the faxing of information within 24 hours of a diagnosis to GPs, in line with the national standards (NHSE 2000b). Many refer newly diagnosed patients to community nurses and continue to update them about significant changes such as the development of metastases. However, improved communication is the responsibility of all health professionals in the multidisciplinary team. There needs to be a commitment from members to work in partnership and to ensure that communication is a two-way process in order to facilitate the best care for patients.

In addition to this close involvement in patient care at diagnosis and throughout their illness, and maintaining effective communication between hospitals and community, the specialist nurse has an important role both in the multidisciplinary team and in liaison between members of the team. As described previously, the team may have many members and is central to treatment planning. The lung cancer nurse specialist may attend different appointments with the patient such as an oncology or surgical appointment, providing emotional support to the patient and also factual information to the doctor. There might then be follow-up in a manner similar to that at the diagnosis, reinforcing important points to the patient and outlining possible events. The multidisciplinary team itself greatly enhances the effectiveness of service delivery by bringing together the different specialities, thereby allowing an exchange of ideas and information in a way that might otherwise not occur. The limitations of each possible treatment option can be explored in the light of best practice. Important aspects of individual patient care can be discussed and, in particular, urgent and difficult cases can be highlighted and acted upon.

Lung cancer nurse specialists may also improve the effectiveness of service delivery through innovative ways of utilising their skills. The development of nurse-led clinics for the purpose of reviewing patients or for the management of symptoms such as breathlessness has been demonstrated to be highly effective (Moore *et al.* 1999).

Another important component of the role of the specialist nurse and one that may also enhance service delivery in the long term is that of an educator of patients, carers and other health professionals. Education is particularly important in relation to communication, and the use of teaching strategies such as role-play enables health professionals to develop skills in a comparatively safe environment (Baile *et al.* 1999). Education must remain a high priority as a means of furthering empowerment, enhancing knowledge and promoting evidence-based practice. Similarly, the remit of the lung cancer nurse specialist must include research and audit, in line with national standards (NHSE 2000b), thereby providing a further opportunity to identify the strengths and weaknesses of the service.

Conclusion

Both the lung cancer nurse specialist and the multidisciplinary team have a valuable contribution to make in terms of increasing the effectiveness of service delivery. The specialist nurse helps to provide an insight into the problems faced by lung cancer patients and plays a significant role in providing support, information and continuity of care to individual patients. Continuity of care is particularly important given the current pressures under which clinicians are increasingly finding themselves, from the growing burden of acute on-calls, reduction of junior doctors' hours and loss of traditional team structures. The development of the lung cancer nurse specialist now provides a model for others to follow when addressing the issue of multidisciplinary working and continuity. This nurse is vital for liaison between the patient and health professionals and between health professionals in the multidisciplinary team and in the community. The multidisciplinary team itself improves communication between specialists and provides an important focus whereby potentially complicated treatment plans can be considered. In essence, the lung cancer nurse specialist and the multidisciplinary team enhance lung cancer service delivery through a complex interplay of improved communication and continuity of care.

Acknowledgements

The authors thank Drs Richard Harrison and Neil Leitch, respiratory physicians, for their advice during the time of writing.

References

Baile, W. F., Kudelka, A. P., Beale, E. A., Glober, G. A., Myers, E. G., Greisinger, A. J., Bast, R. C., Goldstein, M. G., Novack, D. & Lenzi, R. (1999). Communication skills training in oncology. *Cancer* **86**, 887–897.

Bennett, M. & Alison, D. (1996). Discussing the diagnosis and prognosis with cancer patients. *Postgraduate Medical Journal* **72**, 25–29.

Bousfield, C. (1997). A phenomenological investigation into the role of the clinical nurse specialist. *Journal of Advanced Nursing* **25**, 245–256.

CHI (Commission for Health Improvement)/Audit Commission (2001a). *NHS Cancer Care in England and Wales*. London: Commission for Health Improvement.

CHI (Commission for Health Improvement)/Audit Commission (2001b). *NHS Cancer Care in England and Wales. There's No System to the Whole Procedure. Listening to patient views and experiences of NHS cancer services*. London: Commission for Health Improvement.

CHI (Commission for Health Improvement)/Audit Commission (2001c). *NHS Cancer Care in England and Wales. Cancer and Primary Care: The views and experiences of GPs and Community Nurses*. London: Commission for Health Improvement.

DoH (Department of Health) (1995). *A Policy Framework for Commissioning Cancer Services*. A Report by the Expert Advisory Group on Cancer to the Chief Medical Officers of England and Wales. London: DoH.

DoH (Department of Health) (1998). *A First Class Service: Quality in the New NHS*. London: DoH.

DoH (Department of Health) (2000). *The NHS Cancer Plan*. London: DoH.

Fallowfield, L. J., Hall, A., Maguire, G. P. & Baum, M. (1990). Psychological outcomes of different treatment policies in women with early breast cancer outside a clinical trial. *British Medical Journal* **301**, 575–580.

Faulkner, A. & Maguire, P. (1994). *Talking to Cancer Patients and Their Relatives*. Oxford: Oxford University Press.

Hayward, K. (1998). Patient-held oncology records. *Nursing Standard* **12**, 44–46.

Laroche, C. & Lowry, E. (2001). Delivering effective services efficiently: current models of excellence for the provision of an efficient service. In: *The Effective Management of Lung Cancer* (ed. M. F. Muers, F. Macbeth, F. C. Wells, A. Miles). London: Aesculapius Medical Press, pp. 153-160.

Loftus, L. A., McDowell, J. (2000) The lived experience of the oncology clinical nurse specialist. *International Journal of Nursing Studies* **37**, 513–521.

McCann, C. (1998). Communication in cancer care: introducing patient-held records. *International Journal of Palliative Nursing* **4**, 222–229.

Meredith, P., Symonds, P., Webster, L., Lamont, D., Pyper, E., Gillis, C. R. & Fallowfield, L. (1996). Information needs of cancer patients in west Scotland: cross-sectional survey of patients' views. *British Medical Journal* **313**, 724–726.

Moore, S. (2002). A survey of nurse specialists working with patients with lung cancer. *European Journal of Oncology Nursing* **3**, 169–175.

Moore, S., Corner, J. & Fuller, F. (1999). Development of nurse-led follow-up in the management of patients with lung cancer. *NT Research* **4**, 432–444.

NHSE (National Health Service Executive) (1998). *Improving Outcomes in Lung Cancer. The Manual*. London: Department of Health.

NHSE (National Health Service Executive) (2000a). *Referral Guidelines for Suspected Cancer*. London: Department of Health.

NHSE (National Health Service Executive) (2000b). *Manual of Cancer Services Standards*. London: Department of Health.

NHSE (National Health Service Executive) (2000c). *The Nursing Contribution to Cancer Care. A strategic programme of action in support of the national cancer programme*. London: Department of Health.

Smith, S. D. M., Nicol, K. M., Devereux, J. & Cornbleet, M. A. (1999). Encounters with doctors: quantity and quality. *Palliative Medicine* **13**, 217–223.

Standing Medical Advisory Committee (1994). *Management of Lung Cancer: Current Clinical Practices*. London: Department of Health.

Chapter 16

Economic evaluation of advances in the management of lung cancer

Ala Szczepura

Introduction

Lung cancer care, like many other types of medical care, has changed significantly in recent decades; it has become more ambitious, more effective, but also more expensive (Szczepura 2002). The increasing pressure on health care costs has inevitably emphasised the need for economic evaluation of new treatments. Cost increases have been driven by various factors. Principal among these are: demographic trends (i.e. an increasingly elderly population); the development and introduction of new technologies; the associated price effect (i.e. new treatments are usually more expensive than the interventions they replace); and rising public knowledge and expectations (Szczepura & Kankaanpää 1996).

Debates about whether cancer services should provide new drugs or diagnostic facilities, or about the role of hospital versus primary care, or about preventive versus curative activities, are at bottom debates concerning the proper use of resources. Economic evaluation is now viewed as an important tool for dealing with such questions. Increasingly, different agencies are seeking information on the economic impact of new and existing health care interventions. From a strategic perspective, commissioners of cancer services and, more recently, national bodies such as the National Institute for Clinical Excellence (NICE), have been concerned with the health gain which investment in new treatments for diseases such as cancer can buy (Szczepura *et al.* 1993). At the delivery end of cancer care, hospitals and other providers are also increasingly having to ask themselves what their priorities are for future technological and service investment; what new techniques or interventions will bring real benefits to patients and at what cost; and how funders can be convinced that innovations are worthwhile. At the same time, the professionals caring for patients (doctors, nurses and therapists) have been systematically questioning the relative value of the interventions they provide, and embodying this in structured protocols or guidelines (Russell & Wilson 1992). Finally, industry has also come to realise the importance of economic evaluation as a means of informing decision-making about product development, and for positioning products in the market (Rutten & Drummond 1994).

In health, as in every other sector, users want value for money, whether they pay directly or indirectly, in their roles as taxpayers or as buyers of health insurance. Thus the importance of economic evaluation is expected to continue to rise as expenditure on health care increases. In the 1990s, government strategies in the UK and elsewhere focused on cost containment: trying to limit the increase in expenditure on health. However, increasingly, information on benefits gained as well as costs is now considered essential for decision-making.

Health care staff throughout Europe need to improve their understanding of economic evaluation (Szczepura & Kankaanpää 1994). It is essential, therefore, that interested clinicians involved in lung cancer care who currently have little or no knowledge of how such evaluations are carried out, or how their findings can prove useful in practice, should be able to find out more.

This chapter is designed to introduce the reader to some of the basic definitions and approaches to economic evaluation in lung cancer. In particular, the chapter considers the current situation for management of non-small cell lung cancer and highlights the improvements needed in available evidence on costs and benefits in order to be able to assess cost-effectiveness.

Lung cancer diagnosis and treatment patterns

Non-small cell lung cancer (NSCLC) is the most common form of lung cancer, accounting for about 80% of all cases. Small cell lung cancer accounts for the remaining 20% of lung cancer cases. The examples presented in this chapter, therefore, relate to NSCLC, as the most common form of lung cancer.

The UK has a lower 5-year disease-free survival for NSCLC than other Western countries, especially for later stage disease (see Figure 16.1). In England, the age-standardised overall 5-year survival rate for NSCLC is 5.5% and about 80% of patients will die within 1 year (NHS Executive 1998a).

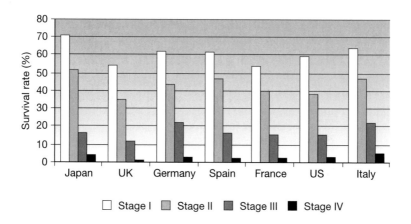

Figure 16.1 Five-year disease-free survival for NSCLC in seven Western countries.

There are no screening tests that have been demonstrated to be cost-effective for the detection of pre-clinical NSCLC disease. Therefore, intervention for NSCLC is primarily concentrated on active treatment or palliative care.

NSLC is most often diagnosed late; two-thirds of patients present with extensive-stage disease with distant metastases, when surgical intervention is inappropriate (Hoffman *et al.* 2000). The examples discussed below are therefore primarily focused on evaluation of the costs and benefits of interventions used in the care of advanced NSCLC patients.

National lung cancer costs

Because lung cancer is the most frequently diagnosed cancer worldwide, and it is associated with more deaths than any other cancer (Osa 1998), the costs to society of this disease are high in terms of both premature deaths and distress. Lung cancer clearly also imposes a heavy burden on health care systems, as the most common cancer requiring treatment. However, data on the burden of disease and national treatment costs associated with lung cancer are limited.

International comparisons of cost of non-small cell lung cancer treatment

NSCLC treatment costs will depend on the medical management strategy adopted, and this in its turn will largely depend on the stage of the cancer. Figure 16.2 shows that, internationally, surgery is generally accepted as the treatment of choice for both stage I and stage II NSCLC (83% and 69% for stage I and II, respectively), whereas chemotherapy (69%) is mainly used for stage IV.

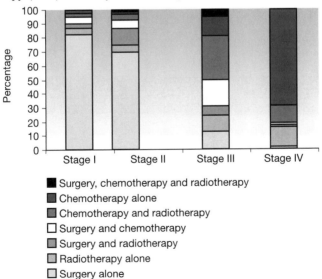

Figure 16.2 International NSCLC treatment patterns versus disease stage (*Source*: Datamonitor 1999, treatment algorithms: lung cancer).

However, at an individual country level the use of *first-line* surgery, chemotherapy and radiotherapy in patients with NSCLC varies from country to country. Table 16.1 shows data for seven key countries.

Table 16.1 Percentage of NSCLC patients treated with surgery, radiotherapy and chemotherapy at first-line (*Source*: Datamonitor 1999, treatment algorithms)

Treatment modality	Japan (%)	UK (%)	Germany (%)	Spain (%)	France (%)	USA (%)	Italy (%)
Surgery	51.8	49.2	40.8	48.5	52.0	35.0	52.1
Chemotherapy	54.1	27.4	70.6	72.1	54.3	56.0	55.3
Radiotherapy	25.7	42.5	29.5	18.3	42.7	55.6	26.6

Note: total percentage is not 100% as therapy double-counted when a combination therapy was used.

The UK is unusual in having a relatively low proportion of NSCLC patients who receive first-line chemotherapy, in contrast with Spain and Germany who report the highest percentage of first-line chemotherapy patients. Similarly, the US reports the lowest proportion of patients undergoing first-line surgery, and radiotherapy is highest in the US, France and UK. Patterns such as these will have an impact on overall treatment costs for the disease.

It is also recognised that the pattern of use of treatments such as surgery, chemotherapy and radiotherapy for a *particular cancer stage* can vary significantly from country to country (Datamonitor 1999). Figures indicate that treatment of stage III NSCLC appears to be the least consistent across countries. This may reflect the shift in therapeutic focus from cure, in patients with stage IIIa disease, to the alleviation of symptoms in those in whom the disease has advanced to stage IIIb. Overall, physicians in all seven countries appear to agree that the treatment of stage IIIb and IV NSCLC should be predominantly palliative to alleviate the symptoms of disease progression. Thus, Figure 16.3 shows that in most countries the vast majority of patients with stage IV NSCLC receive chemotherapy, either alone or in combination with radiotherapy (83% on average). The exception is the UK where a lower use of chemotherapy treatment is reported.

However, international data on total national expenditure on treating NSCLC patients, including radiotherapy, chemotherapy and surgery costs, are generally not available. This means that treatment costs cannot be compared across countries.

Even so, evidence exists that lung cancer treatment represents a major economic burden to society. In the USA it is estimated that one-fifth of all cancer care expenditure is attributable to lung cancer and US$8 billion a year is spent on this type of malignancy (Goodwin & Shepherd 1998). The annual direct cost of medical management of NSCLC is also calculated to be about US$4.6 billion (Shoheiber *et al.* 1996).

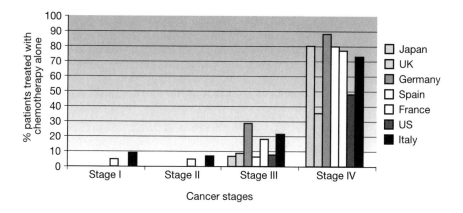

Figure 16.3 Percentage of NSCLC patients treated with chemotherapy across seven countries

In the UK, only crude estimates are available of the financial cost of treating patients with this disease. These indicate that the average cost of treatment for each patient with lung cancer is approximately £4,730 at 1990 prices (NHS Executive 1998b). With an estimated 37,000 new cases per annum in the UK (GLOBOCAN, www-dep.iarc.fr/URL; *Health Statistics Quarterly* 2000 www.statistics.gov.uk/downloads/theme_health/HSQ8Book.pdf), this would equate to an approximate expenditure on lung cancer of £175 million per year (1990 prices). This figure is inevitably now out of date, and current costs are likely to be higher, partly because of increasing chemotherapy expenditure.

International comparisons of chemotherapy expenditure

Although there is a lack of comparable data on national treatment costs for lung cancer patients, some estimates are available for chemotherapy expenditure (treatment algorithms, Datamonitor 1999). Equivalent average cost (i.e. the average chemotherapy drug expenditure per patient with NSCLC in a particular country per full course treatment) has been estimated across the same seven countries (Figure 16.4).

Clearly, calculated chemotherapy expenditure varies significantly from country to country, with the lowest expenditure (average US$674 per patient) recorded in the UK and the highest in the US (US$5,710 per patient). Certain assumptions have had to be made in calculating these figures because data are not available directly; therefore, these chemotherapy expenditure estimates can only give an approximate indication of the overall investment by a country in treating NSCLC patients using chemotherapy.

The differences observed in Figure 16.4 will be driven by a number of factors, including the following: variations in the pattern of use of different standard

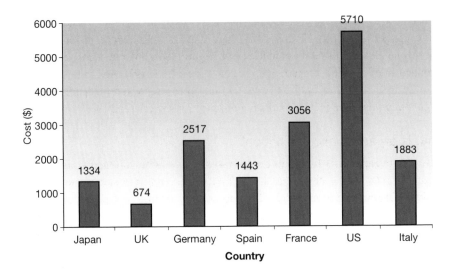

Figure 16.4 Average chemotherapy drug expenditure per patient with NSCLC per full course treatment in seven Western countries (Source: Datamonitor 1999, treatment algorithms).

regimens; the proportions of patients receiving first-line chemotherapy; actual price differentials that exist between equivalent drugs in different countries. For example, given the UK mean drug price as 1.00, the same drugs would be 1.29 in Germany and 2.06 in the US (cost of drug treatment, Datamonitor 1998).

Furthermore, the information presented in Figure 16.4 is likely to underestimate the current cost of chemotherapy in the UK since many of the newer drug combinations were not included in the calculations. In more recent publications, Lees *et al.* (2001, 2002) estimated an average price per patient per full course of treatment in the UK for various of these newer drug combinations as, for example, gemcitabine/cisplatin (US$4,848), paclitaxel/cisplatin (US$6,269), paclitaxel/carboplatin (US$10,138) and docetaxel/cisplatin (US$5,996). However, the authors do not provide percentage use figures for these drug combinations so that a revised UK weighted cost figure cannot be estimated.

From the evidence above, NSCLC treatment costs vary and chemotherapy costs are an important cost driver at the individual patient level.

Economic evaluation of advances in lung cancer care

We will now move on to consider the economic evaluation of lung cancer treatment. Because of the need to limit the examples presented, these will mainly relate to evaluation of treatments for advanced NSCLC, focusing on new chemotherapy regimens but also including a radiotherapy example.

There are increasing options available in terms of possible chemotherapy treatments for advanced NSCLC, and there are also differences in the treatment patterns observed in different countries (see Figure 16.3). Within such a context, the introduction of any new chemotherapy agent for NSCLC will need to be considered carefully in the light of both its costs and any measurable effects, particularly for patients in whom cure is not a realistic option (i.e. stage IIIb and IV).

What is an economic evaluation?

Economic evaluation is linked to *choice* about the possible alternative use of finite resources, even if one choice is simply that of retaining the status quo or 'doing nothing' (Drummond *et al.* 1987). The 'do nothing' option in the case of advanced NSCLC would be best supportive care (BSC). A full economic evaluation addresses the implications of alternative choices on the basis of their respective costs and any benefits (Luce & Elixhauser 1990; Russell 1992). Figure 16.5 depicts the resulting 'cost-effectiveness plane' in which any economic analysis for a new treatment would be undertaken. Clearly, if a new treatment is cheaper and more effective (lower right quadrant) comparison of costs and benefits is relatively simple and the decision made would be to introduce the new therapy. Similarly, if it is more expensive and less effective (upper left quadrant), the new treatment would be rejected. However, if a treatment is more expensive and also more effective (upper right quadrant), or slightly less effective but also less expensive (lower left quadrant), decision-making becomes more difficult.

A number of economic assessment methods are available which can be used as a means of comparing costs and consequences (Drummond *et al.* 1990). The appropriate technique will depend on the types of interventions being compared, the purpose of

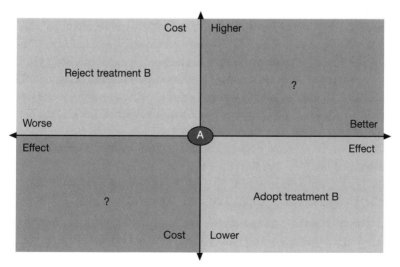

Figure 16.5 The cost-effectiveness plane.

the assessment, and the likely position in the cost-effectiveness plane (Szczepura & Kankaanpää 1996). Four main methods are used:

- cost minimisation analysis (CMA)
- cost-effectiveness analysis (CEA)
- cost-utility analysis (CUA)
- cost-benefit analysis (CBA).

Table 16.2 provides a comparison of the outcomes measured in these four different techniques, and the manner in which results are reported. The table also includes a simple cost analysis.

Table 16.2 Comparison of different methods for comparing costs and benefits

Outcomes are...	Terminology	How reported
...not considered	Cost analysis	Incremental cost of programme B versus A
...assumed not to differ between competing interventions	Cost-minimisation analysis (CMA)	Same
...measured in a natural, clinically relevant unit	Cost-effectiveness analysis (CEA)	Incremental cost per unit, e.g. per ulcer avoided, per life year gained
...measured as quality-weighted survival	Cost-utility analysis (CUA)	Incremental cost per quality-adjusted life year (QALY) gained
...valued in money terms	Cost-benefit analysis (CBA)	Incremental net present value (NPV) of programme B versus A

All the economic evaluation methods in Table 16.2 involve measurement of costs. The first (CMA) is, in fact, limited to measurement of costs, because benefits are assumed to be equal, and is reported in the same way as the cost analysis. In the next section, we will consider the measurement of costs, and examine an example of a cost minimisation analysis. The subsequent section will consider two main methods used to compare the costs and benefits of interventions for advanced NSCLC (cost-effectiveness analysis and cost-utility analysis).

Measuring costs

Cost minimisation analysis (CMA) is the simplest economic evaluation technique. This is used where two interventions have the same outcomes, in which case the intervention which is least costly is the preferred choice.

However, the full costs associated with the interventions being compared need to be measured when undertaking such an analysis. Ideally, these costs should be considered at a 'societal' level. They would then include not only the direct cost to the

NHS of the treatment itself, and any other associated health care costs (e.g. treatment for the side-effects of chemotherapy), but also costs incurred by other sectors such as social care, the voluntary sector or employers (e.g. time off work), plus costs to patients and their families (e.g. travel costs, co-payment). Although economists favour using the broad perspective of society and identifying all costs and all benefits accordingly, this may not represent the true economic interests of decision-makers. Most economic evaluations in health care are therefore limited to health care costs.

The rigour with which different components of care are identified and costed in a study will influence the validity of any final conclusions. Costs that should be included will vary depending on the types of intervention being compared. In the case of chemotherapy regimens, for example, the following costs would be important to consider and should ideally be included in an analysis.

Drug costs

A number of different issues need to be considered when building up a profile of chemotherapy drug costs. Ideally, the cost analysis should:

- specify the drug, or combination of drugs, used
- identify at what doses the drug(s) were delivered, and the number of cycles
- take account of any toxicity or adverse reactions to the drug(s) which cause the dose to be stepped down in some patients, or inadequate response which causes doses to be stepped up in others
- provide an indication of how costs might vary with different numbers of cycles.

Once drug use is quantified, there may be issues about the drug prices used in a cost analysis. Drugs should normally be priced using the British National Formulary (BMA and Royal Pharmaceutical Society 2000). However, where comparator therapies are low cost generics then costing of new therapies might use their discounted price, because this will more accurately represent longer-term costs since the generics are already discounted. Ideally, two or more sets of drug prices should be used in a cost analysis to test the sensitivity of any conclusions to the assumptions made about prices.

Chemotherapy administration costs

The cost of chemotherapy treatment should ideally include the cost of administering the treatment as well as the drug costs. In many cases infusions are administered on an outpatient basis, but in others they may need to be administered over a longer period (e.g. 24 hours), incurring a cost equivalent to a one-night inpatient stay.

Hospital costs (inpatient and outpatient)

In addition to the cost of administering the chemotherapy, there may be a range of associated inpatient or outpatient treatment and diagnostic costs incurred as a consequence of the cancer management strategy adopted. For example, in some cases a significant proportion of patients might receive radiotherapy in addition to their chemotherapy treatment. Patients might also need to undergo surgery for palliative or diagnostic purposes. Outpatient follow-up visits will also be required.

Concomitant medication costs

A further cost associated with chemotherapy will be that of concomitant medications. These might include analgesics and medications for non-haematological toxicity. It is unlikely that such medications are not used, but they may not always be recorded in trials.

Treatment of other chemotherapy complications (e.g. transfusions)

As well as the costs above, there may also be costs incurred because of the need to treat other complications that result from the chemotherapy. Haematological toxicity, leading to bone marrow suppression, is an almost universal adverse effect of anti-cancer chemotherapy. This is potentially serious unless vigorous action is taken. In severe cases, blood transfusions will be required which usually necessitates a hospital inpatient stay.

Home/community care costs

The support provided by various non-hospital health care professionals, including GPs and district or Macmillan nurses, should also be taken into account when comparing different chemotherapy regimens. Estimates of the cost for each type of health care professional can be produced based on the numbers of visits and the unit cost per consultation/home visit (Netten and Curtis 2000). Another community cost may be linked to admissions to hospice care, both inpatient and outpatient. This should, ideally, also be recorded for all patients in a trial.

An example of a cost analysis undertaken by Lees *et al*. (2001, 2002) is shown in Figure 16.6. This compares four combination chemotherapy regimens (gemcitabine/cisplatin, paclitaxel/cisplatin, paclitaxel/carboplatin and docetaxel/cisplatin). The analysis was performed from the UK health care perspective and was based on a head-to-head US trial by Schiller *et al*. (2000). The figure illustrates the difference that inclusion, or exclusion, of particular costs might make to the estimated average cost per patient undergoing chemotherapy. Thus gemcitabine/cisplatin and docetaxel/cisplatin are associated with a lower overall cost than the two other regimens. This is primarily due to lower prices for chemotherapy drugs and lower administration cost; lower administration cost is particularly important for the docetaxel plus cisplatin regimen, counteracting a higher drug cost. In contrast, although the paclitaxel/cisplatin has relatively low drug costs, the administration costs are high, raising the overall cost of treatment. For paclitaxel/carboplatin, the main cost

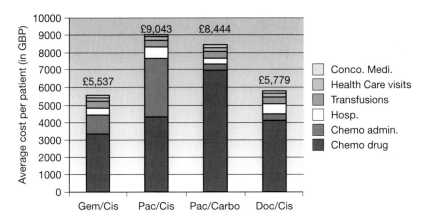

Figure 16.6 Cost analysis for four combination NSCLC chemotherapy regimens.

driver is the chemotherapy agent cost. Otherwise, the cost of transfusions, other hospital costs (inpatient and outpatient), concomitant medication costs, and home/community care costs are not significantly different. This example demonstrates that different types of resource need to be identified and costed if an accurate final conclusion is to be drawn. Best practice would be to include all relevant costs that vary between the therapies being compared.

Comparing costs and benefits

The cost-effectiveness plane in Figure 16.5 demonstrates that, if a treatment is more expensive and also more effective (upper right quadrant), or slightly less effective but also less expensive (lower left quadrant), then decision-making becomes more problematic. Decision criteria will be needed when working in either of these quadrants. In some cases, it may be clear that a new technology is acceptable if, for example, the effect is significantly greater than the additional cost (see Figure 16.7). However, there will be a zone of uncertainty in which it is less evident whether any improvement in effectiveness is worthwhile.

There are three main approaches to comparing costs and benefits in such a situation.

Cost-effectiveness analysis (CEA)

This approach requires a single outcome measure common to both interventions; survival or tumour response rate would meet this requirement for NSCLC. The cost for one unit improvement in the chosen outcome measure is then used to provide an estimate of overall cost-effectiveness. CEA can only be used legitimately to compare treatments for the same condition or patient group, or interventions whose outcomes can be measured in the same units (e.g. life years gained). Although there is no

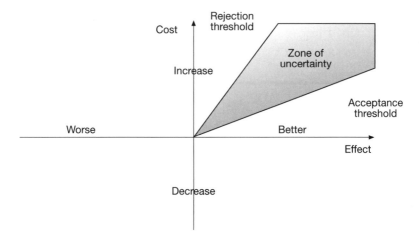

Figure 16.7 Cost-effectiveness decision criteria: zone of uncertainty.

absolute benchmark for an acceptable cost-effectiveness ratio, the cost per life year saved of various widespread interventions such as breast screening (£19,000) provides some indication of acceptable values.

Cost-utility analysis (CUA)

Where interventions differ in terms of outcomes such as survival and quality of life, another approach is to compare these interventions in terms of cost-utility. This requires a single measure which combines these outcome dimensions in a simple index figure: for example, in the form of quality adjusted life years (QALYs). This approach can also be used to compare different types of intervention, such as cancer treatment vs. dementia treatment, and is therefore useful to health care commissioners or policy-makers in that it enables them to know what benefit they would gain if they invest in different health care interventions or programmes. This is the approach favoured by NICE. Once again, although there are no absolute benchmarks, certain informal criteria might be used, such as those shown in Figure 16.8.

Cost-benefit analysis (CBA)

Where the outcomes of the interventions being compared can be quantified in monetary terms (e.g. using a technique such as 'willingness to pay') then cost-benefit analysis can be undertaken. This technique allows costs and benefits to be directly compared in absolute monetary terms. Although the approach has been used to make decisions in some areas, such as the introduction of transplant programmes, it has not been widely used to evaluate other health care interventions. The main drawback of CBA is the difficulty of assigning monetary values to health outcomes, including changes in the length or quality of life.

Evidence	< £3,000 per QALY	£3,000–£20,000 per QALY	> £20,000 per QALY
I	Strong support	Strong support	Limited support
II	Strong support	Supported	Limited support
III	Supported	Limited support	Limited support
IV	Not proven	Not proven	Not proven

I   Evidence from published systematic review(s) of multiple well designed randomised controlled trials (RCTs).
II Evidence from at least one published properly designed RCT of appropriate size and in appropriate clinical setting.
III Evidence from published well designed trials, single group pre-post, cohort, time series or matched case-controlled studies.
IV Evidence from well-designed non-experimental studies from more than one centre or research group.

Figure 16.8 Example of decision-making criteria used in economic evaluation.

Economic evaluation of interventions for advanced NSCLC are mostly limited to cost-effectiveness analyses (CEA), and some examples of these are considered below. Cost-utility analysis (CUA) will also be briefly considered because of its potential value, although this technique has so far had limited application in NSCLC treatment. Cost-benefit analysis will not be considered further in this short chapter. This technique is not widely used to evaluate health care interventions, due to the difficulty of assigning a monetary value to health outcomes, as explained above.

Generally, economic evaluations of NSCLC interventions have typically been conducted retrospectively, often drawing cost data and health outcomes data from different primary studies. However, increasingly, there is more emphasis on incorporating cost analyses into primary studies (e.g. collecting cost and health outcomes data in prospective clinical trials).

Cost-effectiveness analysis and non-small cell lung cancer

A number of cost-effectiveness analyses have been reported in the literature for new treatments used in advanced or metastatic NSCLC. This section will first consider an example where chemotherapy has been compared with the 'minimum' that might be provided, that is, best supportive care (BSC). A second example will then be examined in which various radiotherapy options have been compared. As explained above, CEA requires a single outcome measure common to both interventions; in NSCLC survival or tumour response rate would meet this requirement. The cost for one unit improvement in either of these outcome measures can then be calculated in order to provide an estimate of overall cost-effectiveness. However, even if a new treatment is identified as more cost-effective than an existing treatment, we would still need to decide whether the cost-effectiveness ratio is acceptable, that is, whether a particular level of additional benefit is worth the additional cost.

The first example of a cost-effectiveness analysis is that reported by McKendrick *et al.* (2001) comparing single agent chemotherapy (gemcitabine) versus BSC. This analysis was based on 300 patients with symptomatic, locally advanced or metastatic NSCLC enrolled into a randomised, multi-centre trial comparing gemcitabine plus BSC versus BSC alone (Anderson *et al.* 2000), and was performed from the UK health care perspective. Figure 16.9 shows the direct health care costs associated with this head-to-head trial. As might be expected, the analysis demonstrates that the

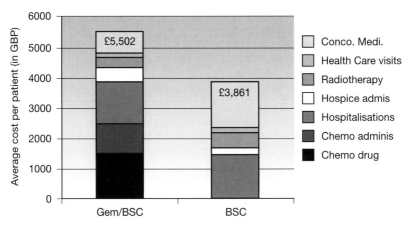

Figure 16.9 Cost-effectiveness analysis: example costs for single agent chemotherapy versus BSC. (*Source*: McKendrick *et al.* 2001)

chemotherapy/BSC combination uses more resources than BSC alone; this is principally due to chemotherapy drug and administration costs. However, the analysis also shows that gemcitabine/BSC is associated with lower resource use than BSC alone for items such as concomitant medications and radiotherapy and surgical procedures. In contrast, the hospice admission resource costs per patient are double for gemcitabine/BSC than for BSC alone. This is due to the increased length of time spent at the hospice per visit, and not to increased numbers of visits to the hospice. Even so, overall, the cost of chemotherapy and its administration dominates the two cost profiles.

Outcome results for the Anderson trial (2000) showed no significant increase in overall survival associated with single agent chemotherapy. However, there were improvements with respect to time to radiotherapy (as a proxy for disease progression) and overall tumour response. The former showed a median progression-free survival of 288 days versus 173 days; and the trial also showed that 18.5% of chemotherapy patients were classified as having a tumour response, compared with 0% of those patients who received BSC alone.

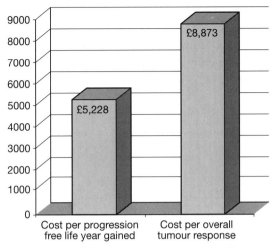

Figure 16.10 Cost-effectiveness ratios: single agent chemotherapy versus BSC.

Two types of cost-effectiveness ratio are shown in Figure 16.10, based on these two outcome measures (disease progression-free life years gained or tumour response). The incremental cost required for gemcitabine/BSC to obtain an extra year of life free of disease progression is estimated at £5,228; and the incremental cost per overall tumour response is £8,873. Improvements in terms of progression-free years are a good indicator of treatment efficacy and would appear to be relatively inexpensive to obtain (£5,228). Although there is no benchmark figure showing the amount that society is willing to pay for this level of benefit, intuitively we would anticipate that this result would fall within the acceptance threshold, as shown in Figure 16.7 (compared with a cost per life year saved of £19,000 for interventions such as mammography). However, if tumour response were used as the outcome measure, there would be less intuitive 'feel' for whether £8,873 per tumour response is worthwhile.

A different example of cost-effectiveness analysis is shown in Table 16.3. This presents the findings of an economic analysis of different radiotherapy regimens for the management of NSCLC patients (Wake *et al.* 2002). This example differs from the chemotherapy example above in that the costs and benefits of a number of different treatments are being considered against the standard treatment (accelerated radiotherapy).

Table 16.3 Selected radiotherapy options for radiotherapy in NSCLC patients

Intervention	Annualised cost	Cost diff vs. standard	Survival difference (years)
Accelerated radiotherapy	£6,547	£0	0.072 (–0.69 to 0.48)
Split-course alone	£8,837	+£2,291	0.45 (–0.14 to 1.45)
Split-course & chemo-therapy	£8,973	+£2,427	1.05 (0.42 to 1.97)
CHART alone	£9,578	+£3,031	0.27 (0.06 to 0.5)

Clearly, the cost of alternative therapies is higher by between £2,291 and £3,031 when compared with standard therapy. However, the benefits are also higher for these alternative regimens, as measured in life years gained, compared with accelerated radiotherapy. Benefits range from 0.27 years for CHART (continuous hyperfractionated accelerated radiotherapy) alone to 1.05 years for split course plus chemotherapy; split course alone provides an estimated average of 0.45 years, but the confidence interval (-0.14–1.45) indicates that this figure is not significantly different from zero. Unfortunately, the analysis did not include values for CHART plus chemotherapy, since data for this combination were not available.

Figures such as those in Table 16.3 can be used to calculate cost-effectiveness ratios based on the cost per life year gained. The results are shown in Figure 16.11 for split-course/chemotherapy versus CHART (the two options with a clear marginal benefit). The figure demonstrates that split-course plus chemotherapy is the preferred option of the two. But it still does not address the question of whether £2,311 is an amount that society would be willing to pay for this level of benefit. As in the chemotherapy example, however, we would anticipate that £2,311 would fall within the acceptance threshold in Figure 16.7.

We now turn to a third form of economic analysis, one that begins to address the issue of *valuing benefits*: cost-utility analysis.

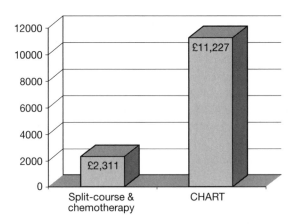

Figure 16.11 Cost-effectiveness ratios: split-course hyperfractionated radiotherapy plus chemotherapy versus CHART. (*Source*: Wake *et al.* Birmingham Technology Assessment Group 2002.

Cost-utility analysis and health-related quality of life in non-small cell lung cancer

As explained above, cost-utility analysis (CUA) is an approach that relies on the measurement of utility; in health this is conceptualised as the value that individuals derive from being in a particular health state. The method is therefore closely linked to the concept of health-related quality of life (QoL) experienced by patients. The main strength of this cost-utility analysis is that it can be used to compare a wide range of interventions and, thus, it can be used by policy-makers to make decisions about investment in competing health care interventions or programmes.

The main rationale for using a benefit measure that includes health-related QoL for a condition such as NSCLC is threefold:

- in NSCLC treatment it is often quality rather than quantity of life which is affected
- traditional clinical measures alone may not reflect the full impact of a treatment on the patient
- QoL provides a measure of 'net outcome', including any health benefits *and* the side-effects of treatment, from the *patient's* perspective.

The quality-adjusted life year (QALY) is the main unit of health care outcome used in CUA. QALYs represent years of life subsequent to a health care intervention that are weighted or adjusted for the quality of life experienced by the patient during those years (Torrance & Feeny 1989). The scale of quality of life used for QALYs can be derived from general QoL measures or other methods of eliciting patient utility for certain states of life (Nord 1992). Quality-of-life weightings for measured states are based on estimates of the public's valuation for these different states of quality of life (utilities). As such, QALYs can be used in a cost-utility analysis.

The dimension of quality of life is typically standardised to a scale ranging from 0.0 (death) to 1.0 (perfect health). For instance, the quality of life of a person who is confined to a wheelchair and who is in moderate distress might be rated as 0.55. A year spent by one person with this quality of life yields 0.55 QALYs; 100 people spending an average of 2 years with this quality of life yields a total of 110 QALYs. Units that are analogous to QALYs include disability-adjusted life years (DALYs) (The World Bank 1993) and healthy-years equivalents (HYEs) (Mehrez & Gafni 1993).

Figure 16.12 provides a demonstration of the concept of a quality-adjusted life year as exemplified for two treatments, A and B. Clearly treatment B offers some

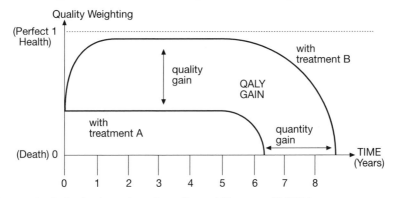

Figure 16.12 Derivation of quality-adjusted life years (QALYs).

advantage in terms of length of life gained, approximately two and a quarter years beyond the six and a quarter provided by treatment A (ca. 36% increase in life years gained, a measure used in the CEA examples presented above). However, treatment B also provides vastly superior QoL during the whole survival period, so that the QALY gain (the difference in the areas under the two curves) is significantly more than 36%: treatment B offers approximately 300% of the benefit provided by treatment A. A similar approach can be applied in the case of advanced NSCLC with the survival axis probably measured in terms of months rather than years.

One advantage of this approach is that it is possible to make comparisons among different health interventions because QALYs are generic units that can reflect changes brought about by different treatments for the same or different health problems. Table 16.4 lists the cost per QALY of a variety of health care interventions. Interpretation of such a league table should consider that the means used to derive costs and QALYs of different interventions vary (Gerard & Mooney 1993).

Table 16.4 Example of cost per QALY league table

Cholesterol testing and diet therapy only (all adults, aged 40–69)
Neurosurgical intervention for head injury
GP advice to stop smoking
Neurosurgical intervention for subarachnoid haemorrhage
Anti-hypertensive therapy to prevent stroke (ages 45–64)
Pacemake implantation
Hip replacement
Cholesterol testing treatment
CABG (left main vessel, severe angina)
Kidney transplant
Breast cancer screening
Heart transplantation
Cholesterol testing and treatment of adults (ages 25–39)
Home haemodialysis
CABG (single vessel, moderate angine)
Continuous ambulatory peritoneal dialysis
Hospital haemodialysis
Erythropoietin for anaemia in dialysis patients (if 10% reduction in mortality)
Neurosurgical intervention for malignant intracranial tumours

---

Cost-utility analysis thus requires a validated method for measuring QoL at different time points in a trial *and* independent valuation of the different QoL states measured. The methodological validity of QALYs and their roles in patient decision-making and setting health care priorities have been widely discussed (Williams 1991; Mehrez & Gafni 1993). Among the methodological concerns are the fact that people's valuations of utility for certain health states can be biased by technical aspects of the ways in which researchers present information describing health states (Smith & Dobson 1992). However, health states measured using certain instruments such as the EuroQol (EQ-5D) have now been valued in a large number of countries (EuroQoL Group 1990).

Measurement of quality of life in non-small cell lung cancer trials

QoL measurement is clearly important in evaluating management of lung cancer. In recent years, considerable advances have been made in developing and validating measures of health-related quality of life in many areas of clinical care (Bowling 1992). QoL measures may be disease-specific (e.g. cancer, arthritis or heart disease) or general (covering overall health). They may be unidimensional (dealing with one dimension such as pain) or multidimensional (a combination of dimensions). They may provide a single aggregate score or yield a set of scores, each for a particular dimension. Measures may be designed to capture a number of dimensions, including: function, mobility, social activity, cognition, emotion, pain and discomfort, sleep and rest, energy and vitality, and health perception and general life satisfaction.

The use of quality of life measures in the evaluation of treatments for NSCLC is still developing. It is probably most advanced in the evaluation of new chemotherapy agents. A review of the literature on disease-specific QoL measurement in NSCLC chemotherapy studies has recently been undertaken for the period 1966–2003 (Szczepura and Clay 2004). Searches were carried out on Medline (1966–2003), EMbase (1980–2003), OLGA-qol (and other sources including Cochrane, the NHS National Research Register (NRR), 'Health and Psychosocial Instruments' and sources accessed through the Internet). These identified a total of 606 relevant articles, ranging from papers considering the concept of measurement of QoL in NSCLC to reports of trials of chemotherapy (alone or in combination with other interventions). Examination of these identified nine validated instruments that are reported to be in use for measuring QoL in advanced NSCLC studies; the most frequently used were: the European Organisation for Research and Treatment of Cancer Quality of Life Questionnaire C30 (EORTC QLQ-C30) and the lung cancer module (EORTC QLQ-LC13), Functional Assessment of Cancer Therapy-Lung (FACT-L), and the Memorial Symptom Assessment Scale (MSAS).

Examination of the literature also identified a number of emergent themes. These include the following:

- large numbers of early articles indicating the need for QoL outcome measures to be included in trials, but little evidence that QoL measurement has actually been integrated effectively or consistently into later studies
- a poor standard of reporting in many QoL studies; that is, lack of detail on instruments used and their validity, time points at which QoL was measured, drop out rates, how missing data is handled, etc.
- a lack of clarity over the reason for including QoL outcome measurement in a study; that is, whether the information is for clinicians, for patients or for policy-makers
- where QoL measurement is described, there is an observed lack of consistency in the instruments used

- confusion over whether some instruments exclusively measure health-related quality of life, with symptoms and toxicity measures included in the instruments.

Particularly important for economic evaluation, the main QoL measures used in trials have not incorporated a valuation stage and therefore instruments cannot be used to produce a single index figure (for cost-effectiveness analysis) or a utility value for the QoL experienced by individuals (on a scale of 0 to 1.0).

Conclusions

The ultimate aim of economic evaluation is to inform decision-making, either clinical, managerial or policy-making (Institute of Medicine 1985). However, a note of caution needs to be sounded here. At best, economic evaluation can only *inform* the decision-making process; it should not be viewed as removing the need for careful thought and judgement or as providing 'the answer'. Indeed, sometimes its role is simply to clarify the precise nature of the choices that must be made (The Netherlands: Ministry of Welfare, Health and Cultural Affairs 1992).

At the heart of most choices in health care lies the need to compare any measurable benefits provided by a medical advance with the additional resources associated with its use. As the case studies presented in this chapter illustrate, outcome measurement in economic evaluation may need to go beyond simple clinical impact; quality of life is evidently an important measure. However, the examples presented in this chapter also illustrate that in order to evaluate new therapies for NSCLC improvements are required in the evidence-base available for making decisions, in terms of both improved cost information and also more consistent measurement of treatment benefits such as QoL. Several key issues need to be addressed, including:

NSCLC cost studies:
- cost studies are generally lacking for NSCLC and are often poorly carried out
- there is a lack of consistency in the types of cost included in 'economic' studies
- generalisable, routine NSCLC care costs in the service setting in different countries are unavailable.

NSCLC treatment benefits:
- very few trials of NSCLC include measures of quality of life
- when they do, there is a lack of consistency in the instruments used to measure QoL
- where QoL is measured, it is usually not with a view to comparing benefits with costs.

The lack of robust NSCLC treatment cost studies and limited prospective collection of appropriate outcome measures is being addressed by a large, pan-European, prospective observational study (ACTION) which will recruit patients with stage IIIb and IV NSCLC who are receiving first-line chemotherapy (Szczepura *et al.* 2004). Up to 1,500 patients will be enrolled across seven European countries. Resource use will be monitored to include chemotherapy drug use and administration, concomitant medication, treatment complications, hospitalisation days and physician visits. Patients will be followed for 18 months or until death. Outcome measures evaluated during the study will include survival, tumour response, symptoms (Lung Cancer Symptom Scale) and general quality of life (EuroQol: EQ-5D). Recruitment commenced in Germany on 7 April 2003.

In conclusion, this chapter has necessarily had to limit itself in terms of the examples provided. It has therefore focused exclusively on NSCLC (excluding discussion of small cell lung cancer). It has also primarily considered examples linked to chemotherapy, although this decision might be rationalised by the fact that it is in this area that most emphasis has been given to date on economic evaluation of new therapies, and use, or consideration, of quality of life measures is more evident in this area. However, the methods discussed above are equally applicable to other advances in the management of lung cancer, including developments in radiotherapy, surgical innovations, screening and staging modalities, and new biological approaches to therapy.

References

Anderson, H., Hopwood, P., Stephens, R. J., Thatcher, N., Cottier, B., Nicholson, M., Milroy, R., Maughan, T. S., Falk, S. J., Bond, M. G. *et al.* (2000). Gemcitabine plus best supportive care (BSC) vs. BSC in inoperable non-small cell lung cancer: a randomized trial with quality of life as the primary outcome. UK NSCLC Gemcitabine Group. Non-Small Cell Lung Cancer. *British Journal of Cancer* **83**, 447–453.

Bowling, A. (1992). *Measuring Health. A review of quality of life measurement scales.* Buckingham: Open University Press.

BMA (British Medical Association) and the Royal Pharmaceutical Society of Great Britain (2000). *British National Formulary (BNF 40)* September 2000. London: British Medical Association and the Royal Pharmaceutical Society of Great Britain.

Datamonitor (1998). Executive Brief. Cost of Drug Treatment at first-line 1998. Data on file Eli Lilly and Company Ltd.

Datamonitor (1999). Treatment algorithms 1999: Segmenting the lung cancer population. Data on file Eli Lilly and Company Ltd.

Drummond, M. F., Stoddart, G. L. & Torrance, G. W. (1987). *Methods for the Economic Evaluation of Health Care Programmes.* Oxford: Oxford University Press.

Drummond, M. F., Stoddart, G. L. & Torrance, G. W. (1990). *Methods for the Economic Evaluation of Health Care Programmes.* Oxford: Oxford University Press.

EuroQoL Group (1990). EuroQol; a new facility for the measurement of health-related quality of life. The EuroQol Group. *Health Policy* **16**, 199–208.

Gerard, K. & Mooney, G. (1993). QALY league tables: handle with care. *Health Economics* **2**, 59–64.

Goodwin, P. J. & Shepherd, F. A. (1998). Economic issues in lung cancer: a review. *Journal of Clinical Oncology* **16**, 3900–3912.

Hoffman, P. C., Mauer, A. M. & Vokes, E. (2000). Lung cancer. *The Lancet* **355**, 479–485.

Institute of Medicine (1985). *Assessing Medical Technologies.* Washington, DC: National Academic Press.

Lees, M., Aristides, M., Botwood, N., McKendrick, J., Maniadakis, N., Wein, W. & Stephenson, D. (2001). Economic evaluation of Gemzar/cisplatin relative to other new agents for non-small cell lung cancer (NSCLC) in the UK. *Value in Health* **4**, 86–87 (abstract).

Lees, M., Aristides, M., Botwood, N., McKendrick, J., Maniadakis, N., Wein, W. & Stephenson, D. (2002). Economic evaluation of gemcitabine alone and in combination with cisplatin in the treatment of nonsmall cell lung cancer (NSCLC). *Pharmacoeconomics* **20**, 352–337.

Luce, B. R. & Elixhauser, A. (1990). *Standards for Socioeconomic Evaluation of Health Care Products and Services.* London: Springer-Verlag.

McKendrick, J., Botwood, N., Aristides, M., Lees, M., Maniadakis, N., Wein, W. & Stephenson, D. (2001). Economic evaluation of Gemzar and best supportive care (BSC) relative to best supportive care alone in the treatment of non-small cell lung (NSCLC) cancer in the UK. *Value in Health* **4**, 86 (abstract).

Mehrez, A. & Gafni, A. (1993). Healthy-years equivalents versus quality-adjusted life years: in pursuit of progress. *Medical Decision Making* **13**, 287–292.

The Netherlands: Ministry of Welfare, Health and Cultural Affairs, Government Committee on Choices in Health Care (1992). *Choices in Health Care.* Rijswijk, The Netherlands: Ministry of Welfare, Health and Cultural Affairs.

Netten, A. & Curtis, L. (2000). *Unit Costs of Health and Social Care.* Canterbury, UK: Personal Social Services Research Unit, University of Kent.

NHS Executive (1998a). *Guidance on Commissioning Cancer Services: improving outcomes in lung cancer. The Research Evidence.* London: Department of Health.

NHS Executive (1998b). *Guidance on Commissioning Cancer Services: improving outcomes in lung cancer. The Manual.* London: Department of Health.

Nord, E. (1992). Methods for quality adjustment of life years. *Social Science and Medicine* **34**, 559–569.

Osa, K. E. (1998). Epidemiology of lung cancer. *Current Opinions in Pulmonary Medicine* **4**, 198–204.

Russell, L. B. (1992). Opportunity costs in medicine. *Health Affairs* **11**, 162–169.

Russell, I. T. & Wilson, B. J. (1992). Audit: the third clinical science? *Quality in Health Care* **1**, 51–55.

Rutten, F. & Drummond, M. (1994). *Making Decisions about Health Technologies: A Cost-Effectiveness Perspective.* York: Centre for Health Economics, University of York.

Schiller, J., Harrington, D., Sandler, A., Belani, C., Langer, C., Krook, J. & Johnson, D. H. (2000). A randomised phase III trial of four chemotherapy regimens in advanced non-small cell lung cancer (NSCLC), *36th Annual Meeting of the American Society of Clinical Oncology,* New Orleans, LA, Abstract #2 (www.asco.org/prof/me/html/00abstracts/p/m_2.htm, accessed 28/09/01).

Shoheiber, O., Schrogie, J. J. & Johnson, N. (1996). Non-small cell lung cancer: a cost of illness study. *Pharmacotherapy* **16**, 136.

Smith, R. & Dobson, M. (1992). Measuring utility values for QALYs: two methodological issues. *Health Economics* **2**, 349–355.

Szczepura, A. (2002). Healthcare outcomes: gemcitabine cost-effectiveness in the treatment of non-small cell lung cancer. *Lung Cancer* **38**(Suppl. 2), 21–28.

Szczepura, A. K. & Kankaanpää, J. (1994). Interests in health care technology assessment (HCTA) and HCTA training needs in eight European countries: COMETT-ASSESS. *Social Science and Medicine* **38** (Economic Appraisal Special Issue), 1679–1688.

Szczepura, A. K. & Kankaanpää, J. (eds) (1996). *Assessment of Health Care Technologies: Case Studies, Key Concepts and Strategic Issues*. Chichester, UK: John Wiley.

Szczepura, A. & Clay, D. (2004). Time to stock-take: a systematic review of the value of Quality of Life (QoL) studies in non-small cell lung cancer care. Internal report, Centre for Health Services Studies, University of Warwick, UK.

Szczepura, A. K., Sidhu, K., Cobb, B., Cooper, R. & Geller, R. (1993). Setting priorities in UK health care - and the new NHS R&D strategy. In *Setting Priorities in Health Care* (ed. M. Malek). Chichester, UK: John Wiley.

Szczepura, A., Cullen, M., Anderson, H., Pimentel, F. L., Riska, H., Solberg, O. G., van den Borne, B.E.E.M., Thomas, M., Frimodt-Moller, B., Kielhorn, A. *et al.* (2004). The Assessment of Cost and ouTcomes of chemotherapy In an Observational setting in patients with advanced Non-small cell lung cancer (ACTION) study: rationale and design. *Lung Cancer* **43**, 113–115.

Torrance, G. W. & Feeny, D. (1989). Utilities and quality-adjusted life years. *International Journal of Technology Assessment in Health Care* **5**, 559–575.

Wake, B., Taylor, R. & Sandercock, J. (2002). *Hyperfractionated/accelerated radiotherapy regimens for the treatment of non-small cell lung cancer. A systematic review of clinical and cost-effectiveness*. Birmingham: West Midlands Health Technology Assessment Collaboration.

Williams, A. (1991). Is the QALY a technical solution to a political problem? Of course not. *International Journal of Health Services: Planning, Administration, Evaluation* **21**, 365–369.

World Bank (1993). *World Development Report 1993: Investing in Health*. New York: Oxford University Press.

Index